AMBIGUITY OF THE SACRED
PHENOMENOLOGY, POLITICS, AESTHETICS

SÖDERTÖRN
PHILOSOPHICAL STUDIES 12
2012

Ambiguity of the Sacred

Edited by
Jonna Bornemark
& Hans Ruin

SÖDERTÖRN
PHILOSOPHICAL STUDIES
12

Södertörn University
The Library
SE-141 89 Huddinge

www.sh.se/publications

Printed by E-print, Stockholm 2012

Södertörn Philosophical Studies 12
ISSN 1651-6834

Södertörn Academic Studies 49
ISSN 1650-433X

ISBN 978-91-86069-47-6

Contents

Introduction

Western modernity is defined sociologically in part by the separation of politics and religion, and the establishment of a secular sphere of public life. According to the Enligthenment ideal, religion should be a private matter that should not influence the political sphere, where a rational construction of the community and the state should take place through argument and deliberation. The establishment and upholdning of this secular sphere is today a focal point of political tensions, throughout the world, also in supposedly "modern" societies where the very delimitation of the secular is under constant debate. This phenomenon is continuously analysed and explained from many different perspectives, historical, sociological, and economical. But often the most elusive aspect of it seems to evade thematization, namely the very meaning of the sacred, and of its distinction and interdepency vis-à-vis the secular or profane.

In the early phenomenologies of religion, notably those of Rudolf Otto and Mircea Eliade, the sacred—and the holy—was a central theme and to some extent their defining topic.[1] This was not incidental. The very word "sacrality" implies the existence of something beyond the reach of rational elucidation and explanation, but also what should be protected from being approached disrespectfully. It is a word that in itself would seem to signal a *limit*. If somehow "real," it calls for and implies respect, awe, and even fear. If not "real," it seems to shrink down to nothing at all, and it becomes unclear what it means to study it in the first place. What is left for rational study would then be the different practices and comportments that develop

---

[1] Following Levinas some interpreters of the phenomenom of the holy has recently sought to draw a strict line between the holy and the sacred, or "sacral," where the latter somehow designates a more destructive or negative side of the holy. Such a distinction may be motivated in certain cases, but it can easily hide an unreflected theological motivation, that needs to be thought through as well.

around what is taken to be sacred, holy, or taboo in and by a specific culture. A key text which establishes the distinction as such in a sociological framework was Emile Durkheim's 1912 study on the *Elementary Forms of Religious Life*, which instituted the strict separation between the sacred and the profane as sociological categories. But in this type of approach the very phenomenality of the sacred often dissappears from view and is again obscured. In contrast, the phenomenological perspective insisted on the possibility of traversing this aporia of the sacred, by focusing on it not as the hypothetical existence, or non-existence, of a something beyond rational explanation, but as an experiential category, a field of *meaning* which could be thematized in a systematic way.

What the phenomenological analyses of Otto and Eliade could contribute were thus descriptive classifications of the lived meaning of the sacred, or the *hierophantic*, in terms of a distinctive sphere of human experience. They could explicate patterns of intentionality, both as psychic comportment and as the very organization of space and time.[2] For Eliade the sacred constituted the very defining trait of religion, and it was around the experience of sacrality and its distinction from the "profane" that he built many of his analyses. The relative merit of these early phenomenological analyses lay in their ability to explore patterns and structures of meaning and intentionality in a way that was more true to how they were actually manifested and "lived."

The refusal to take a stand on the ultimate reality of the sacred was consistent with a Husserlian program of "bracketing" the phenomenon under scrutiny. At the same time it was also what generated much criticism from scholars in religious studies for implicitly giving way to quasi-theological modes of thinking and thus giving up on the ambition of finding rational and scientific explanations. Phenomenology of religion in this earlier form was often questioned and disputed as methodologically

---

[2] See Rudolf Otto, *The Idea of the Holy*, translation J. Harvey (New York: Oxford UP, 1958), and Mircea Eliade, *The sacred and the profane*, translation Willard Trask (New York ; Harcourt Brace, 1959). See also the more recent essay by Randall Studstill "Eliade, Phenomenology and the Sacred." in *Religious Studies* 36 [2000]: 177–194, which gives a summary of Eliade, and the later critical discussion of his work in contemporary religious studies. For a collection of texts in phenomenology of religion that deals with this thematic, and that includes texts by both Otto and Eliade, see *Experiences of the Sacred. Readings in the Phenomenology of Religion*, eds. S. Twiss & W. Conser (Hannover: Brown UP, 1992).

outdated. It was considered not only to lack explanatory value, but also to be naively essentialising and unsensitive toward the role of language and toward cultural differences in general.

This dispute on the relevance and value of a traditional phenomenological approach has continued up till this day in the field of religious studies.[3] From the viewpoint of philosophy and modern phenomenology and post-phenomenology the situation looks somewhat different. What was perhaps most problematic in the older forms of phenomenology of the sacred was not then its lack of explanatory force, nor its theological bias, but rather its unreflected presuppositions that the sphere of the sacred or hierophantic was clearly demarcated and self-contained, that it could be isolated in its self-same essence by a conscientiuos phenomenological gaze. What is called for today is rather an approach that can address not just the dichotomous structure of the sacred—as both fascination and terror, to recall Otto—but the fundamentally *ambiguous* nature of the phenomenon itself. The traditional dichotomy still rests on a stable essential structure of meaning, on a something that appears in a doubble guise. But the ambiguity of the sacred concerns the ambiguity of sacrality as such, an inner instability and polysemy belonging to the very notion of the sacred. The meaning of the sacred needs to be thought through again in an unprejudiced manner. It needs to be traversed, activated, and critically assessed. This way we can perhaps begin to see and understand sacrality as a more mobile, transformative and essentially ambiguous sphere of human experience with subterranean links to politics, desire, language, and aesthetics, to questions of rights and obligations, sacrifices and transgressions.

Through a post-Heideggerian deconstructive phenomenology, shaped also by an encounter with psychoanalysis, and cultural anthropology, the phenomenon of the sacred has opened itself to such different avenues of exploration. In his seminal lecture "On Religion" from the Capri conference in 1994, Derrida pointed to the ambiguity of the phenomenon of the sacred, how it designates purity, exclusiveness, transcendence, pointing toward a life beyond life, and how it through a logic of supplementarity in the end

---

[3] For a good overview of the discussion, see Douglas Allen's article on "Phenomenology of religion" in the recent *Routledge Companion to the study of religion* (London: Routledge, 2010).

also implies death and sacrifice, ultimately a sacrifice of the self.[4] Following this and other leads, the interest in phenomenological approaches to the sacred is again growing.[5] It is discussed as a category for thinking the uncalculated event, as a category for difference, and for transcendence, often in conjunction with discussions of the return of religion as such.

In such discourses the distinction between the descriptive and the normative is sometimes also intermixed, as the sacred and holy is charged with an aura of hope and even redemption, of a fragile kind, but still as a project of redeeming it in and for an age that in so many ways would seem to have left it behind. In the face of such hopes of somehow "resurrecting" or "saving" the sacred, it is also important to continue to explore its meaning and experience in all its multiplicity, to make ourselves acquainted with its vicissitudes and possibilities, perhaps in order to move beyond this category itself. It may be that ultimately the very meaning of the sacred rests on something else, on the enigma of the transition between life and death, or on the finitude of human reason and perception. Perhaps it is a category that needs neither to be dismantled nor resurrected, but instead to be revealed more fully in its own latent presence and foundation also in a time that regularly believes itself to have left it behind. In short, we need to reopen the question of the sacred, in its phenomenon and its phenomenality, in its coming into presence, as well as in its disappearance.

The puritanism animating the desire to establish once and for all a secure border between the spheres of the sacred and the secular today stands in the way of exploring its multifacetted phenomenality. What is needed is therefore not the rehearsal of an enlightenment credo to keep the spheres intact, but to find new ways of further investigating the polarized dichotomy of the secular and the sacred, to explore both the ethical potential and the latent violence involved in phantasms of cleanliness and separation. The goal should then be to critically investigate the roots of

---

[4] Jacques Derrida "Faith and Knowledge." in *Religion*, edited by J. Derrida and G. Vattimo (Cambridge: Polity Press, 1998), § 40f. (68 f).

[5] See, e.g, Espen Dahl *In Between. The Holy Beyond Modern Dichtomies* (Göttingen: Vandenhoeck & Ruprecht, 2011), which contains an excellent summary of traditional phenomenological approaches to the problem of the holy, as well as a defense for a new phenomenological approach. A somewhat earlier attempt to reassess the emergence of the phenomenon of the holy in late modernity was *Das Heilige. Seine Spur in der Moderne* (Bodenheim: Athenäum, 1987), edited by Dietmar Kamper and Christoph Wulf.

fanaticism, and the inner complicity of redemption and destruction, activated in the thought of the sacred. But in doing so one should also be attentive to the transformative potential of the concept, the ways in which it can permit us to rethink the humanity of human, as itself a source and a focus of sacrality.

In 2010 a symposium was organized at Södertörn University in Stockholm with the title "The Ambiguity of the Sacred: Phenomenological Approaches to the Constitution of Community in Religion, Politics and Aesthetics." The idea was to bring together scholars from a wide range of disciplines, from philosophy, religion, theology, social science, and aesthetic disciplines, to engage in a multidisciplinary discussion around different aspects of sacrality. Commentaries were prepared to all the invited speakers in advance by a scholar from a different discipline. The goal was to show how the theme of the sacred traverses traditional lines of demarcation and opens up new ways of bringing polical, philosophical and aesthetic issues to bear on what is still often believed to belong strictly to the sphere of religion and a uniquely religous experience. The essays presented in this volume all originate from this encounter.

In the first contribution, "Sacredness as a Social Strategy," Muniz Sodré discusses the power of the sacred as a social and political strategy among Afro-Brazilians in Brasil and other parts of Latin America. The sacred is described as ambiguous in itself, as both the most impure and the most pure. As a positive power it provides the possibility of transcendence and of transformation, whereas as a negative power it implies prohibitions and violations. Both sides are at work in the syncretistic religiosity of Afro-Brazilians, which contains strategies of social liberation as well as strategies to ensure the continuity of the group of African descendants. However, this does not result in a monoculture, but in a plurality of strategies and identities. The symbolic interpretation of the world includes rituals, gestures, dances, foods, beliefs, etc., through which the world is linked together by proximity and a relation of micro and macro cosmoses rather than by cause and effect. Through proximity the individual becomes part of the symbolic process and gains her identity as well as a collective consciousness. In this way, Sodré argues, it also produces both social effects and provides political strength.

In his commentary to Sodré, Mattias Martinsson poses the question of religiosity and liberation within a more explicit Marxist framework. This is a tradition that has understood religion as an obstacle to liberation, and

Sodré's position would in this sense be a long way off from any Marxism. Nevertheless, Martinsson argues, a more nuanced understanding of Marxism would instead imply a close link between the two. Such a link could be developed not least through Sodré's separation between religion and religiosity, through which the sacred acquires a progressive character, and as a certain form of religiosity a secular political potential.

Jacob Rogozinski's contribution "'You Shall Kill the One You Love': Abraham and the Ambiguity of God." addresses the significance of the sacrifice of Isaac. It focuses on one of the most debated texts in the Old Testament concerning the ambiguity of God, a story that throughout its reception has motivated questions about the relation between religion, faith, and ethics. What kind of God demands the sacrifice of his own child? And can any faith justify such a murder? How could this ambiguity of the divine be understood? One way has been to understand it in terms of two different divine orders, the God of Moriah who demands murder, and the prohibition against murder deriving from the God of Sinai. Rogozinski instead shows how the story plays different roles in Judaism, and in Christianity and Islam. He criticizes Levinas's reading for not taking the ambiguity of the divine into account, and for not doing justice to the Jewish interpretation. The latter understands the God who demands murder as listening to the devil and thus as something satanic. This does not, however, lead to a dualistic understanding of the divine, but focuses instead on the different names of God in the story as signifying an inner differentiation of God.

In her response, Elena Namli focuses on how God relates to human beings, and on the role of the humans as willing and acting creatures. She argues that here we stand before an ambiguity pertaining to human action itself. As such it is an ambiguity central to ethics that should be kept alive and not be seen as a riddle to be solved. She defends Levinas's interpretation, referring also to biblical scholars who claim God's command to be the only source of morality in the Old Testament. Morality is thus removed from the discussion of contradictory divine commands. Instead she claims that morality is always relational, which again puts the focus on the free choice of Abraham.

In the subsequent contribution, "Ambiguities of Immanence Between Stanislas Breton and Louis Althusser (or, Why an Apostle Recycles as an Exemplar of Materialist Subjectivity)," Ward Blanton analyses how St. Paul has exerted such a strong fascination among political philosophers today and how he connects Christianity to secular materialism. The article centers around a reading of the French philosopher and theologian Stanislas Breton and his philosophical Paulinism and his Paulinian reading of Louis Althusser's materialism. Here Paul gives voice to an immanent religion beyond a religion of external limits and commands, thus reshaping the relation between the secular and the religious. Breton points to an indispensable void within every system, a void that ideology obsessively tries to fill once and for all. Instead of ideology, Breton suggests a "meontology" built on an immanent void at the center of every identity, and he uses the image of the Pauline cross to point to this gap and to criticize every representation of the Absolute. The cross emerges as the name that escapes all modern systems.

In his commentary, Hans Ruin continues the discussion of the role of Paul and Pauline theology within the so-called turn to religion in phenomenology. He also highlights the ambiguous role that Paul has played throughout Christianity, not least in relation to the creation of Christian anti-semitism. To the the cross as an emptying we should also add the cross as a symbol of power and violence. As such the cross gathers, more perhaps than any other symbol, a fundamental ambiguity of the sacred, as salvation and threat in one figure. But as a sign of an emptying of power, a *kenosis*, it marks a genuinely founding rapture and a primordial revolutionary moment. In this sense Paul can justly be said to invent a new kind of subjectivity related for example to Althusser's "interpellated" self.

In "Minimalist Faith, Embodied Messianism: The Ambiguity of the Sacred and the Holy," Bettina Bergo investigates the limits of phenomenology. She focuses on forms of consciousness that transcend the object-oriented intentionality, raising the question what it means within phenomenology to be alive. She notes the ambiguity of this concept, that philosophies of life and vitalism have often resulted in dangerous endeavors. In her attempts to find a way between formalism and vitalism, Bergo discusses the limits of faith in Jean-Luc Nancy and Gérard Granel. She contrasts the Christian concept of faith with Jewish messianism as discussed in Levinas, and as a possibility to think transcendence, a living subject and passivity together. She shows that Levinas in *Infinity and Totality* follows Husserl rather than Nietzsche and Bergson, and gives priority to the universal form—and formalism—of intentionality. The later Levinas on the other hand prioritizes a deep passivity, similar to Granel's pre-intentional sacred world of light, but whereas this world is deeply solitary, Levinas's messianism insists that we are connected to each another before we are perceiving subjects, and in this way escape the dangers of vitalism.

In a commentary on this text, Jonna Bornemark focuses on the relation between formalism and vitalism, and discusses the limit or the in-between as an alternative way out of the problem that Bergo has set up. Bornemark understands the limit-drawing event as the interconnection between life (or formlessness) and intentionality (or form), and their common genesis. She also discusses some of the political consequences of this separation in secular and religious societies respectively, which either tends to over-emphasize formless life, or that which can be measured by object-intentionality.

The relation between religion and politics is also the topic of Fredrika Spindler's contribution. In "An Unresolved Ambiguity: Politics, Religion, Passion in Hobbes and Spinoza," she shows that both Spinoza and Hobbes understand religion as a purely human phenomenon, but argues that it nevertheless plays an important role within politics. Both argue for a separation between religion and politics. However, where Hobbes reduces the role of religion to issues of domination, Spinoza leaves open a space for a reflection not only on how religiosity plays a role in the political, but also for its possible potential with respect to knowledge, since the source of religion lies in imperfect human knowledge. Both Hobbes and Spinoza understand religion as a strong social force and argue that political authority must necessarily use this ideological material for its own benefit. But Spindler shows how Spinoza's analysis is more sophisticated. As opposed to Hobbes, Spinoza claims that it is impossible for the state to rule over opinions and convictions and that any legislation countering the desires of the multitude with too much violence will be overthrown and thus invalidated.

Karolina Enqvist, in her commentary, embraces Spindler's attempts to read Spinoza as a political thinker. She continues this line of thought through a reading of two Spanish philosophers, María Zambrano and Vidal Peña García, and their works on Spinoza. Enqvist emphasizes the impossibility of perfect knowledge in Spinoza, which opens up for an irrational thinking as the way to best "preserve in being," and that this is where questions of religion, thinking, and materialism coincide. In this way Enqvist wants to radicalize Spinoza's position, as one where his whole project becomes religion.

The limitation of human knowledge is central also in Päivi Mehtonen's "Nominalistic Mysticism, Philosophy and Literature," in which she discusses the position of the language philosopher Fritz Mauthner. Mehtonen starts out from the statement that avant-garde aesthetics and poetics are based on the loss of an external object. She investigates the role of medieval mysticism in Mauthner's skeptical and atheistic critique of language. With Mauthner she also speculates on the possibilities of a philosophical language in the process of its de-ontologization and separation from metaphysical concerns, connecting it to the avant-garde question: What replaced the loss of the realist object? Mauthner understands word-realism as a relic of a religious world-view and instead develops a medieval nominalism that points to the limits of language and explores the contingency of history. He also proposes a theory of three understandings of language: Language as adjectival word, as substantive word, and as verbal word. The first produces a purely aesthetical world, the second the world of a naïve realist, and the third a world of relations and change. Mauthner's nominalist critique of naïve word-realism paves the way for an experimental language and an avant-garde revolution of an adjectival world. Thus it also opens up the question of a modernist aesthetic sensibility and the problem of the sacred, if and how it can be captured by language.

Jon Wittrock raises the question if Mehtonen only wants to point toward Mauthner's role in intellectual history, or if he is considered to have a political relevance today. He discusses the relation between the possibility of progressive politics and a radical critique of instrumentality (and the substantive word) in thought and language, and how Mauthner can help us in such a task. If the political means a distribution of resources, then it remains within instrumentalization, he argues. If, however, it has its ground in a conceptualization of desire as such, then Mauthner could help us in such a task.

In the final contribution Marcia Sá Cavalcante Schuback gives a different interpretation of the sacred, which she understands as a name for the abyssal and mysterious difference and identity between life and death. As such we are always within the sacred. It is not something we can choose to take part in, rather it is without entry and exit, as a gift always already given and thus what always has to be received. She describes the current atmosphere of nihilism and absolute immanence as a no way in, no way out. She investigates the relations between and common source of the sacred and profane, religion and philosophy. Ultimately the phenomenon of the sacred is described as pointing to an appearing that is not an appearing of things, but rather the appearing of appearing as such. This dimension exceeds the possibility of our full conceptual grasp, and we are left to acknowledge the beauty of its fragility. The wonder of beauty breaks down the order of things, not in order to take us somewhere else, but rather into the midst of things. For Cavalcante wonder is the attunement to the place where the sacred and philosophy touch and intersect.

The conference and the production of this volume is part of a three year research project on phenomenology and religion which has received generous support from Axel and Margaret Ax:son Johnson Foundation.

Stockholm, December 2011

Hans Ruin
Jonna Bornemark

Sacredness as a Social Strategy

MUNIZ SODRÉ

For orthodox theology concerned primarily with the transcendence of God or else with "the wholly Other," "sacredness" has always been an uncomfortable concept. However in the history of some Latin-American countries there are notable cases in which sacredness appears as a social strategy among the economically and politically underprivileged social strata. As an example of this, I will here describe how in Brazil the descendents of slaves have turned, throughout the centuries, their African pantheon of liturgical communities into valuable assets to interact with the global ruling society, and thereby also providing new ways of looking at humanity.

The idea of the sacred is closely linked to the idea of secrecy. *Sacer* is originally a separate portion of land, the area marked by men with a taboo, wherein human immanence (as in a territory), coexists with a transcendence that can be associated with a god or a deity. *Dewio*, the Indo-European semantic matrix for "god," means shining. It is the sunlight. There seems to be some universality in this semantic reference, since the idea of divinity is often associated with light, or the offspring of light.

The sacred in the sense of "separate ground," and as a place of exception, is a site to reserve for closer and deeper connections with the light in all its manifestations and varieties of irradiation, from obscurity to the fullness of its luminosity. The sacred thus contains the possibility of full sunlight, but also the virtuality of the shadow, in short the latency of something that withdraws or is confined to silence (*mysis*, in Greek).

"Separating" comes from the Latin *secernere*, from which originates the word *secretum* (secret), meaning precisely the separate. In the rites with strong symbolic significance the more "separate" or mysterious the meanings of gestures and words are, the greater is the holiness. It is even

15

greater when the secret involves the liturgical human embodiment in all its modulations of existence, including sexuality. Thus we can understand why the sacred within Christian radicalism has been refered to as "the colored mud of eroticism."

The sense of the sacred was originally extended to the human body, insofar as it is understood as a microcosm and not as an object separated from the person (no one "had" a body as such before the 16th century, rather he "was" a body). Being a microcosm means being inextricably linked to the community and the cosmos (heaven, animals and plants). If a person is subjected to a whole community and to a higher cosmic order, the boundaries of the flesh do not mark the limits of an indi-vidual. Everything is interconnected. Just as there could be sacred places within the community, so too did a personal body contain sacred places, in the form of taboos or interdictions.

Of course, the theological rationalization of the human connection with transcendence tends to limit, if not put an end to, the full dimension of the sacred. Monotheism in itself is averse to all that appears as diverse or obscure, because when you multiply the references, you lose the power of centralization of belief. Not for nothing Spinoza defines polytheism as a "polite atheism."

The presence of obscurity is a source of ambiguity in the concept of the sacred. Durkheim spots an ambiguity in the coexistence, inside the religious sphere, of the pure and the impure:

> Therefore, the pure and impure are not two separate genera but two varieties of the same genus that includes all sacred things. There are two kinds of sacred, one auspicious, the other inauspicious. And not only is there no discontinuity between the two forms, but the same object can pass from one to the other without changing its nature. The pure can be made impure and vice versa. The possibility of there transmutations accounts for the ambiguity of the sacred.[1]

The concept of the sacred carries with it a positive sense of transcendence elaborated in positive theology (where we find the identification of the sacred and the divine), but also the weight of prohibitions and violations, and a search for stability before the confrontation with death. It is why the

---

[1] Émile Durkheim, *The Elementary Forms of Religious Life*, translation Carol Cosman (New York: Oxford University Press, 2001), 306.

sacer, as Freud also said, is both holy and accursed. In the positive sense, the specific radicality pertaining to the sacred is replaced by the idea of "divinity." This abstraction is better carried out by the universalism of the great religions than by the restrictions of the body and the sacrifices involved in polytheism. In modernity, the bodily sacred is to some extent contained in the idea of "the unconscious."

Nowadays, it is the passage from continuity to discontinuity that shows the visceral connection between the sacred and the erotic. Bataille, as a primary example, describes how sexual activity brings discontinuous beings into play, that is, beings distinct from each other, single and alone in their experiences of engagement, birth and death. Between one and another there is a gap in communication, which cannot be suppressed, but whose vertigo can be felt—it is the fascination of death. It is death, however, that shows duration: when two people come together to breed a third one, the amalgam is deadly to the essence of the separate (sperm and egg-cell, procreator and their offspring), but allows the continuation of two separate beings.[2]

Bataille says:

> On the most fundamental level there are transitions from continuous to discontinuous or from discontinuous to continuous. We are discontinuous beings, individuals who perish in isolation in the midst of an incomprehensible adventure, but we yearn for our lost continuity. We find the state of affairs that binds us to our random and ephemeral individuality hard to bear. Along with our tormenting desire that this evanescent thing should last, there stands our obsession with a primal continuity linking us with everything that is.[3]

Now if we put aside the institutional aspects of religion and focus on the feeling evoked by the word *sacer*, as the inner and of the sacred as a secret, we can see the erotic as an aspect of a human being's inner life, and also as pointing to a sense of the religious. Unlike the purely reproductive sexuality, eroticism appears in consciousness as a questioning of the inner life, therefore as an existential questioning. In the erotic quest, the spirit can be said to escape the subordination imposed by the reality of the mortal

---

[2] Cf. Georges Bataille, *L'érotisme* (Paris: Minuit, 1957), translation Mary Dalwood *Eroticism – Death and Sensuality* (San Fransisco: City Lights Books, 1986) and *Théorie de la religion* (Paris: Gallimard, 1973), translation Robert Hurley *Theory of Religion* (New York: Zone, 1989).

[3] Bataille, *Eroticism*, 15.

body, reaching far into the sacred beyond gods and mythical deities, into the substrate of reality.

This search does not seek the natural end of reproduction of life, but something close to death, which is the deep sense of continuity caused by the replacement of the discontinuity, of the isolation of being. That's why, says Bataille, eroticism is "the adoption of life even in death." This is fully "religious"; in the sense of a radical and intimate experience, the ultimate meaning of which is the fusion and removal of limits. But it is religious as well in the sense of the turnover of interdiction and transgression, which makes possible both the sacred and the erotic. Trespassing, says Bataille, suspends the decree without suppressing it and that is the basis of both the erotic feeling and the religious feeling.

A Secular Sacred

In the Afro-Brazilian communities we find a secular sacred pattern which is neither lacking the secret nor the eroticism of the gods. Historically, the liturgical communities that gave rise to the profusion and popularity of cults of African origin in Brazil were the result of a fusion of different elites, dignitaries and priests of the ancient worship of deities who were brought to Brazil as slaves, following inter-ethnic wars and slave raids on the African continent. Thus, for example, the city-state of Ketu was conquered and razed to the ground by the king Ghezo, who sold batches of captives to the Portuguese.

The people of Ketu (Yoruba) arrived in Brazil in captivity but without slave morality, having rather the language of the Muslim jihad, of war. As the revolts were not successful, the black elites developed instead other forms of assertion and dissent, wherein religiosity took the lead.

The term "religiosity" seems appropriate, since it does not apply to "religion" in the European sense of a monopoly of universal faith by an ecclesiastical institution. Weber makes a distinction between religious rituals and religions of redemption, but takes into account the special character of monotheistic or polytheistic beliefs of the collective beliefs, being aware that there even may be a religion without divinities (like Buddhism). The word "religiosity" softens meanings attributed to strict religion, since it contains other variables such as magical practices, and even strategies of social liberation. In the case of Afro-Brazilian cults, these are religious-mythical-historical strategies (religious rituals that worship both cosmological principles and ancestors) in order to ensure the continuity of a human group, the descendants of Africans, in the hard conditions of slave diaspora.

This kind of strategy implies that, around the liturgical communities of African origin, popularly known as Candomblés, there developed a unique model of social organization among black people. This has given the city of Salvador-Bahia, for example, such noticeable traces of black singularity that it has become known around the world as "Black Rome." This archetypal African pattern is able to radiate to other areas.

There does not exist, as is well known, a homogeneous African paradigm: there is some talk of forty-five and even fifty different "Africas." However the diversity of socio-economic realities and cultural traditions converge on a common ground, rather than in a mystical approach, known as "animism" by the theological rationalism of the West. It is in fact a radical experience of the sacred.

Afro-Brazilian cults demonstrate the presence of a complex paradigm of civilization, different from the European paradigm that focuses on the powers of capitalist organization and linguistic rationality. At the center of the worldview of these cults there is the recognition of the here and now of existence, of special forms of concrete interpersonal relationship, a symbolic experience of the world, of the emotional power of words and actions, and of the power of getting things done as well as a joy before reality.

All this stems from a symbolic pact, that is, a network of signs and alliances legitimizing an intercultural consensus (among the various ethnic groups of African origin as well as among white people) that was historically established in the early republican days. None of this can be understood by means of a mere anthropological bias, since the symbolic pact springs from a political collective action. Politics lies in the mobilization of social assets for the consolidation of intra-group alliances and in a tactical approach to the global hegemonic society.

There is a peculiar political act in the transmission of assets pertaining to black liturgy. No cultural heritage that may be socially operative is transmitted as a static package of data, but rather as something that we must re-enter in history by means of reviving it and giving it new contours. Heresies, dissolutions, and bans can be part of a dynamic of that nature.

In the case of the liturgical black community, what is transmitted is the symbolic pact around the *Arkhe*, that is, a consensus on the mythical powers and representations that are projected in the language—enacted, issued, sung—of the community as well as in the affective ways (faith, belief, joy), of articulation of experiences. *Arkhe* is not the nostalgic old, nor an appeal to the primal past. It is rather all that eludes purely rational attempts of apprehension, as a fundamental something that is not fully remembered, something that is partially missing but that is all the same symbolized through the worship of cosmological principles (the deities) and ancestors who impersonate ethical principles.

More specifically, the memory of *Arkhe* consists of a cultural repertory of prayers, greetings, songs, dances, foods, legends, parables and cosmological symbols transmitted through mystical initiation inside the black liturgical community and within reach of global society. All of it requires a secret experience, which does not exclude at all the possibility of descriptions and interpretations by anthropologists and writers.

The Brazilian reinterpretation of an African cultural heritage has always been at the same time ethical, religious, and political. The black tradition has been historically included in the Brazilian society to promote the civilizing of slaves and their descendants. The symbols and the cultural effects of a paradigm (meaning the African *Arkhe*, manifested in a set of values, which articulates ethical values, ceremonies, sacrifices, and hier-archy) have always been representations supposedly able to act as dynamic instruments for the socialization of black and poor people.

However, we should distinguish Blacks from Afro-Brazilians. The latter are not to be defined only by color, but rather by mystical and existential involvement in liturgical communities (*candomblés* or *terreiros*). Community should thus be comprehended as a symbolical horizon for inter-subjective relations, which one might define as deep affective bonds and as an ethical engagement in a political and existential project.

The *terreiros* did not emerge by historical accident, but rather as an extension of an African paradigm, where communitarian exchange and negotiation are fundamental features. They are ways of complementing and restoring the ethical-communitarian foundations of traditional African civilization values.

Instead of a cannibalistic translation of differences (as it was suggested by modernist writers), Afro-Brazilian liturgical communities have been trying to show since the 19th century that social and cultural differences can approach each other by way of meaningful analogies. A dialectical way of thinking does not make itself necessary here. Exclusive differences should be replaced by inclusive ones converging on a sort of fractal proximity that should be understood as a changing of details and minor aspects of everyday life toward more tolerant forms of human understanding. The force of a communitarian presence creates a practical humanism, which one may comprehend as an opening to social and cultural differences within the same political territory.

I have suggested calling those unique intercultural translation strategies "seduction," which is something opposed to the production of order, that is, a radical opposition to the utilitarianism inherent in Western metaphysics.[4] To seduce (coming from Latin *seducere*) in a liturgical sense, means changing someone's position or deflecting from one's finality. Afro-Brazilian religious lucid practices have always been an affirmative way for the presence of another civilization paradigm in Brazil, and at the same time a cultural strategy meant to avert the ruling classes' consciousness from its supposedly absolute and universal truth.

Afro-Brazilian culture therefore stands for a substantial symbolical platform permitting afro-descendants to turn obstacles into assets on their way through the barriers and the hindrances that had been laid out by the white ruling society. Afro-Brazilian culture is a symbolical way (based on rituals and different from written ways) of interpreting the world. In a ritual (that is always also a cultural strategy), gestures, dances, foods, beliefs, rhythm and many other symbolical assets, link themselves together without any cause and effect connections, but rather by proximity.

However we should not see proximity as a shortening of physical distances, but rather as an ethical category. People can be physically or electronically close to one another and still have no proximity. As a matter of fact, proximity has to do with one's participation in the symbolical process which then leads to the identity and collective consciousness of a social group. It states that communion does not result from community, conversely community may follow something that we might call communion. It is thus a symbolical approach, not a spatial concept at all. Through proximity, cultural differences seduce each other, just like musical notes on a stave, in helping to produce conciliation or at least a reasonable balance of opposite terms.

---

[4] Cf. Muniz Sodré, *A Verdade Seduzida – por um conceito de cultura no Brasil* (Rio de Janeiro: Francisco Alves, 1990).

In order to cope with ethical proximity or propinquity, we should look for understanding in the concept of social sensitiveness. First of all, in regard to the imposition of social structures, we are compelled to take into account that the power pertaining to social institutions does not rest merely on the replacement of subjecting contrivances by subjected ones. The creative force in society comes about continuously whatever its goal may be: to perpetuate or to establish new social structures.

Herein lies man's faculty of feeling, namely sensitiveness, as something that affects and rebounds upon us in a positive manner. The Greek verb *aisthanomai* (translated into Latin as *sentire*) is the proper word to refer to man's conscious exterior and interior sensations. Sensitive perception is the spiritual faculty related to what Plato and Aristotle refers to as *aistheta*.

Aesthetics is a modern notion. However Baumgarten, who created it as "a science of the sensitive way of having knowledge of an object," did not limit the concept of art to what is nowadays interpreted as "the fine arts."[5] By inventing the expression "aesthetics," instead of the possible alternative "philosophical poetics," he meant to point out a gnoseology of the sensation or of the sensorial perception, which was supposed to be irreducible to logical knowledge.

By means of an "epistemology of sensitivity," that ascribed to Beauty—an intrinsic mark of truth in sensation—a cognitive value, Baumgarten's direction was in opposition to Kant's, as seen in the Kantian doctrine that sensuous appearances are nothing more than a pedagogical and temporary source of knowledge. Beauty, as Baumgarten asserts, is not only the sensuous dimension of a concept, but the privileged way to reveal certain objects, that grant to the aesthetical an autonomous knowledge. Yet even though the fine arts may serve as a privileged form of representation, they do not exhaust the domain of aesthetics, namely as the "art of perceiving" or the poetics of perception, and thus a way to the knowledge of sensuousness in a broad sense.

Going back to their conceptual origins may guide us on the issue of social effects of sensuous appearances, that reach into real, possible and imaginary realms. We are indeed affected all the time by volumes, colors and rhythms, as well as by sentences and narratives. Sensuousness is a kind of persistent

---

[5] Cf. Alexander Gottlieb Baumgarten, *Aesthetica* (Hildesheim: Georg Olms Verlag, 1961 [1750]).

sound that drives us with no clear separation between reality and imagination. In such a realm we cannot apply structures and laws to establish the ontological unity of the world, because herein we find ourselves in a continuous drift between personal and collective strata of experience.

Sensuousness lies at the heart of politics whenever one thinks about social visibility. The black struggle to establish and to accept the interpreted or translated reality was political. It was visualized as a faith in cosmological and sacred entities as well as in honorable ancestors. In fact, the duty to the liturgical community and the ethical values—the continuity of the founding principles—are fundamental, and yet susceptible to change based on spatial-temporal variation.

The political aspects of that historical movement often escape the unsuspecting ethnologist, who is usually focused on the description of the traditions and rites, as if they were cultural "survivals," if not cultural mystical anachronisms. There are many analysts who are driven by a purely culture-based logic and who neglect to see the political role of the reconstruction of signs in the form of chants, rituals, dances and so on. They cannot see how they contribute to the establishment of a new position in regard to the conflict between the universalism of the political state and a particular culture, and hence how they serve to free political action on behalf of a socially and economically subordinate group.

Therefore it is analytically short-sighted and culturally naive to believe that the theoretical issue of the sacred is solved only in the symbolic dimension, as is usually the case in anthropological analysis. Alongside the mythical-religious phenomena we can trace a collective affirmation, claims for recognition of identity and strategies of power—concerning the hegemony of representations—that are clearly political.

It is therefore appropriate to speak of religiosity (not religion in its Roman sense) or of Afro-Brazilian cults as an "experience" (in the sense that Walter Benjamin gives to that word) of active and collective relationship with History on behalf of afro-descendents in its manifest form (historical memory) as well in latent form (myths, imagery, intergenerational transmission). It differs, therefore, from a religious "grasp on life" which is a private relationship to the event of transcendence. In fact, religion as a sphere of privacy is a liberal trick to resolve its contradiction before politics in the modern public space.

Thus, the Afro-Brazilian cults can be seen in the light of late-modern culture. When God and fate remain associated with the belief of the majority population, separate spheres such as the sacred places backed by community values, enable new kinds of group activities in search of new social roles.

It is true, that in the practical action of cults it is not a matter of *Realpolitik*, it is not an activity that concerns the legal and constitutional systems of power, guaranteed by the absolutism of the written representation. It is rather a set of actions within the sphere of the sensuous, where the existence of spiritual entities implies the existence of another paradigm of civilization, that is political in itself. In other words, what ensures and justifies the sacred black liturgy is a peculiar way of thinking sovereignty within a territory controlled by the apparatus of a State.

Religion, Religiosity and Political Sacredness
Remarks on Muniz Sodré's Paper

MATTIAS MARTINSON

As I know too little about the situation of African-Brazilian groups I cannot and will not respond to Professor Sodré's interesting paper by commenting on the concrete political issues that he addresses. Instead what I can and will do is to reflect on a number of theoretical, conceptual and political philosophical issues which came to mind when I was confronted with Sodré's text.

There are indeed several theoretical undercurrents in the paper, although very little is said explicitly about its inspiration and position in a broader political theoretical field. In this short response, I will limit myself to one such undercurrent, namely, what I interpret as a hidden trace of a conversation with Marxism on religion and liberation. I will enter the discussion from that specific angle, generalize a bit and draw out some consequences that seem to be of interest for a discussion on religion, politics and the sacred.

Within a general Marxist framework, living religion is treated more or less as a symptom of social injustice—an indication of the wrong state of things. Religion might very well help people to bear and endure oppression, but in itself religion can never liberate them from the oppression as such. Hence, religion will always in the end be a significant part of a general practice of *legitimatizing* the oppressive forces: to use God in order to endure oppression is to accept and give in to *status quo*. Stated differently, in Marxism true liberation has nothing to do with religious relief. It is entirely related to fundamental changes in the material base of society. When such change really takes place, religion will necessarily become redundant and pointless.

At a first glance, Professor Sodré appears to take a route more or less opposed to this standard form of Marxism. In his paper, religiosity and the sacred are viewed as true possibilities at the core of the social struggle *for* recognition of particular identities and *against* the "global hegemonic society." This can be interpreted as a clear dissociation from the standard Marxist position.

However, looking more closely one can also trace a positive connection to the standard form of Marxism. This similarity is hidden, as it were, in Sodré's distinction between *traditional religion* and *religiosity*. According to this distinction, *religion* in its typical form is heavily institutionalized, fundamentally clerical, and Western/Roman. Furthermore, since it supports a "private relationship with the event of transcendence," religion is also closely intertwined with Western consumerist rationality.

This seems to mean that institutionalized European religion (which has been the theoretical pattern for the concept of religion in general) in a somewhat paradoxical way supports liberalism and its drive towards privatization. Towards the end of the paper Sodré even claims that religion in this sense is a "liberal trick."

Religiosity, on the contrary, is understood as a "radical experience of the sacred." It is intimately connected to magical practices, mythical strategies and a living liturgical communality—characteristics that stand up against the privatized Western form of religion. Therefore, it comes as no surprise that Western rationality often has considered *religiosity* (beyond or free from a religious institution) to be primitive and irrational. According to Sodré, this religiosity has been undermined effectively in the Western theological context and filed away under the label "animism."

This general distinction between religion and religiosity is not uncommon in the broader debate. At least since Friedrich Schleiermacher, it has been frequently suggested that religiosity has to do with the fundamental conditions of human existence, while religion is the social power-structure that does not correspond fully to the human experience. However, Sodré's argument is somewhat different, not least as he relates the religiosity of African-Brazilian groups to a fundamentally social experience, far from the existential inwardness of religiosity in the Schleiermacher-tradition.

From a Marxist point of view, then, one could perhaps say that Sodré separates the institutionalized form of religion and its private religiosity— one that constantly falls in to the logic of the oppressive capitalist system—

from *another form of religion* that does not fall prey to the logic of *Marxist* critique. This "other" religion should rather be taken into consideration as a real and active force in the struggle for social change, at least in the African-Brazilian context discussed in the paper. Sodré also takes a critical stance against Western ethnology and anthropology of religion; disciplines that focus on cultural description just to conclude that African-Brazilian religiosity is an anachronistic leftover, rather than something different or significant in its specific political context.

Consequently, if viewed in the framework of a Marxist theory of religion, Sodré seems to suggest that we should discard the Western form of religion as well as the dominating liberal forms of theology *and* religious studies, in order to connect the reflection on social struggle in the African-Brazilian context with a reflection on the "active and collective relationship with History" that springs from these groups' way of experiencing the sacred. Given such a "Benjaminian" change of perspective, religiosity (not religion) might become a truly significant force in the process of political recognition, justification and liberation of African-Brazilians.

One important prerequisite in professor Sodré's attempt to take this form of religiosity seriously is to give the notion of the *sacred* a progressive character. As I have already mentioned, the concept of religiosity that he promotes has to do with the African-Brazilian experience of the sacred, which is connected to their collective-historical experience—not to the private-existential sphere. This is also the key to the important concept of the "secular sacred" promoted in the paper. If I have understood Sodré right on this point, the idea of a secular sacred would mean, on the one hand, that "secular" is a fundamental category for *any* adequate notion of the political. (Sodré argues that it is important to settle "whether we can talk about the secularization of the sacred," which would be same as "reducing the sacred to the human dimension, with political power." This way of putting it echoes the standard form of Marxist materialism: only profane secular forces can be taken into consideration in the political struggle.)

On the other hand, however, the form of secularization connected to the African-Brazilian experience of the sacred seems to be radically *different* from the secularity of the liberal West, which ultimately discards the division of labor between a political and religious life. Thus, if Marxism tends to neglect the true force of religiosity and replace it with a wholly secular perspective, Sodré recognizes this specific form of religiosity, which supports a truly secular political potential.

Now, if this exposition in relation to Marxism is relevant at all (if there actually is an implicit Marxism in the paper), then it would be interesting to discuss the supposed distinction within the notion of the secular and its relation to religiosity. Dialectically speaking, if the "Western secular" is a result of secularization of a certain form of oppressive apolitical or non-political religion, will the secular not inherit certain distinct aspects of that division of labor that makes it politically insufficient in itself? If that is so, what then is the point of a "secular sacred"? I mean, what good comes from the secular if the notion itself supports a privatized liberal form of life that stands up and against the experience of the sacred in the African-Brazilian context?

From a more explicit Marxist point of view, it could perhaps be stated that the dialectical-materialist perspective is secular in a general sense, but does not this secularity have to be qualified further, in terms of a critical or post-bourgeois secularity? The question, then, is whether the secularization of the sacred proposed in the paper can be viewed as a post-bourgeois secularity? If the answer is yes, then one can once again ask how relevant the concept of the secular is in the political context under consideration. Is not the sacred a kind of driving force for the proposed political perspective, and does not the proposed relationship between the sacred, religiosity and the political open up a new perspective that goes beyond the very notion of secular (given its standard bourgeois, capitalist interpretations)? If that is the case, one could also ask if the distinction between religion and religiosity can be so strictly kept in terms of the institutionalized *Western* form and its "other." I really think that a modified Marxist perspective on religion is important to develop. But is Western religiosity *just* a liberal trick in contrast to a politically good religiosity, or does it have interesting aspects as well? Could *it* even learn something from African-Brazilian religion, I mean, learn something about its own political potential *as* religion?

You Shall Kill the One you Love
Abraham and the Ambiguity of God

JAKOB ROGOZINSKI

1 And it came to pass after these things, that God did test Abraham, and said unto him, Abraham: and he said, Behold, here I am. 2 And he said: Take now your son, your only son Isaac, whom you love, and go into the land of Moriah; and offer him there for a burnt offering upon one of the mountains which I will tell you of. 3 And Abraham rose up early in the morning, and saddled his ass, and took two of his young men with him, and Isaac his son, and clave the wood for the burnt offering, and rose up, and went unto the place of which God had told him. 4 Then on the third day Abraham lifted up his eyes, and saw the place afar off. 5 And Abraham said unto his young men, Stay here with the ass; and I and the lad will go yonder and worship, and come again to you. 6 And Abraham took the wood of the burnt offering, and laid it upon Isaac his son; and he took the fire in his hand, and a knife; and they went both of them together. 7 And Isaac spoke unto Abraham his father, and said, My father: and he said, Here I am, my son. And he said, Behold the fire and the wood: but where is the lamb for a burnt offering? 8 And Abraham said, My son, God will provide himself a lamb for a burnt offering: so they went both of them together. 9 And they came to the place which God had told him of; and Abraham built an altar there, and laid the wood in order, and bound Isaac his son, and laid him on the altar upon the wood. 10 And Abraham stretched forth his hand, and took the knife to slay his son. 11 And the angel of the Lord called unto him out of heaven, and said, Abraham, Abraham: and he said, Here I am. 12 And he said, Lay not your hand upon the lad, neither do you any thing to him: for now I know that you fear God, seeing you have not withheld your son, your only son from me. 13 And Abraham lifted up his eyes, and looked, and behold behind him a ram caught in a thicket by his horns: and Abraham went and took the ram, and offered him up for a burnt offering in the stead of his son.

Genesis 22, 1–19

Known as the "sacrifice of Abraham" or, in the Jewish tradition, as the *Aqedah,* the "binding" of Isaac, this text confronts us with the essential ambiguity of God. What is at stake here is the limit of faith: could any faith justify murder, including the murder of one's own child? And *who* is the God who could order that murder? Could we believe in this God? It is not only Abraham, but every reader of this story who is put to the test. For the text remains profoundly enigmatic. At first, we cannot understand Abraham's submission to the terrifying order, his silence; especially if we remember that, before the destruction of Sodom, he did not hesitate to oppose God in the name of Justice. We know that Abraham's "obedience" has been valued by Christianity and Islam (but not by Judaism). However, his obedience raises the question of the relation between faith and ethics. For the ethics of the three monotheisms is grounded on the Revelation of the Ten Commandments, and the sixth one states the prohibition of murder. Did Abraham know this statement? According to the Jewish tradition, Abraham already knew the Torah, even if this Law would be given to Moses several centuries after. In any case, the story of Isaac's binding would lose any meaning, if it is not considered in the context of the prohibition of murder. So, we find a contradiction between two divine orders: by obeying God, Abraham breaks God's Law, he sets God to God himself. Who is the God of Abraham? Is he the God of Moriah or the God of Sinai? What could be a God who "tests" in such a cruel way his believer? If he is the All-knowing, he must have known beforehand the result of the test. Is he a perverse God? Is he God himself? Could this trial be a kind of devilish temptation? Moreover, we know that Isaac is not an ordinary child: he is the "child of the Promise," this Promise that God has inscribed in Abraham's name, which makes him *Av-raham,* literally: the "father of multitudes." By ordering the killing of Isaac, God seems to contradict himself, to become faithless to his own Promise, and he will contradict himself again by cancelling the first order. In that sense, the text not only confronts us with the ambiguity of God, but, more radically, to his madness. Above all, it could seem scandalous that he has intervened only once to save a single child. The Jewish tradition has emphasized this scandal, especially during the dark times of persecution. To quote a Hebrew Middle-Age poem, which calls on the silent God in such a way: "For only one *Aqedah* and which, moreover, turned well, there was a commotion in the sky, and the angels, the Cherubs, the Seraphs gathered and swirled—and now so much and so much of *Aqedoth* happen under thy eyes, so many innocents are slaughtered, and Thou keep silent?"[1]

The story of Isaac's binding has been interpreted in different ways by the modern thinkers. It often aroused indignation, for instance for Kant and Hegel. In *Fear and Trembling*, Kierkegaard deals with it in a different manner: for him, the case of Abraham shows to us that faith is an "incredible paradox," "capable of making of a murder a holy action, which is pleasant to God." According to him, ethics and faith are two separated spheres, and we can pass from ethics to faith only by a "leap." Indeed, he defines ethics as the reign of the general, of "what is applicable to everyone"; whereas faith is "this paradox according to which the individual is over the general." In the sphere of faith, every ethical norm or law is suspended: because faith is a singular relation to God, an "absolute relation to the Absolute," to "an absolute Different, without any distinctive clue." God is the absolute exception which justifies all exception. "If faith is not this, then Abraham is lost": he is only a murderer or a madman. Does it mean that any believer should imitate Abraham, by committing himself infanticide for God's sake? Certainly not: it would be, says Kierkegaard, the "most horrifying misunderstanding." The absolute singularity of Abraham's experience is incommunicable, impossible to imitate—and "it is by faith only that we resemble Abraham, not by murder." However, it is obvious that Abraham's faith is an inseparable part of his trial. Otherwise, if God had not required his son's life, the paradox of faith would have been annihilated, and Abraham would not have been Abraham. This "paradoxical" conception of faith, as suspension or transgression of the ethical norms, is not foreign to the Bible, and we can find several examples of it, like the theft of the birthright by Jacob, the murder of the Egyptians by Moses, the scandalous acts of the prophets or of Jesus Christ himself. None of them however reaches the radicality of Abraham's trial, with the threat of an annihilation of the Promise it implies.

Unlike the Christian and Islamic commentators, the Jewish tradition has sharply rejected any interpretation of Abraham's story which could justify murder by invoking an arbitrary order of God. For that reason, some Rabbis tried to look for a "sin" which could rationally explain Abraham's

---

[1] Quoted by André Neher in his beautiful book *L'exil de la parole* (Paris: Seuil, 1970), 227; *Exile of the Word*, translation David Maisel (Philadelphia: The Jewish Publication Society of America, 1981).

trial as a "punishment." They alleged that God wanted to punish his attitude to Ismael and Agar, exiled by him in the desert, either his territorial compromise with the Cananean king Abimelekh. Here the Jewish tradition involves itself in the fatal slope of theodicy: it tries to justify the unjustifiable. In the same way, some Jewish thinkers have "justified" the Nazi Holocaust as a divine "punishment" of the sins and unbelief of their people.... Here, again we find the perverse, the sadistic God who is presupposed by most of the common interpretations of Abraham's sacrifice. Nevertheless, it is possible to defend from a Jewish point of view an ethical interpretation of the episode, without accepting the postulate of a divine infliction. This reading has been assumed by Levinas. He opposes his conception of a faith ruled by ethics to the "hardness" and "violence" of Kierkegaard's thought which would announce Nietzsche and Heidegger. "This hardness of Kierkegaard rises at the precise moment when he 'overcomes' ethics," by entering a religious stage that no ethical law could justify: "so begins the contempt for the ethical foundation of Being."[2] According to Levinas, this claim to overcome ethics is based on a counter-sense: Kierkegaard identifies ethics to the abstraction of the General, where the singularity of the Ego is lost. He does not perceive the primordial ethical relation between I and the Other, a constant singular relation where the face of the Other calls the Ego to its infinite responsibility. From this ethical perspective, the episode of Isaac's binding can receive another signification: Kierkegaard has not understood that "the attention lent by Abraham to the voice which brought him back to the ethical order by forbidding him the human sacrifice is the highest moment of the drama. That he obeyed the first voice is surprising. That he had, in spite of this obedience, enough distance to hear the second voice, here is the most important."

This analysis raises at least two questions. Levinas tries to move the emphasis from the first call to the second, as if the second alone carried the entire meaning of the story. Is it true? Does the second call succeed in erasing the scandal of the first? It is apparently the same God who commands successively the murder and the prohibition of murder, the break of the Covenant and its confirmation. By refusing to hear the first call, Levinas does not take into account the ambiguity of this God.

---

[2] Emmanuel Levinas, *Noms propres* (Fata Morgana, 1976), 106–113; *Proper Names,* (Stanford University Press, 1997).

Moreover, he seems "surprised" by Abraham's obedience to the first call and he presupposes that Abraham could hold a certain "distance" from the divine injunction. However, what would be obedience to God who would not be unconditioned? In Levinas's ethics, our exposition to the Other is too unconditioned, as a "devotion without promise," a "gift without return," without any kind of distance or reserve. In a certain sense, the Levinassian Other who commands an absolute sacrifice of myself is not so different from the God who imposes to Abraham his terrifying trial. But Levinas's ethics is situated from the point of view of the sacrificed and not of the sacrificer: as if Levinas was speaking instead of Isaac himself, bound on the altar and agreeing on his sacrifice. There is nevertheless a difference between the Biblical narrative and his ethics: the Other which requires my total devotion is not God, but the Other Man: *"le tout-Autre, l'absolument-Autre, c'est autrui."* So, we find again, barely transposed, all the ambiguity of Abraham's God in Levinas's Other, which is at the same time the imploring face of my victim and the "grinning hateful face of my persecutor."

We can remark too that Levinas refuses to name "God" as the author of the first call. He holds faithfully to the main Jewish tradition which has not accepted that God could break his own law by commanding a murder. But, in that case, *who* is the source of the call? The author of such an evil injunction can only be the Evil One, and this was already the teaching of the Talmud. In Treatise *Sanhedrin* (89b), the Rabbis assert this:

> After what words did God put Abraham to the test? After Satan's words. Because it is written 'Abraham made a big feast the day of the weaning of Isaac.' Then Satan addressed the Holy One, blessed is He, and said to Him: 'Master of the Universe, you offered a son to this hundred-years-old man and during this feast he did not even think of offering you a turtledove.' God answered him: 'But if I said to him: bring me your son in offering, he would sacrifice him immediately.' At once follows the verse: and God did test Abraham and said to him: 'take now your son, your only son....'

This attempt to overcome God's initial ambiguity is characteristic of rabbinical Judaism. As we know, the figure of the Devil does not appear in the Torah. As it is held in a strict monotheism, the most native tradition of Judaism refuses to admit a principle of evil which would be different from God and would oppose to him. "I form the light and I create the darkness; I bring the peace and I create the woe. It is Me, the Lord, who make all this." The God who speaks here with the words of Isaiah (45, 1–7) appears deeply ambivalent, because he includes *in him* the origin of darkness and woe, what the Torah names the wrath of God. At length, this essential ambiguity has become unbearable: so this dark side is dissociated from God and presented as his "Opponent," in Hebrew: *Satan*. This character appears only in some late texts of the Bible, like the Book of Job, where he is the Tempter who obtains from God that he lets him torment Job to test his faith. Unlike Judaism, where Satan will never come to the fore, this dissociation will increase in Christianity: by assuming that "God is love," that he is absolutely good, this religion tends to project totally his dark side in an opposite principle and to make it a kind of anti-God (even if Satan remains under the sway of God).

This dualist or Gnostic tendency, which crosses the whole history of Christianity, is not quite foreign to Jewish tradition, as we can see in the passage of the Talmud which I quoted. This text indeed projects on Abraham's story a scheme forged earlier in the Book of Job: it is to answer to the challenge of the Devil that God would have decided to test Abraham. But this theodicy succeeds in saving God's goodness only by limiting his omnipotence and by breaking his unity. As with all the Gnostic "explanations" of evil, it only removes the difficulty. The problem arises then in knowing why God could be tempted by his Opponent, and why he allows the Devil to test so cruelly Job, Abraham, and the multitudes of humbled and tortured victims of human history. A God who agrees so easily on evil, a God who seems the passive accomplice of Satan, does he not have in himself something satanic? This could confirm what R. Caillois has defined as "the essential movement of the dialectic of the sacred": "any power which represents it tends to break up: its first ambiguity is resolved into conflicting elements [...]. But hardly these poles arose from the distension of this ambiguity, that they provoke each from their part, precisely as they possess the character of sacred, these same ambivalent reactions which had made them isolate one from the other one."[3] So the initial ambiguity of the God of Israel reappears in both opposite principles which result from the split. We know that the Evil One "sometimes appears as an Angel of Light"—but if the Devil keeps the trace of his divine origin, on the contrary God often behaves as a devilish

---

[3] Roger Caillois, *L'homme et le sacré* (Paris, Gallimard, 1939, re-edited 1988), 48; *Man and the Sacred*, translation Meyer Barash (Urbana: University of Illinois Press, 2001).

Tempter. A dialectic which could be illustrated by the tragic encounter of the Inquisitor and the witch: while her executioner tortures her in the name of a God of goodness and love, the witch invokes the sombre figure of Satan as a principle of revolt and freedom….

Abraham's paradox so locks us into apparently insuperable aporias. If we try to exonerate God by considering the trial of Abraham as the punishment of a sin, we make of God a merciless torturer and we justify a priori the worst injustices of human history. If we assert that God requires the sacrifice of his son to test his faith, such a perverse God is no better than the Devil. But if we refuse to accept that, if we attribute to the call a diabolic origin, we derive then towards a Gnostic dualism, and we still do not understand how God can authorize the Devil to tempt Abraham…. Is there any possibility of leaving the aporia, of asserting the divine origin of the call without demonizing the God of Abraham, or of maintaining the initial ambiguity of God without cleaving his attributes? To answer these questions, it is necessary to come back to the letter of the text. It would be indeed possible that its successive translations have occasioned a deep misunderstanding of its meaning. What does God ask exactly of Abraham? Does God ask Abraham to lead his son to Mount Moriah in order to "offer him in 'olah"? Never in this passage do we find the term qorban, which means a ritual sacrifice. The Hebrew word 'olah does not hint at the killing of a victim: it means literally "rise." We thus deform the text when we translate this term to mean "burnt offering," as in all of the English translations, or to "holocauste," as in most of the French ones. The only French translation which follows the Hebrew, that of Chouraqui, transcribes the term into the French "fais-le monter en montée" ("make him rise in a rise"). To translate the expression into German, Buber and Rosenzweig forged the term Darhöhung which means at the same time "exposure" and "elevation" (in the sense of a spiritual experiment). These translators remained faithful to the Jewish tradition, at least to the traditional interpretations which insist on the non-sacrificial meaning of this narrative. Indeed, in the midrash (or rabbinical comment) called Genesis Rabbah, God declares: "I have never asked to Abraham to immolate his son." And Rashi, the great medieval commentator, specifies: "He did not say to Abraham: 'immolate him', because the Holy One, blessed is He, did not want that he slaughters him, but only that he makes him rise on the mountain as an offering. And after he would have made him rise, He would say to him: 'Make him come down!'"

Nevertheless, we should note that the word *'olah* appears very often in the other books of the Torah, for instance in *Leviticus,* where it obviously has the meaning of a "burnt offering." More precisely, it is a *total* sacrifice by the fire, a "holocaust," where the animal victim is completely burned in the offering to God. But nothing proves that this word has the same meaning in Abraham's story. So, the order given to Abraham can have a sacrificial sense or a very different one, and nothing in the context allows us to decide. The divine order seems essentially equivocal, as were the Greek oracles, and its ambiguous character reveals an ambiguity of God himself. Abraham decides, however; he chooses without hesitating the sacrificial meaning. Offered to various interpretations, the call reveals here the secret desire of the addressee. It reveals Abraham's desire of murder, a desire which he refuses to assume, which he projects onto the Other, in the divine message. It is of course necessary to resist any temptation to "psycho-analyse" Abraham, by deciphering his unconscious desire. At least, this narrative teaches us which conception Abraham has of God. By inter-preting the call in such a way, he shows us that he remains captive in a mortiferous relation to the divine. He imagines God as a tyrant who denies his own Promise and requires a holocaust, an absolute sacrifice, a total gift without sharing. We have heard of this fierce god, who demands the life of the firstborn sons: his worship was celebrated by the heathen tribes of Canaan. His name was Baal or Moloch, and the Torah never ceased in denouncing his cult as an abomination. When he gets ready to sacrifice Isaac, Abraham proves that he did not really break with idolatry, that he still confuses God with Moloch.

What is an idol? A god "made by man's hand," a human, or a too human representation of God? Any idolatry is an alienating projection, an image of myself projected onto the plan of the Other and which appears to me *as if* it was coming from the Other. Marion is right to define the idol as an "invisible mirror." When the human glance stretches out towards the divine, the idol is this visible figure which stops the glance by reflecting it, by sending it back to it its origin: "the idol masks the mirror because it fulfils the glance [...]. Because it offers to the glance its first visible, the idol stays as an invisible mirror."[4] It is for that reason that the idol "goes

[4] Jean-Luc Marion, *Dieu sans l'être* (Paris: Chicago: Fayard, 1982), 21 and 37; *God without Being,* translation Thomas A. Carlson (University of Chicago Press, 1995).

towards its twilight, because in its dawn it already reflects only a foreign brightness." It is also for that reason, let us add, that every idol is sacrificial (including the modern idols of politics and of spectacle...). The projection which constitutes my idol is an alienating identification, a primordial sacrifice of myself: it is my flesh, my life which I illusively transfer to my image in the mirror; and the idol will not stop requiring new sacrifices. Idolatry is not a false religion which it would be possible to set against the true one, as Marion considers possible to oppose the falsity of the idol and the icon as "true image" of the Invisible. For any icon can become an idol. The idolatry, or rather the *idolization,* is one of the most originary modes of my relation to the Other. It happens on this surface of projection, this invisible screen where I project my own phantasms, which disfigure the face of the Other and forbid me any access to the Other. Nobody said it better than Augustine: the adorers of images "see a mirror, but they stop there: they do not see through the mirror the One who must be seen through the mirror; so, they do not see that this mirror which they see is a mirror, in other words an image."[5] If I want to discover the Other in truth, I shall have to go through the idol, which means at first to recognize it as a false image of myself.

What is at stake in Isaac's binding becomes clearer: in its ambiguity, the biblical text summons us to choose, to decide between an idolatrous and sacrificial representation of the divine and another, alternative, conception. Who is the God of Abraham? Once more, the letter of the text gives us a decisive indication. At the beginning of the episode, when it is said that "God did test Abraham" the Hebrew name for God is *Elohim.* Then, at the climax of the story, when Abraham is on the verge of killing Isaac, the call which stops his hand is not from *Elohim* but from the Holy Name, the unpronounceable name of God: YHWH (translated in English by the periphrasis *the Lord*). How should this change of name be interpreted? Some scholars choose to classify the texts of the Torah according to the various names given to God: these would then belong to different sources which would have been later collected in a unique text. In this passage, the change of the divine name intervenes however in the very core of the narrative, when the sacrificial order is evicted by the prohibition of murder,

---

[5] Augustines, *De Trinitate,* II-24; *On Trinity,* translation Steven McKennaz (Cambridge: Cambridge University Press, 2002).

and this caesura gives all its impact to the narrative. It is possible to consider it as a first revelation of this unspeakable "Name" which will later be revealed to Moses atop Mount Sinai. A still indirect revelation, because it is not revealed to Abraham, but only to the reader —but it is however a true revelation, where is unmasked another dimension of the divine. For the Jewish tradition, each of his names reveals one of God's faces: if *Elohim* is the name of his "attribute of rigour," his "attribute of mercy" is called YHWH. According to the *midrash Exodus Rabbah,* "the Holy One, blessed is He, says to Moses: 'is it my name which you want to know? My name is according to my works [...]. When I judge creatures, my name is *Elohim.* When I suspend the sentence, my name is *El Shaddaï.* When I am merciful to the world, my name is YHWH.'" But what is the "rigour," what is the "justice" of a god who requires a holocaust? We have to approach otherwise the difference of the divine names. *Elohim,* which has the grammatical shape of the plural, is a common name: it is the generic name of the divinity, but also that which indicates in the Bible the *heathen ones.* It derives probably from the root *alah,* which means "to adore." It is so the name of the undifferentiated divine, of all the entities which men can adore. At this level, no demarcation is possible still between the sacred and the holy, between the idol and the invisible Other. According to some other authors *El,* or *Elohim,* comes from a Semitic radical meaning *Power,* creative and procreative strength, which is found, too, in the name of the ram, *eyl* (and, several centuries later, in the name of the God of Islam). He is sometimes called *El Shaddaï,* the Lord of the Mountain, the High and Almighty God, or maybe the Destroyer (from the root *shadad* which designates the power to master and destroy).

To these cosmic attributes of the divine, these symbols of a powerful strength which the God of Israel shares with Baal ("the Lord") and Moloch ("the King"), or even Zeus ("the Bright"), opposes the name YHWH. Here, we do not have to deal any more with a common name, but with a proper, absolutely idiomatic one, which has to remain for that reason secret, unpronounceable, except in the most intimate relation which binds him to who invokes him. Who is thus YHWH, and in whom does this name distinguish itself from those of the idols? Just before revealing to Moses his unspeakable Name, YHWH expresses this enigmatic sentence: "*Ehyeh asher ehyeh.*" Instead of reading it as an ontological thesis ("I am the One who is," "I am the Being itself") as did the mainstream of Christian theology, the Jewish tradition has always understood it as the assertion of a *being-with.*

According to Rashi, God announces to Moses that *"I shall be with you* in this distress *as I shall be* with your people in all distresses to come." So, the unspeakable Name does not appear as the universal attribute of a cosmic power, but in a singular relation between one I and another I, as the certitude of a support, the promise of a community. He does not appear as the almighty Master who requires an absolute obedience, but as the one who frees from servitude ("It is me, YHWH, your *Elohim,* who made you escape out of Egypt, out of the house of slavery"). He does not fill up the glance by showing the glorious image of a First Visible, but he forbids on the contrary the cult of images and any attempt to represent the divine in the visible. Finally, far from requiring of his believers a total sacrifice, he is the one who forbids murder and refuses holocausts.[6] The Jewish tradition has tried to bind the first five commandments to the five following ones: so, the first one, the affirmation of the divine name YHWH, is directly connected with the prohibition of murder. As says a *midrash* (*Mekhilta haKodesh*), "On one of the tables of Law was written: 'It is me, YHWH' and on the other one: 'Thou shalt not commit murder'—so the Torah teaches that who spreads the blood strikes the image of God." We understand henceforth why the call to holocaust was coming from *Elohim*; whereas the second call, which orders not to kill Isaac, is the call of YHWH.

What is the relation between these two divine names? Is it only two manners of naming the same God as suggests the expression "I am YHWH, your *Elohim*"? Or would one of these two names be *more-true,* closer to God's truth than the other? In his *Philosophy of Revelation,* Schelling analyzes the story of Abraham and the change of divine names. According to him, *Elohim* opposes to YHWH as the "still indistinct," non-revealed God to the "differentiated God," who reveals himself by being named. But this revelation is not immediate: it supposes a dark ground against which God strives to come to the light. So, the true God can appear only through that primordial obscure God from whom he is inseparable. "The true God, writes Schelling, is only the one who appears and he thus presupposes continuously *Elohim* as the substratum, the medium of his apparition."[7]

---

[6] Cf. Isaiah 1, 11–16: "'The multitude of your sacrifices, what are they to me?' says YHWH. 'I have more than enough of burnt offerings [...]. They have become a burden to me [...]. Your hands are full of blood; wash and make yourselves clean. Take your evil deeds out of my sight!'"

[7] F.W.J. Schelling, *Philosophy of Revelation,* 29th lesson, SW, t. XIV, 123.

There would be thus an inner differentiation, an ambiguity of God which belongs to the very process of his Revelation. Is it identical to the fundamental ambiguity of the sacred, to its auto-differentiation between the opposed poles of purity and impurity? This ambivalence, however, is inherent to the sphere of the sacred; while the duality of *Elohim* and YHWH would make us pass from the sacred to the holy, from the sacrificial idol to the God beyond any image or idol. However, by reducing *Elohim* to an idol, do we not risk breaking the unity of the God of Abraham and Moses?

There is a character in the narrative about whom we have not yet spoken, and which will help us to better understand the relation between the two divine names. It is the ram which Abraham sacrifices (but to which God?) instead of his son. We know that the Hebrew name of the ram, symbol of strength, and of phallic power, has the same root as *El-Elohim*. By sacrificing the ram, would it be *Elohim* himself whom Abraham immolates? This is the hypothesis which Lacan defends. His argument is based on the Freudian theory of the murder of the primordial father. According to Freud, the animal-totem worshipped and ritually sacrificed by the clan is a substitute for the father of the primitive horde, who would have been murdered by his sons. The gods of archaic religions, including the God of the ancient Hebrews, would be sublimatory representations of this despotic *Urvater*. This hypothesis helps us to understand why every idol demands sacrifices: the idol is the god-totem, substitute for and image of the murdered Father. By offering victims to him, the sons try to allay his anger, that is to say their own culpability, and they repeat infinitely on new victims the initial murder. To this sacrificial religion, based on anxiety and culpability, Freud sets the purely ethical cult of the Egyptian God *Aton*, which Moses would have vainly tried to impose on the tribes of Israel. It is this forgotten figure of the Father which would have later come back to constitute, under the name of YHWH, the God of Jewish monotheism. Behind the duality of the divine names, Freud distinguishes two different sources of religion, two versions of the Father. Lacan extends this analysis by distinguishing the imaginary and the symbolic Father: the Œdipian rival, who is the castrating and incestuous *Urvater* of the horde, and the signifier of the Name of the Father, warrant of a symbolic Law which forbids incest and murder. He reinterprets in this context Abraham's story.[8] If the ram "rushes towards the place of the sacrifice," it is because it is a metaphor of the imaginary Father, of the fierce *Urvater* who "comes to greedily raven" Isaac's blood and flesh. But "the One whose name is unpronounceable designates him for the sacrifice" instead of Isaac. It is indeed the animal-totem of his people, its *Elohim,* that Abraham offers in sacrifice after having heard the call of YHWH. Here, continues Lacan, "is marked a sharp demarcation between God's enjoyment (*la jouissance de Dieu*) and what is, about him, designated by a tradition as desire." Instead of sacrificing his son to God's cruel enjoyment, Abraham sacrifices the God of enjoyment in the name of another version of the Father, what opens to him the way to the truth of his desire as structured by the Law. God's ambiguity would take root in the radical ambiguity of the Father, who is at once structuring and traumatic, principle of subjectivation and of derangement. Here all the efforts of the psychoanalyst consists in cutting through this ambiguity.

It is necessary to take time to question this Lacanian interpretation of the *Aqedah*: of this gesture where Abraham, playing God against God—or the Father against the Father—sacrifices a sacrificial idol in the name of a God who proscribes sacrifice. This means, paradoxically, protecting the structure of sacrifice (and thus of the idol) in the very movement which would have to surmount it…. When he separates the two poles of the paternal function, when he distinguishes the "God of truth" from the "God-totem," the "God-symptom" of religious neurosis, does Lacan not, despite everything, try to protect the Father? That is to protect God's place (but which God?) in the field of psychoanalysis. Does he not return then below the Freudian criticism of religion? Between the two modes or the two sources of religion, could one of them reveal to us the truth of any religious illusion, of *its own* illusion? Is the paternal function capable of bearing without getting rid of such antagonistic versions of the Father? Finally, by transferring the ambiguity of the divine to that of the Father, does Lacan not content himself with removing the aporia, just as Levinas did by transferring the ambiguity of God to the face of the Other Man? So many questions which I shall not claim to have answered here. I shall have to content myself, to conclude, by returning one last time to the Hebrew text: to this Mount Moriah where the

---

[8] In his interrupted seminar on *The Names of the Father* (1964). See also, about this topic, the remarkable book of Francois Balmes *La nom, la loi, la voix* (Paris: Eres, 1997).

unspeakable Name is given to hear. It is so that the Jewish tradition has understood this word: *mori-yah*, literally, "vision of Yah," that is to say of YHWH, whose Name is given here, even before his messenger namely addresses Abraham. The *vision of YHWH*: an expression which is itself ambiguous, according to both senses of the genitive. It could indicate the place of the interrupted sacrifice as that where *YHWH sees* (but what does he see there? the truth of Abraham's desire? that of his own desire?), and also as the enigmatic place where the invisible YHWH would give himself *to be seen*. In any case, "Moriah" would be the secret signature which inscribes in the narrative the revelation of the Name and enjoins us, in an infinite reading, to decipher it.

You Shall not Commit Murder
The Ambiguity of God and the Character of Moral Responsibility

ELENA NAMLI

Jacob Rogozinski's very insightful reflection on the issue of the ambiguity of God offers us an opportunity once more to contemplate the biblical narrative of the "sacrifice of Abraham" or "the binding of Isaac." I appreciate especially the comparative approach within the article. Working with a number of narrative contexts and emphasizing the different names of God and his human counterparts, Rogozinski points out the importance of traditional readings of the Bible, as well as their somewhat risky self-evidence.

As an ethicist and theologian, I would like to elaborate on one feature of the ambiguity addressed by Rogozinski. I hope I do not over-interpret his argumentation by claiming that one crucial dimension of the ambiguity at stake is that it is of a radically practical character. This ambiguity is not about the theoretical (speculative) concept of God; it is about God who relates himself to a human being and about a human being making a volitional decision, a decision about how to act (before God). Call it faith, as in the case of Abraham, call it despair, as in the case of Job (or Isaac), or call it rejection, as in the case of Ivan Karamazov "returning his ticket to God," but in each case it is a matter of engaged and practical ambiguity. I believe that Kierkegaard and Levinas, as well as Kant, are useful here due to their recognition and clear articulation of this practical character of the ambiguity of God, ambiguity in a discourse of the act, not just of speculation.

For example, Kierkegaard's idea of the suspension of morality, upon which Rogozinski touches in his article, is productive because the suspension is not a speculative, theodicy-like justification of God approving or even expecting an immoral act (such as murder in the story of Abraham and Isaac). Instead, it is a human being who is the subject of the suspension. The suspension of Kierkegaard becomes meaningful only when a human being takes morality very seriously and then confronts a situation where God demands or seems to demand an immoral act.

In the heritage of Levinas, we can find a suspension of the religious into morality.[1] While Kierkegaard claims that faith suspends morality, Levinas seems to hold that a radically responsible moral position transcends faith, or at least the faith understood as human beings' submission to God's legislative power. To cite Merold Westphal:

> The ethical is the teleological suspension of the religious. One advantage of this formula is that by appearing to be exactly the opposite movement to the one Kierkegaard presents, it invites comparison with the nineteenth century's most powerful critic of the philosophical reduction of the other to the same […] A teleological suspension is not a reduction. It does not say that X is nothing but Y. It is rather an *Aufhebung*. It says that X can only be properly understood in relation to Y […] Thus a teleological suspension does not eliminate; it relativizes. The object of a teleological suspension is negated in its claim to autonomy, to self-sufficiency and completeness […][2]

It is of importance here that the ambiguity of God does not disappear, but becomes the very condition of such a suspension. I agree with Rogozinski that it is of crucial significance to keep the ambiguity of God alive, and not to rationalise it by transferring God's ambiguity into some other sphere, or by projecting it onto someone else. Not least through his use of Jewish traditions which focus on the different names of God in the story of Abraham and Isaac, Rogozinski elaborates on the possibility of maintaining focus on the ambiguity of God himself. I would like to challenge the approach of the article on two points, however. The first point is that of morality understood in terms of divine commandments, and the other is Rogozinski's critique of Levinas.

If I understand correctly, Rogozinski describes Abraham's choice in terms of the morality of God's commandments. Rogozinski states in his

---

[1] Merold Westphal, "Levinas's Teleological Suspension of the Religious" in *Ethics as First Philosophy,* ed. Adriaan Peperzak (New York and London: Routledge, 1995), 151–160.
[2] Ibid., 153.

article that "[…] the ethics of the three monotheisms is grounded on the Revelation of the Ten Commandments." The question then arises of how Abraham, who knew the commandment "you shall not commit murder," must respond to God's command "you shall kill your son." I appreciate Rogozinski's comparison, in analysing the story of Abraham and Isaac, with the story of Sodom. Why did Abraham oppose himself to God in the story of Sodom? Why did he obey God when it came to Isaac? Was this the same God? Was this the same Abraham? Was this the same morality? At least one important difference appears within the comparison. In the story of Sodom, it is God who was going to punish and sacrifice, while Abraham raised the issue of justice with his God. In the story about Isaac, Abraham was asked to sacrifice a part of himself, his only son, the future of his people. There are therefore two different subjects of morally judgeable acts in these two stories: God in one and Abraham in the other. This circumstance can in fact function as an explanation of the different behaviour of Abraham and even of God. If we assume that Abraham could have seen Isaac as a part of himself rather than a particular individual, another difference with the story of Sodom appears. In that narrative, the object of Abraham's moral concern was the stranger. My point is, therefore, that it is debatable whether the story of the binding of Isaac is a story of justice in the first place. But if it is, how should we interpret it? God, or someone who may be God, commands Abraham to kill. God (assuming it is the same God) had previously prohibited killing. How should Abraham decide?

According to my interpretation of the dilemma of Abraham, a choice between morality and God is not a choice between two different commandments. If we ground morality in the commandments of God, all ambiguity can be eliminated. We may be justified in simply taking the last given commandment and letting it override the earlier one. This is the well-known model within different traditions of religious and secular law. It has been rightly criticised due to the risk of the replacement of law and morality by the very power of the legislator. A lot of socially constructive criticism of religion is built upon the rejection of the problematic idea of God's unbounded will as the main source of morality. If the will of the divine lawgiver is the only source of morality, then it is difficult to prescribe moral responsibility to human beings. Sometimes it has been argued that in the context of the Old Testament, the divine commandment theory must be seen as the very rationale of religious ethics. Rogozinski seems to join this tradition. However, there are biblical scholars who are strongly opposed to this interpretation. John Barton is one of those who maintain that the dimension of the divine commandment is only one among a number of ethical approaches in the Old Testament.[3] He suggests that within the Old Testament, God's commandment is not seen as the only source of morality. I believe it is possible to extend this argument and claim that the Old Testament God is not the only source of moral law; he is rather a counterpart within it, which is why he listens to his prophets, at least sometimes.

Levinas saw this clearly. He was not disturbed by God's omnipotence in relation to moral law, proclaiming instead that human beings share all moral responsibility. God's law is not a complete set of commandments, but a result of dynamic relations with other persons. That is why I do not agree with Professor Rogozinski when he suggests that Levinas plays down the ambiguity of God by transferring it onto the face of the Other Man. The ambiguity of God's commandment to Abraham is still present, but its practical character is of another kind. It is not only a question of God commanding differently; it is a question of morality, which is understood radically and relationally. If God is the only source of morality, then the problem of evil is about God. How is it possible to remain faithful to God who creates an unjust world and who seems to expect human beings to commit unjust acts? Ivan in Dostoevsky's *The Brothers Karamazov* summarises very effectively this kind of critique of every traditional theodicy. Ivan rejects the unjust world and returns his ticket.[4] But if morality is relational, then the binding of Isaac is still Abraham's choice, and Ivan Karamazov is not justified in his decision to return the ticket.

According to Levinas, the law, both legal and moral, is relational and includes the personal responsibility of all parties. God's law is not an exception, and it always demands active positioning on the part of the human being. Standing before God entails the expectation that the human being will obey the law. At the same time, she must co-create the law in the very moment of her moral decision. In Levinas's own words, "Jewish wisdom teaches that He Who created and Who supports the whole universe cannot support or pardon the crime that man commits against man. [...] Judaism

---

[3] John Barton, *Understanding Old Testament Ethics. Approaches and Explorations* (Louisvelle: Westminster John Knox Press, 2003), 15–30.

[4] Fyodor Dostoevsky, *The Brothers Karamazov*, translation Richard Pevear and Larissa Volokhonsky (New York: Farrar, Straus and Giroux, 1990), 244–246.

believes in this regeneration of man without the intervention of extra human factors other than the consciousness of the Good, and the Law."[5]

Contrary to Rogozinski, I believe that this very troublesome position of human beings does not play down the ambiguity of God. God's ambiguity is still present, but it does not justify human beings in resigning from moral responsibility. Every confrontation with a God who violates justice calls for an active response on the part of human beings. There is actually one thing which is played down in Levinas, and that is God's omnipotence, but neither Levinas nor Dostoevsky regarded omnipotence as something God could not sacrifice.

---

[5] Emmanuel Levinas, *Difficult Freedom. Essays on Judaism*, translation Sean Hand (Baltimore: The Johns Hopkins University Press, 1990), 20.

Ambiguities of Immanence Between Stanislas Breton and Louis Althusser (or, Why an Apostle Recycles as an Exemplar of Materialist Subjectivity)

WARD BLANTON[1]

Immanence, an Apostle, and Some Paradoxes of Paul's 'Return'

Of what is it a symptom that an ancient mystical apocalypticist, the self-appointed "apostle of Jesus Christ," returns in our time as a crucial indication of a self-consciously *materialist* philosophy or as a philosophy, precisely, *of the profane*? There is an intellectual perplexity evoked by these apparent cases of mistaken identity that has yet to play itself out in a re-working of genealogies of philosophy and biblical interpretation that might really understand it. Why does the ancient apostle Paul incite contemporary philosophers to name him as an exemplary case of a materialist philosophy

[1] I would like to thank the British Academy for funding my project, 'Of political and mystical bodies: St. Paul in the archive of Stanislas Breton', allowing me to spend the summer of 2008 in the Breton archive at the Catholic Institute in Paris. I have been lucky enough to present aspects of my thinking about Breton, Paul, and Althusser at conferences at the University of Amsterdam (Death and Beyond), the University of Copenhagen (Religion and Political Thought), the University of Oslo (Jesus in a Period of Cultural Complexity), the Van Leer Institute in Jerusalem (The Theological Turn: Scripture and Contemporary Philosophy), Södertörn University in Stockholm (The Ambiguity of the Sacred: Phenomenological Approaches to the Constitution of Community in Religion, Politics and Aesthetics), and the University of Glasgow (Religion and Public Life Colloquium), and I am very grateful to organizers of these events. Some of the pieces of this essay occur in substantially revised form in Ward Blanton, "Dispossessed Life: Introduction to Breton's Paul" in Stanislas Breton, *Saint Paul* (Insurrections: Critical Studies in Religion, Politics, Culture), translation Joseph Ballan (New York: Columbia University Press, 2010).

of the event (Alain Badiou, Slavoj Žižek) or a political philosophy of *the profane* (Giorgio Agamben)?

If we are witnessing today a short-circuiting of distinctions between the 'religious' and the 'secular'—and how else would we understand the phenomenon of Paul returning as the guarantor of an effort to think, to ground a contemporary philosophical materialism—then it is not merely coincidental that Paul has reappeared as a particularly forceful index of this scrambling of received codes. As a *topos* within modern philosophical traditions, for example, Paul has functioned as a very ambiguous border-figure between these two territories. Jean-Michel Rey articulates some of the issues best when he entitles his excellent book about Paul as a peculiar political figure within modern European literature, *Paul ou les ambiguités.*[2] Rey's portrayal of Paulinism against the backdrop of Herman Melville's exploration of the ambiguity of the sacred in *Pierre or the Ambiguities* (1852) seems particularly apt, as Rey's book makes clear. The real forceful-ness of Rey's exploration of generally forgotten strands of Paulinism within modern literary and even revolutionary texts emerges, after all, in its capacity to show how "Paul" has come to occupy the site of several essential and interrelated aporiae within the self-definition of modern European culture. Shall one read Paulinism as faithful to or betraying its own cultural, religious, or ethnic heritage, and, in any case, which cultural option would one tend to valorize, and which would one tend to denigrate? Are the mythologized cultural heroes of European literature those who preserve or preservingly reinvent their own cultural tradition or those brash enough to subvert it? Closely related to this stock of questions (which Rey explores in many pithy chapters), should we read Paul as the consummate spokes-person for the permanency of the religious or a proclaimer of religion's end and overcoming? And, why, in the European philosophico-political trad-ition, is *that* striking ambiguity so perennial, so perennial that Derrida will eventually refer to it as a "little machine" in its automaticity, as if religion is here built to 'return' in just that moment when it is overcome and left behind?[3] To add only one more (repetitively) ambiguous Pauline scenario,

---

[2] Jean-Michel Rey, *Paul ou les ambiguities* (penser/rêver)(Paris: Éditions de l'Olivier, 2008).

[3] Jacques Derrida, "Faith and Knowledge: the Two Sources of 'Religion' at the Limits of Reason Alone" in *Religion* (Cultural Memory in the Present), eds. Jacques Derrida and Gianni Vattimo (Stanford, CA: Stanford University Press, 1996), 6, 35.

is Paul's dropping out from hegemonic political categories and the consequent consolidation of an experimental (and originally non-representable) "political" body a useful way to imagine democratic futures—or is this move precisely that form of ultimately otherworldly or utopian non-engagement that will only ever result in disastrous evacuations of recognized, inherited political spaces? Just as the love affair between Pierre and Isabel in Melville's novel remains stranded in an ambiguous (and even undecidable) space (separating inherited European norms and 'new world' innovations, basely incestuous transgression and supreme indications of transcendent love, revelations of the truth of Pierre's cultural inheritance and tragic cases of mistaken identity), Rey invites us to see how Paul the apostle stands in for awkward perennial ambiguities in the self-constitution of modern European culture.

My own work has oriented itself around the way a decidedly modern (and one might say secular) concern, to think in purely immanent terms, has itself repeatedly participated in the resurrection or recycling of Paulinism as, precisely, an exemplary name for immanence. Initially, this repeated, even mechanically reproduced (so Derrida), paradox of modern self-definition is a surprise to witness inasmuch as the effort to think philosophically the death of God has so often become inseparable from a philosophical repetition of Paulinism as an archetypal tableau of the Western religious tradition. Surprising or not, however, the repetition or refrain appears with regularity. We must not forget, for example, the way Spinoza's incorporation of the otherworldly divine into the world (the famous *deus sive natura*) in his *Theologico-Political Treatise* so frequently relies on moments of identification with a (Stoicized) voice of the apostle, as if the critique of transcendence and the criticisms of "the dead letter" had become the same thing. As Spinoza repeated, "his doctrine was the same as ours."[4] Hegel repeats the gesture when he presents his philosophy as a

---

[4] Cf. Benedict de Spinoza, *A Theologico-Political Treatise* (New York: Dover, 1951), 40, 53, 58f., 65, 67f., 80, 158, 163f., 176, 198, 201. For more recent readings comparing Paul and Roman Stoicism, see Emma Wasserman, *Death of the Soul in Romans 7: Sin, Death, and the Law in Hellenistic Moral Psychology* (Tübingen: Mohr Siebeck, 2008); Troels Engberg-Pedersen, *Paul and the Stoics* (Louisville, KY: Westminster John Knox, 2000); and *Cosmology and the Self in the Apostle Paul: the Material Spirit*. Oxford, UK: Oxford University Press, 2010); Runar Thorsteinsson, *Roman Christianity and Roman Stoicism: a Comparative Study of Ancient Morality* (Oxford, UK: Oxford University Press, 2010);

Paulinist mode of thinking immanent to the risky openness of being as such, other modes of thinking (from the measured limits of Kant's critical reason to the merely empirical and reconstructive efforts of the biblical historian) as non-Pauline legalism and subservience.[5] Likewise, I show in *Displacing Christian Origins* some of the ways Martin Heidegger's early work was not simply 'influenced' or 'oriented' by his understanding of early Christian experience. Rather, on several occasions in his early work it is in the same moment as Heidegger uncovers *phenomenological immanence* that he presents *himself* as a kind of *Paulus redivivus*. In just this respect, however, we may say that Heidegger's resurrection of the apostle (at the moment of overcoming static metaphysical or religious transcendence) is the rule rather than the exception in a long tradition of modern political and philosophical thought that founded itself on the critique and over-coming of heteronomous or external limits and commands.

It is within such a lineage that I want to consider how another effort to think immanence conjures a return of the apostle. Here I want to stage an encounter between Stanislas Breton's philosophical Paulinism and aspects of Louis Althusser's materialist models of ideology and the freedom of revolution. Breton was a lifelong friend and intellectual ally of this great Marxist thinker, and staging an encounter between the Paul of one and the "aleatory materialism" of the other allows us to understand better what at first appeared to be a perplexing confusion of categories in more recent efforts to think philosophically materialist notions of the subject by way of an ancient apostle. These wires, so to speak, have been provocatively short-circuited before.

---

and Niko Huttunen, *Paul and Epictetus on Law: a Comparison* (London: T&T Clark, 2009).

[5] Here the intensely Augustinian and Lutheran tale of Paul as the "origin of Christianity," with its structurally necessary denigration of Judaism as both another religion and merely "legalistic," becomes more apparent. This formally or structurally generated anti-Semitism haunts the story of Paulinism from Hegel well into the 20th century and even recent philosophical readings of Paul do not always recog-nize how to escape from it. I explore some of these aspects of the various Paulinisms of Hegel in the first two chapters of *Displacing Christian Origins: Philosophy, Secularity, and the New Testament*.

Breton as Philosophical Reader of Paulinism

As we would expect, Breton's philosophical encounter with Paul is one that eludes strict historical method.[6] When Breton speaks of Paul and allegory, for example, the philosopher uses two texts (from Ephesians and Hebrews respectively) which are, he fully acknowledges, not generally imagined by contemporary biblical scholars to be written by Paul himself.[7] Nevertheless, he invites, can they not "seem to form a kind of preface to any introduction to the allegorical method"?[8] Paulinism stands in for a kind of effective history of the Pauline legacy, a shifting, developing, and contested or ruptured legacy that, for all these reasons, affords an archive which, for the thinker, opens up a multiplicity of ter-ritories for expansive conceptual exploration and invention. In this case, for example, Breton's caveats about historical authorship are imme-diately followed by a beautiful discussion of time plunging into eternity, of the Christ of Ephesians—caught up in such a plunge of the contingently historical into the permanency of the structural—becoming the "copula of the universe," the mediating hinge between subject and predicates in a rhapsodic movement of cosmic reconciliation of (in the words of the letter to the Ephesians) of the "all in all." Breton's philosophical reading of this

---

[6] For those who are not familiar with contemporary historical research on Paul, it may be useful to recommend three books that I find to be some of the most important touchstones for a historical understanding of the figure. For specific readings of Pauline texts, I find unsurpassed the work of Dale B. Martin, *The Corinthian Body* (New Haven: Yale University Press, 1999); and Stanley Stowers, *Rereading Romans* (New Haven: Yale University Press, 1997). For more general and introductory comments, I recommend E. P. Sanders, *Paul: A Very Short Introduction* (Oxford/New York: Oxford University Press, 2001); and David Horrell, *An Introduction to the Study of Paul* (London/New York: Continuum, 2000).

[7] The distinction between authentic and inauthentic letters of Paul has been a set piece of university discourse about this literature for almost two centuries, in fact. For general discussion, see the introductions of Sanders or Horrell. For a more general historical framework explaining the appearance of pseudepigraphic productions in the Pauline tradition, see the reconstruction of John Dominic Crossan and Jonathan Reed, *In Search of Paul: How Jesus's Apostle Opposed Rome's Empire with God's Kingdom* (San Francisco: Harper, 2004).

[8] Joseph Ballan's excellent English translation of this text has not yet gone to press, forthcoming as Stanislas Breton, *Saint Paul*, Insurrections: Critical Studies in Religion, Politics, and Culture (New York: Columbia University Press, 2010). Therefore I will include references to the French page numbers of Stanislas Breton, *Saint Paul* (Paris: Presses Universitaires de France, 1988), 28.

passage solicits thought to consider this textual Christ in philosophical modes we might have otherwise missed. Of course, by wiring ancient metaphysical (and, I am quick to note, sometimes anti- or post-metaphysical) axioms into the apocalyptic and mystical world of Paulinist insurgency, metaphysics (as well as the limits of metaphysical reasoning) lights up with a strange new hue as well.

As Breton writes of the Christ of the letter to the Ephesians becoming the copula of a universal philosophical system: it is in the energy of a circuit or "loop-like construction" of action that—once narrative time is plunged into structures of eternity—"mimes ... the aseity of self-sufficiency of the Absolute" (28). Breton is speaking here of the way Ephesians 1.9-12 imagines a teleological movement of divine intention, planning, and effective carrying through of an action to gather into God, by way of a cosmic Christ (Breton's "copula of the universe"), *ta panta* (all things) (28f.). As is typical of him, however, here we see Breton squeezing together mystical and philosophical texts tighter still, forcing each, as it were, to bleed into the other. Compressing his religio-philosophical construction further, Breton adds the final twist: when, he tells us, religious narrative mimics ancient philosophical structure (and vice versa), readers are confronted with a play of gestures in which a tele-ological reading of the structure of the universe explodes into life, precisely, as a "semantic order," as if the "meaning of Being," or the struc-tures of ontology itself, could be read in the forceful imperative of a speech performance like "let there be light!" (30f.)

I am unpacking this moment in Breton's reading as it exemplifies an intensity of interpretive juxtaposition and mutual explication of intellectual traditions that characterizes Breton's Paul book generally. To keep up with Breton, readers must endeavour to be agile, for in forging such connections, quickly and schematically, this philosophical Paulinist takes us from statements of a Pauline disciple (say, the author of Ephesians), back into Paul (Romans), and then out again into Classical Greek philosophy (Aristotle) and its mystical interpreters (Meister Eckhart), finally arriving at a subtle commentary not only on Martin Heidegger ("the meaning of Being") but also on Louis Althusser (for whom emergence into being and subjection to the performative speech act of sovereign power occur simultaneously). To think with the Pauline legacy, Breton's reader finds, is to grapple also with ontologies and theories of power and subjection in which a *being* in the world emerges only *in, with, and through* a yes-saying to a substance best understood in terms of a *performative speech act*—'Let there be light!'—or, as in Louis Althusser's famous example of the policeman addressing someone in the street: 'You there!' When the light switches on, or when that someone turns to the authority to answer, 'You mean me?', then reality starts to appear *as* summoned (in Althusser's terminology, interpellated) by the call that is itself the movement of self-reinforcing power. At Breton's instigation, now listen to an Althusserian depiction of power's revelatory function in the "call" of ideology, this time keeping predestinarian Pauline texts in mind. In an interview with Fernando Navarro, for example, Althusser discussed the issues:

> There is a paradox here. It is as if, when I believe in a notion... I were not the one who recognizes it and, confronted by it, could say: 'That's it, there it is, and it's true.' On the contrary, it is 'as if', when I believe in an idea, it were the idea that dominated me and obliged me to recognize its existence and truth, through its presence. It is 'as if'—the roles having been reversed—it were the idea that interpellated me, in person, and obliged me to recognize its truth. This is how the ideas that make up an ideology impose themselves violently, abruptly, on the 'free consciousness' of men [sic]: *by interpellating* individuals in such a way that they find themselves compelled 'freely' to recognize that these ideas are *true— compelled* to constitute themselves as 'free' 'subjects' who are capable of recognizing the true wherever it is present, and of *saying so*, inwardly or outwardly, in the very form and content of the ideas constitutive of the ideology in question. ...That is the basic mechanism that transforms individuals into subjects. *Individuals are always-already subjects, that is to say, always-already-subject to an ideology* (emphasis added).[9]

As Breton is pointing out so clearly, the basic circuitry of Althusser's construal of subjects as effects of power issuing as a call to individuals is comparable to the surprising Pauline move in Ephesians or Romans 9 to imagine the individuality and qualities of individuals as *effects* or machinations of sovereign power. Breton's reading allows us to feel the rhythms of Althusserian notions of ideology in Paulinist conceptions of pre-destination. By the same token, of course, and perhaps more surpris-ingly, Breton invites us to intuit a form of Pauline sovereignty and Paulinist allegory (with their respective visions of the "aseity" of the divine) in Althusserian notions of ideology. Wiring all these links back into his construction of Paul,

---

[9] See the interview "Philosophy and Marxism" in Louis Althusser, *Philosophy of the Encounter: Later Writings, 1978–87* (London/New York: Verso, 2006), 281.

readers of Paulinist texts of predestination and mysticism are therefore led to the heart of a logic in which, as Meister Eckhart had it, "the being (of things) is the verb by which God speaks all things in speaking to them," or even, "(the creatures) are the adverb of the Verb" (30f.). Ontology shifts entirely into the space of Paulinist predestin-ation and discussions of "calling," part of a larger mode of thinking about the world in which performative speech act, the call and response of power, constitute the world as it is. Paul the apostle now converses with Althusser, the great inventor of an aleatory materialism in which 'ideology' is no longer simple 'false consciousness' (which would imply the existence of a world *without* summoning interpellation) but rather *the mode in which worldhood exists*, namely, as emerging from the practices of interpellated subjects.

As Paul Ricoeur could still lecture in the 1975, it is perhaps surprising in light of some of Althusser's earlier writings to see how Heideggerian his later reworking of materialism seems.[10] Perhaps so! However, we should not miss the way in which, already in earlier statements about ideology like this one, Althusser was fascinated to think the relationship between economic base and superstructure—the former still providing "determination in the last instance" to the latter—in a way that was not merely "descriptive." And with this passing beyond analysis that is mere "description" of a state of affairs, Althusser's thinking begins to be lured away from the noun to the verb (as it were), to the question of the *modes of relation* between these related structures, to an actively and essentially relational sphere in which related structures solicit and respond to one another. And even in these earlier writings this sphere was better accessible to a mode of phenom-enological description than to mechanistic or topological meta-phors. Descriptive modes open up ways of matching effects (Althusser mentions censorious bans on cultural works as an example) to causes (a repressive State apparatus operating to maintain the status quo). But this possibility of matching layers or instances of the self-reproduction of the society is, strictly speaking, distinguishable from the emergence of what Althusser calls "a very special kind of obviousness," that phenomenological space in

---

[10] Paul Ricoeur, *Lectures on Ideology and Utopia* (New York: Columbia University Press, 1986), 115: "[…]Althusser reminds us of Heidegger in the hermeneutic circle, though I doubt he had that at all in mind. (Althusser hardly seems very much Heideggerian; Heidegger must be the worst of all ideologists for someone like Althusser.)" On the contrary, really, in light of Althusser's "aleatory materialism."

which one declares, 'Yes, that's how it is, that's really true!' To say the same thing somewhat differently, this move toward the "special kind of obviousness" inhering in new subjective forms can also be read as part of what Etienne Balibar describes as Althusser's "conceptual break with any expressive causality, the decisive step towards *materialism*," or towards a kind of immanence in relation to the self-reproductive force of the social itself rather than to second order *descriptions* of it.[11] Ironically (given the frequent hand-wringing and criticism about Althusser's panoply of mechanistic, functional, or process metaphors), it is the move away from expressivist hermeneutics (in which ideology would be a symbol of structures appearing or existing elsewhere) that allows Althusser to afford a material density to ideology itself.[12]

In light of Breton's invitation to consider Althusser with Paul, we should note the fundamental sense in which an exploration of the "obviousness of obviousness" is integrally related to Althusser's desire to move from "descriptive theory to theory as such," as if entering into the life of power

---

[11] Warren Montag describes a similar movement in Althusser toward immanent critique and immanent description by showing Althusser's deployment of Spinozist immanence against the *hermeneutical* tradition. I have set up an encounter between Althusser's late aleatory materialism and Breton's Paul in ways that are (genealogically speaking) closely related to Montag's very interesting recent discussions (to my knowledge unpublished except in Spanish) of Spinozistic immanence as a repetition of an Epicurean materialism in "Lucretius Hebraizant: Spinoza's Reading of Ecclesiastes" (cf. Warren Montag, "Lucretius Hebraizant: La lectura de Spinoza del Eclesiastés" in *Spinoza contemporaneo*, eds. Galcerán and Espinoza, Madrid: Tierradenadie ediciones, 2009). See also, Warren Montag, "Spinoza and Althusser Against Hermeneutics: Interpretation or Intervention?" in *The Althusserian Legacy*, eds. E. Ann Kaplan and Michael Sprinkler (London/New York: Verso, 1993), 51–58.

[12] The umbilical link between the Spinozistic making-immanent of a God function and the paradoxical intensification of the question of the call and response of a "revelatory" "encounter" is a theme I will develop at greater length elsewhere. For the moment, I only note the general reduction of causes to effects: "No Cause that precedes its effects is to be found in it [i.e., aleatory materialism], no Principle of morality or theology (as in the whole Aristotelian political tradition: the good and bad forms of government, the degeneration of the good into the bad). One reasons here not in terms of the Necessity of the accomplished fact, but in terms of the contingency of the fact to be accomplished." Louis Althusser, *Philosophy of the Encounter: Later Writings, 1978–87*, 174. I have developed some of the links between secular immanence and the "return" of religion as an analytic form and critical archive in Ward Blanton, "'Reappearance of Paul, "Sick"': Foucault's Biopolitics and the Political Significance of Pasolini's Apostle" in *Journal for Cultural and Religious Theory* (10.2, 2010).

rather than picturing it from the outside. Small wonder that Althusser himself refers to the Paul of Acts:

> As St. Paul admirably put it, it is in the 'Logos', meaning in ideology, that we 'live, move and have our being.' It follows that, for you and for me, the category of the subject is a primary 'obviousness' (obviousnesses are always primary): it is clear that you and I are subjects (free, ethical, etc.). Like all obviousness, including those that make a word 'name a thing' or 'have a meaning' (therefore including the obviousness of the 'transparency' of language), the 'obviousness' that you and I are subjects—and that that does not cause any problems—is an ideological effect, the elementary ideological effect. It is indeed a peculiarity of ideology that it imposes (without appearing to do so, since these are 'obviousnesses') obviousness as obviousness, which we cannot *fail to recognize* and before which we have the inevitable and natural reaction of crying aloud (aloud or in the 'still, small voice of consciousness'): 'That's obvious! That's right! That's true!'[13]

Like Heidegger's efforts in his early *Phenomenology of Religious Life* to think everyday temporality as such apart from extraneous metaphysical models, Althusser also is led back to the religious archive for images able to keep pace with the machinations of immanent, everyday obviousness.

Moreover, it is particularly in the context of *this* juxtaposition of Paul and Althusser that Breton's central reflections on the kenotic, emptying, or hollowing "call" that is a Pauline proclamation of a crucified messiah become significant as a mode of subverting the otherwise always-already effective link between power and subjectivity. In Breton's philosophical appropriation of Paul is the scandalously unsettling, even "stupid" (cf. *mōria* in 1 Cor 1) identification with the crucified messiah that names a potential detachment, unhinging, or bracketing of the "special kind of obviousness" by which our world, or any world, solicits our participation, incites affirmation, thereby becoming what it is. This appropriation of the Pauline *topos* of the crucified, which drove Breton's life-long philosophical engagement with the apostle, participated in Breton's efforts to theorize an unpredictable *gap* or *void* in all knowledge, all identity, and all forms of cultural or political power. By trafficking in this radical Pauline image of stark *dispossession* within the heart of all possessive identity—a messiah dead on an apparatus of imperial control—Breton hoped to make

---

[13] Louis Althusser, "Ideology and the State" in *On Ideology* (London: Verso, 2008), 45f.

way for a philosophical thought that could bore a hole through the completion of all projects of expert knowledge. In this respect, we may say of Breton's *oeuvre* what he liked to say of Paul's, namely, that, *rather* than the certainties of knowledge, his philosophical writing attempted to remain always and ever a testimony to a "founding rupture ('*rupture instauratrice*')" within thought itself.[14]

Founding Rupture: Paulinism and Void-talk[15]

Those accustomed to the usual platitudes about religion or theology being the last hope for modernity's escape from an otherwise soul-searing nihilism will be surprised to see the way Breton finds in the apostle an exemplary thinker of "the nothing," of all those hollows or voidances that creep into or magically appear within otherwise internally coherent structures of thought and cultural practice, all those modes of the "very special kind of obviousness" which makes worldhood and subjects. This category of the irrepressible void, however, was an integral part of Breton's work throughout his career, and it is precisely as a participant in thinking through this category that Paul remained an obsession for the philosopher. Always interested in mathematics and set theory, for example, Breton's early *Theory of Ideologies* orients a thinking of all structures of thought around the way all countable elements within any given ensemble or category must necessarily participate in a kind of zero degree, an "empty part" that is inseparable from "the totality" of the set.[16] The zero degree or empty part is "in the grammar of ensembles an indispensable sign for our operations."[17] Breton sometimes described this null, empty, or zero degree element within the ensemble as a kind of in-difference within the identity of the system, neither integrated inside nor safely outside of the system and yet utterly indispensable, a *sine qua non* of the countable ensemble in its hanging together *as* a system. The "neuter" or "neutral" part in the estab-

---

[14] Stanislas Breton, *La Pensee du Rien* (Kampen: Kok Pharos Publishing, 1992), 113.
[15] Apologies to Rosemary Radford Ruether for playing on the title of her classic *Sexism and God-talk*.
[16] Stanislas Breton, *Théorie des Idéologies* (Paris: Desclée, 1976), 34.
[17] Ibid., 44.

lishment of identity, this nullity forever disturbs all totalizing self-enclosure or self-grounding of identity as such.

In a different context and much later, Breton summarized the same issues as a fundamental problem for any metaphysics oriented around *identity*. Indeed, the problem of the impossible but structurally necessary moment in the construction of identity is described by Breton as an "evil genius" within the system of identity:

> What would be the logical formula for a statement as banal as the following: 'There are French philosophers'? Retranslated into simple language, this equivalence would take the following form: 'a determinate set', described by the quality 'French philosopher', is not empty, or distinguishable from the set 'zero.' Thus one has to pass through zero in order to arrive at an existential judgment. The zero set, however, is defined by the entire number of objects which, not being identical to themselves, can only be contradictory. Ontological difference [between Being and beings] only seems thinkable through this detour which confronts us with sheer nothingness. The impossible becomes a necessary condition. These strange propositions, which I will allow to develop freely here, join the by no means less strange metaphysics that controls the access to Being through its opposition to 'nothing(ness),' which means its opposition to the absolutely absurd.[18]

Significantly, however, it is not simply that Breton reads set theory or that he finds the self-grounding of all countable sets, like "humanity is humanity," to be perennially haunted by the supplementary assertion, "and nothing else."[19] There is in this haunting of or voidance within the ensemble "a minimum of division" in its very identity, and Breton suggests the haunting *sense* of this "minimal" gap in the identity of a given cultural set-up can produce extraordinary effects. There can emerge, for example, an obsessive passion to purify "humanity" as if by way of a violent extension of this imperative to "nothing else," identity becoming resolved only by way of a violent exclusion of what will count as "not" humanity. As Breton describes it, one way to cope with the ineluctable "empty part (*la partie vide*)," the "indispensable void (*la vide indispens-*

---

[18] See the transcript of the 'Alterities' conference in 1986 in which Breton tried to articulate his own more and less metaphysical modes of thinking difference and alterity alongside those of Pierre-Jean Labarrière and Jacques Derrida ("Difference, Relation, Alterity" translation Pierre Colin, *Parallax*, 2004, vol. 10, no. 4, 42–60), 43.

[19] Breton, *Théorie des Idéologies*, 35f.

able)" within every system is to find in it a kind of intolerable "limit" internal to the ensemble (ibid.). Ideology, or simply a represent-able ensemble or cultural set-up, finds within itself an irreparable desire to *pierce through* appearances, the fragile stability of the ensemble's identity, and this in order to encounter this "void" directly. As Breton puts it, this impulse can result in the demand to sacrifice the ensemble itself for the sake of a pure encounter with the excess 'beyond' its limits, and in such instances those within the cultural ensemble may be driven to acts of profound "enthusiasm" in their desire to rid themselves of this minimal voidance within the ensemble, within the heart of their collective project. This "lucid folly" (whose status as either "satanic or divine is of little importance," as Breton liked to say) is itself "incompatible with life" in the sense that the "enthusiasm" to rid oneself of this minimal gap in identity may well drive our lucid fools to a point of intransigence at which point "a diplomacy wearied with youth" may simply "nail them to the cross" (35). Whether or not this "lucid folly" drives one to acts of martyrdom or profoundly violent exclusion, Breton's approach suggests that one is always or structurally liable to the lure of ecstatic, impossible moments.

These last lines already begin to suggest the relevance of Breton's engagement with set theory as a theory of violence for his understanding of Paul. The relevance hinges on the way Breton's *own* way of responding to the structural possibility of voidance is different from reactionary or revolutionary violence (both reactions to the same threat or lure of the directly encounterable void or the void as substratum). Crucially, Breton goes on in his theory of ideologies to propose that the "pale substratum," the void both sustaining and haunting the ensemble "does not exist."[20] This way of reading "nothing" here is critical, as it implies that all efforts to pierce *through* the identity of an ensemble, the appearance of a cultural form, in order to achieve the serenely self-subsisting essence of the beyond, are doomed to failure.[21] There is no direct encounter with the *nihil* for the

---

[20] Breton, *Théorie des Idéologies*, 118.
[21] Much more could be said about these issues in relation to Breton's work, though such discussions would exceed the scope and interests of an introduction. But the rejection of the nothing as a substratum or outside of ideology are crucial and affect rather intimately the occasional critique of Breton as a Hegelian or neo-Platonic philosopher of identity. We should also not miss the way recent critiques of Gilles Deleuze, as neo-Platonic or Scotist thinker of the indifferent One, are answered in the same way: with a rejection of the substantiality or role as substratum of the void. See the excellent

would-be revolutionary or reactionary sacrifice, as neither active nor passive sacrifice can *save* identity—past, present or future—from this haunting void. It is not possible, for example, to *eliminate* the haunting of cultural mode or ensemble by the "nothing else" that lures cultural conservatives to supreme acts of suppressive violence in their efforts to fill the gap that seems constitutively to endanger the given cultural identity. The void into which one may throw threatening terrorists of all sorts is an abyss that can never be filled, as the constitutive *threat* of the negation of an ensemble is a wound that can never be healed. In this respect, Breton's work is very close to the discussions of ideology in Slavoj Žižek, as both imagine that what the limit to identity prohibits—the access this limit also forecloses (to the new, the beyond, the purified, unscathed or saved)—is reflective or *internal* to the system itself.[22] Breton will suggest, therefore, that the martyrological or persecutorial passion of enthusiasm—the obsession with finally solving or grounding the ensemble in question, with finally conjuring it into full presence—is itself merely a form of the "death instinct," a longing for the release of cultural life from its limits, in death or in a way that is (as Breton suggests above) "incompatible with life."

reflections on Deleuze and the future of emancipatory philosophy in Kenneth Surin, *Freedom Not Yet: Liberation and the Next World Order*, New Slant: Religion, Politics, and Ontology (Durham, NC: Duke University Press, 2009), 238f. Nor should we miss that a similar concern not to reify the void as the substratum of the One is a driving concern behind Alain Badiou's critique of Gilles Deleuze, which *plays itself out also as the particular sort of Paulinism* Badiou finds in the ancient apostle. cf. Alain Badiou, *Deleuze: the Clamor of Being*, Theory Out of Bounds (Minneapolis: University of Minnesota Press, 2000); and Badiou's (Paulinist) rejection of a 'fourth' discourse of mysticism about the unspeakable One:

> For Paul, the fourth discourse will remain a mute supplement, enclosing the Other's share in the subject. He refuses to let addressed discourse, which is that of the declaration of faith, justify itself through an unaddressed discourse, whose substance consists in unutterable utterances. ...I believe this to be an important indication, one that concerns every militant of a truth... I shall call 'obscurantist' every discourse that presumes to legitimize itself on the basis of an unaddressed discourse." Alain Badiou, *Saint Paul: the Foundation of Universalism*, Cultural Memory in the Present (Stanford, CA: Stanford University Press, 2003), 52.

[22] In this sense, Breton's discussions of the inconsistent and ontologically ephemeral (yet structurally profound) nature of the "empty part" or "zero" level of ideology are comparable to the later Lacanian discussions of the Real. cf. Žižek's discussion of the two roles of the "real" in Lacan's early and later work in Slavoj Žižek, *The Sublime Object of Ideology* (London/New York: Verso, 1989), 161ff. Zizek's own work, it may be added, has moved toward a more structurally/internally generated model of the real over time (see, e.g., *The Parallax View* Boston: MIT Press, 2006), 25f).

Mad Rhapsodies of the Paulinist God

How then do we cut through ideology, once we read ideology as the very substance of subjectivity and that "very special kind of obviousness" we enjoy so much? Crucially, at pivotal moments in his early discussion of such structural models, Breton's theoretical structures elide themselves into a Paulinist narrative, and this as Breton proceeds with his elucidation of a theory of ideologies. (Of course, to return to my earlier point about the inability of the historical narrative 'Paul' to remain safe against the tides of philosophical thought, this is *also* to say, *vice versa*, that the religious narrative begins to slide into a theory of ensembles and their reliance on a 'zero' level!). Moving somewhat closer to his full disclosure of a *Paulinist* critique of ideology, Breton writes that, within Paulinism, the cross signifies the pale void that renders inoperative the fullness of any ensemble or cultural form, that is, of all ideology *tout court*. In this respect, Breton's emptying or kenotic function of the Paulinist cross functions in a similar way to the ineluctable "remainder" or remnant Giorgio Agamben finds in Paul, a topic that becomes operationalized in Agamben's Paul in the messianic "call" that hollows, renders inoperative, or (following the Paul of 1 Corinthians 7) "as if it were not" (*hōs mē*).[23]

Given these underpinnings, it is no surprise that Breton's Paulinism usually brings with it sharp critiques of triumphalist and repressive Christian institutions and culture, with the philosopher adding on this occasion that the void-function likewise renders inoperative both the all-consuming and self-enriching God of "integrative theologies" and the cultural tectonics of a Christian "hermeneutics" that has repressed "the

---

[23] Compare the majority of Agamben's book on the remainder/remnant (which orients itself not so much on Romans as in 1 Corinthians 7 where the messianic pressuring of temporality forces an activity "as if" one were "not" what one is) to Rudolf Bultmann's earlier (Heideggerian) fascination with the Pauline category, neither boredom nor anxiety exactly but functioning similarly at a quasi-ontological level Giorgio Agamben, *The Time that Remains: a Commentary on the Letter to the Romans* (Stanford, CA: Stanford University Press, 2005); Note the crescendo of Bultmanns famous exposition of Paulinism in Rudolf Bultmann, *Theology of the New Testament* (New York: Scribner's, 1951), v. 1: 351f.. As we seek to establish (generally missed) encounters between disciplines, interests, and temporalities, one should note also the emancipatory exploration of these categories in the work of Vincent Wimbush, *Paul the Worldly Ascetic* (New York: Mercer University Press, 1987).

poverty of its origin."[24] Those who would be faithful to the Paulinist logic of the cross, he asserts, must remain faithful to thinking all beings, and indeed being itself, in a way that is "meontological," that is *not* (*me*-ontological) a science of self-grounding *identity*.[25] With this move from harmonious self-possession to the "founding rupture" (*"rupture instauratrice"*), Breton begins to make clear the ontological revolution or "turning" involved in a Paulinist appropriation of the cross, as well as to make clear how it is that this Paulinism affords an inexhaustible source for the *critique of ideologies*. Ever deferring and subverting the ontological identity that could provide justification or warrant for the triumphalist "evolutions of the city of God" or the legitimizing ideologies of the state, the meontological cross will be for Breton the unsettling thought that is at once a Pauline story of the crucified messiah and also the indication of an immanent, universalizable voidance that plagues all identity. And it is perhaps the indeterminacy of the mutual affectation of this isomorphism that names something essential about reading Paul with the philosophers (47f.).

More should be said about the critical function of Breton's Paul, however. Notice the way Breton's reading of the cross bleeds over into an Althusserian statement about the permanency of an ideological state's 'zero level' of repression and exclusion. Althusser once declared in relation to Heidegger that the zero level of an ideological state is the Heideggerian "there is" of factical being, always already thrown, specified, organized *as* a singular state of affairs which, for this very reason, seems to solicit a *destruktion*, a deconstruction, a revolution.[26] And, just between these

---

[24] Breton, *Théorie des Idéologies*, 47.
[25] Ibid. While it would carry us too far afield to explore the link between the "materialism" of Althusser's "aleatory encounter" and Breton's "meontology." suffice it to say that the crucial link is here, with the thought of contingency (the swerve or clinamen of "aleatory encounter") and Breton's thought of the "crucified" or brutally suppressed messianic function. Both alike provide a ground that disturbs the harmonious (but atomistic) fall of atoms in the void (for Althusser's materialism) or the enjoyment of atomised worldhood and its "special kind of obviousness" in Breton.
[26] Note the way that Althusser is at pains to include Heidegger in his repressed history of materialism, primarily because Althusser sees in Heidegger's *es gibt* or *il y a* of the facticity of everyday life a profound statement about the originary *contingency* from which emerges this everyday. "A philosophy of the *es gibt*, of the 'this is what is given', makes short shrift of all the classic questions about the Origin, and so on. And it 'opens up' a prospect that restores a kind of transcendental contingency of the world, which in turn points to the opening up of Being, the original urge of Being, its 'destining', beyond which there is nothing to seek or think. Thus the world is a 'gift' that we have been given,

echoes, Breton insinuates the Pauline story of the crucified messiah, a kind of permanency of the crucified and a kind of eternity of that moment whereby, through identification with the crucified, the "nothings" would become "something," thus "destroying" the *paradeigmata* of the world that first deprived them of their being in the first place (I am borrowing the Pauline language of 1 Corinthians 1 and Romans 12).[27] Making similar connections, Breton writes:

> At origin, and I have no doubt that it is a question of origin, 'there is' (*il y a*) the judgment of the Cross. This judgment divides humanity in what would be, according to the etymology of *Krisis* translated again by the German *Ur-teil*, a decision-separation: on the one hand, those who exist according to the noble values of wisdom and power; on the other the anonymous and undifferentiated ensemble of those who, by reason of constraint and not of essence, do not accept those values. But Christ [sic. Actually the argument works much better from Breton's beloved 1 Corinthians 1] pronounced himself without equivocation for what does not exist. The God he evokes tolerates no wavering; this God can be spoken of or affirmed through neither classical philosophic categories nor in the traditional attributes discerned by a religion.[28]

One does not encounter the divine precipitate of this crisis, in other words, either by deduction from generalities or from the induction of particulars. Indeed, none of the "justifications," so many niceties, of power's knowledge and wisdom, will lead you to the (as it were, revelatory) encounter, or stabilize you once you are there. What then? This is the encounter open

---

the 'fact of the fact [*fait de fait*]' that we have not chosen, and it 'opens up' before us in the facticity of its contingency, and even beyond this facticity, in what is not merely an observation, but a 'being-in-the-world' that commands all possible meaning." Althusser, *Philosophy of the Encounter: Later Writings, 1978–87*, 170; cf. 190.

[27] I am also echoing this particular language of Paul as an evocation of the language of the "neutral" in Roland Barthes, which also has strong echoes with Breton's lifelong reflections on weakness and void as a paradoxical (and, as both would point out, scandalous) form of power. While the comparisons and the ongoing vivacity of their formulations are a topic for a different context, note the immanent antagonism implied in Barthes' linguistic focus: "...let's recall that the subject of our course, the Neutral, is what baffles the paradigm: the paradigm is the law against which the Neutral rebels..." Roland Barthes, *The Neutral: Lecture Course at the College de France (1977–1978)* (New York: Columbia University Press, 2005), 42. In this respect, Breton shows us what Barthes never says clearly, that Paulinism constitutes a significant part of the archive of the rebellious neutral.

[28] Breton, *The Word and the Cross*, translation Jacquelyn Porter (New York: Fordham University Press, 2002), 54.

only to the partisan, *those who side with the 'nothings'* in a struggle against those wisdoms and powers which constitute themselves on the exclusion of these (now named, particularized, emerging) nothings. Two further aspects of Breton's Paulinist critique of ideology should be pointed out here, as what has said so far may suggest that it is a simple, formal paradox that implies (even as it disavows) a zero level within all cultural acts of counting-as. Worse, such an easy going formalism lends itself in turn to a sense that the paradoxes in view are (just as simply) useful tools available for those already disposed to criticize formations of power. But this is to miss the almost anarchic and free forcefulness of cultural transformation Breton has in mind, a forcefulness he articulates in different ways on different occasions with depictions that are decidedly more visceral, gut-wrenching, and dark than mere formalisms might suggest. In this respect, we should not miss the way Breton's darker modes (wherein, for example, 'Christianity' has its original inspiration in a nightmare and where freedom is largely an illusory obfuscation of our real function within relations of power) are more decidedly Pauline modes (on the one hand) and hovering at the deep level of ontological commitments (on the other).

Consider, for example, a kind of introspective self-examination and summary of his work that appeared in 1990, when Breton drew an explicit link between "meontology" and the (Heideggerian) "ontological difference," that philosophy of thinking the difference between being and beings as, precisely, *difference*, a *gap* from which representable beings *cannot be saved*.[29] Here Breton goes one step further in his theory of these pluriform "signs" of the "cross," reading Paulinism in light of the work of Rudolf Bultmann, early 20th century biblical studies colleague of philosopher Martin Heidegger. For Breton, the important thing about Bultmann is the

---

[29] See Stanislas Breton, *Philosopher par passion et par raison* (Grenoble : Éditions Jérome Million et les Auteurs, 1990), 8f.

While Sloterdijk does not generally remark on the profound links between Paulinism and precisely the *break* with religion imagined to mark the work of the young Heidegger, it is nevertheless the case that his own reflections on Heidegger in the aptly named *Nicht Gerretet* (Unsaved) constitute an important point of comparison for Breton's reading of Paul. See Peter Sloterdijk, *Nicht Gerretet: Versuche nach Heidegger* (Frankfurt am Main: Suhrkamp, 2001). My own analysis of the intimate union of, precisely, Heidegger's effort to step outside of theology or religion *and* his own early turn toward Paulinism appears in a chapter entitled, "Paul's Secretary: Heidegger's Apostolic Light from the East" in Blanton *Displacing Christian Origins: Philosophy, Secularity, and the New Testament* (Religion and Postmodernism).

way he suggests that the voidance of the Paulinist cross is that which makes possible a critique of reification, fetishization, or the "magical instrumental-ization" (through "ritual technique") of all representations of the Absolute. The cross, as Breton explains Bultmann, is that which renders the Absolute inoperative, unavailable for all such economic gestures, and this because of its own "subtraction" from all determinate contexts.[30] As such, the cross is the name of that which escapes a modern system in which, increasingly, the only mode in which anything can exist is by way of effective production, an activity modernity accomplishes by organizing ends through measured means, this being the modern mode of being Breton glosses as the "will to power." Repeating his earlier definition of both cross and set theory, and this in his own book about ideology and the critique of power, Breton summarizes these ideas as Bultmann's "heroic meontology." As we will see, one of the reasons it is "heroic" for Breton is because Bultmann was (theoretically at least) willing to sacrifice for this thought of the Paulinist cross a "possessive instinct," a rendering inoperative of the culture of private property that Breton takes very seriously in all of his writings (94).

Breton is clear about such a dynamic throughout his own expansive and diverse 'meontological' writings. On the one hand, the cross annuls sacrifice. He already suggested as much in his discussions of the lure of the metaphyisical "pale substratum," for which adherence to ideological formations will sacrifice either the formation itself (in revolutionary violence) or all those who seem to threaten it (in an endless conservative sacrifice of 'terrorists'). In either case, one is only attempting to localize and annihilate the spectre of the void that haunts the formation, thus making fully present and fully safe the identity of the system as such, finally avoiding its void. In this respect, Breton's Paul explores similar political logics as does Alain Badiou's remarkable work of theatre, *The Incident at Antioch*.[31] Thus, in a striking repetition of the haunting early Christian line, whoever *saves* life in this (sacrificial) way only loses it: one finds that the kingdom or revolutionary utopia does *not* arrive despite the execution of all those 'obstructions' thought to have blocked it; or, one finds that the systemic *place* of the executable

---

[30] Breton, *Théorie des Idéologies* 93.
[31] The play was the subject of a recent conference at the University of Glasgow, "Paul, Political Fidelity and the Philosophy of Alain Badiou: a Discussion of *Incident at Antioch*" (February 13–14, 2009). The publication of Susan Spitzer's English translation of this play is forthcoming with Columbia University Press.

'terrorist' is *itself* never sacrificable, despite the sacrificial execution of countless terrorists. To put it differently, the placeless and unrepresentable *nihil* that haunts a structure cannot be exorcised by any effort to *localize* this threat, to place this placeless space in Guantanamo Bay or to concretize its unrepresentable trauma by filling it with unrepresented—and it still seems, (legally) unrepresentable—human beings.

At the same time, however, the unsacrificeable sacrifice *does* make difficult demands of a different sort for Breton. He speaks frequently of the gapping or "distancing" effects of the voidance of "the cross" in all its guises. Following an aged philosophical tradition of "training for death," Breton's "nothing" urges us to see beyond the "reification" of subjects and objects as they have come to exist in our time or that of others.[32] This necessarily ascetic openness to seeing our world 'negated' in this way, *this* form of losing of our lives for the sake of the inaugural rupture, however, is *also* a way of gaining a sense of a *creative* pulsation of life yet to come, indeed a pulsation Breton describes as "the auto-construction of the spirit, the specific autonomy of the [world] soul and of the birth of the world."[33]

This is important to say, as this productive movement, this dispossessed life, is what Breton sometimes calls "the rigor of the negative" the paradoxes of which (between loss and excess, death and life) are unavoidable (8). In ways reminiscent of Walter Benjamin's "messianic" figures, in Breton the minimal difference indicated by reference to a "void" within the field of the visible may be read as a kind of wink, a slight alteration in appearance that *is also* an indication that the world of appearances is or could yet be otherwise. Like Benjamin's messianic time, the revolutionary transvaluation of all values, the changing of *everything*, is a potential of a minimal, evanescent

---

[32] For an extended exploration of the motif, see Jacques Derrida, *The Gift of Death*, translation David Wills (Chicago: University of Chicago Press, 1995), 12ff.

[33] Breton, *Philosopher par passion et par raison* (Grenoble: Editions Jérome Millon et les Auteurs, 1990), 9. This is the kind of phrase which summarizes very nicely the ambiguously (post)metaphysical nature of Breton's work. The movement of being is auto-telic, returning to itself, but only inasmuch as it is producing a form of alterity and negation of identity. Breton was criticized by Derrida and others for phrasings that sound all too Hegelian, as perhaps does this one. Nevertheless, in keeping with what Derrida would himself say of Hegel (namely, that we would never be done reading and re-reading him), Breton said fairly often that the best way to think the limits of metaphysics was by eschewing the illusion that one had stepped outside of them!

tweak of appearance.[34] In the thinker's (and more aptly, as it is the figure Breton almost always has in mind, the *cultural critic's*) openness to the messageless message of the wink, however, a truly excessive being may yet donate what Breton often designates as "that which it neither is nor owns." To return to the issue of the "peculiar kind of obviousness" that is our more or less pre-scripted place within a given world, here we see Breton exploring modes of thinking "cross" as that which insinuates—weakly, with a mere wink or even as only a form of dreamy madness—a solicitation to a world in which everything will be changed.

But we must still say more here in order to make the depth of Breton's commitment to a Paulinist ontology of the crucified clear. For Breton, in other words, the *scandal* and *stupidity* of the failed messiah in the first two chapters of 1 Corinthians (which organized Breton's thinking so profoundly) was not simply a tactical inversion of worldly categories, with apparent or reified wisdom being brought low by way of the excluded. It was, more profoundly for Breton, how divinity, or how truth, appears as such. And with that simple gesture of intensification or generalization of the Pauline statements about the crucified in 1 Corinthians 1, 2, we open up the door to an ontology (and perhaps a meontology) from which no one remains unscathed. One must say emphatically, for example, that for Breton the Paulinist divinity does not remain *outside* such assertions or the wrenching exertions of paradoxical inversions of value. The identification of the divine with the crucified for Breton then names the crossing of multiple intersections. In its pathological attachment to the moment of a crucified messiah, divinity finds itself inflicted with the most hair raising case of what Breton sometimes calls "mad love," impassioned attachment that unhinges the coordinates of pre-established identity. At the same moment of this intensely erotic investment, however, there is for Breton an uncanny distancing effect that settles into the otherwise personal attachment, this dual and paradoxical movement is summarized perfectly by Breton as a "shadow cast by a personal relation converted into the *a priori* of generalized perception." There is thus a strange, simultaneous dual

---

[34] The association between appearance and messianic temporality in Benjamin is a common exploration. Note the Bergsonian link between ephemeral "image" and opening to radical revaluation in his famous "Concept of History" essay in Walter Benjamin, *Selected Writings*, Vol. 4, 1938–1940 (Cambridge, MA: Belknap Press, 2003), 390, 397.

movement: a "mad love" that distends and transforms the desiring self in relation to the beloved; and—at the same time—a settling back of this singular love into a 'distanced' or formal structure. Breton goes on to further elaborate this strange double movement constitutive of his philosophical reading of Paulinism by adding: "The paradox, if there is one, is the coincidence of a mad love and *another folly*, also divine, which strips that love of its too-human resonances or consolations" (emphasis added). Echoing Paul's peculiarly paradoxical pronouncement that "I no longer live but Christ lives in me," Breton generalizes the Paulinist cross and its crossing or dispossessing of identities as that "sublime point where man [sic] ceases in some way to be man" and "where God in some way ceases to be the God common to religions."

Existing at the intersection of two forms of madness, at this crossing of a dual movement in the Paulinist cross God is no more a coherent identity than the human. This is an important point, as unlike a long history of Christian theologizing, for Breton's Paulinist faith in the crucified divinity is not a realm of security against the dispossessing movements of mad love, an inflection of a metaphysical tradition with serious political implications. Representing neither the transient human nor the stable ground of metaphysical structure—but rather caught between two forms of madness—for the Paulinist there remains only a lived surging of a transformative insurgency into the *paradeigmata* of a cultural set-up. Not (predictably, safely) representational, with the Paulinist there is rather a singular process of cultural transformation that is a riskier, if freer, kind of gamble. Pressing these aspects of Paulinist narrative back into the philosophical structures of the unavoidable void of the neutral, Breton brings together all the strands of our discussion by summarizing Paul's argument in 1 Corinthians 1 this way:

> To press the Greek text, which uses two substantive adjectives in the neuter, it would be helpful to translate the passage in the following way: 'underneath the Apollonian face we give God [i.e., 'wisdom'], there is a nocturnal passion putting him 'outside himself' by madness (*to moron tou theou*) and impelling him toward the 'infirmity' of an abasement (*to asthenes tou theou*). Under these dramatic images there breaks through a free energy separating them from all our thoughts of divinity, whether common or learned. The faith whose infirmity participates in that of the Crucified puts the sign of the Cross over all our too-facile beliefs. Yet Paul declares without a little enthusiasm that that infirmity and that madness liberate a power that is stronger than that of men and a wisdom

wiser than their wisdom. He could have added that 'she who has ears to hear' will wonder about her capacity for understanding.[35]

The dispossessing madness of love within Paulinist divinity—that which, Breton tells us, names the cessation of a sort of God—finds an answer to its own echo in the Paulinist believer who measures the neutrally unhinged and therefore unmeasurable expression of God in the only way possible: intensive, self-forgetful enthusiasm. If there is a freedom of a decidedly Pauline thought of the cross, a freedom in the impossible naming of the execution of a messiah as a revelation of the strength of the divine, it is in the explosion of this space of a void, the dispossessed, unmeasured, or unjustified nature of which does not temper its forceful emergence. This moment of freedom is inextricable, therefore, from that writhing tangle of limbs and identities Breton will, throughout his work, name only the "nocturnal passion" or "nocturnal upsurge" of God, nights and movements from which no one in the Paulinist universe emerges unchanged.

The pressing question, in this sense, is never really one of the universal validity of notions of resurrection, 1st century christological or pneumatological conviction, or the Jewish orthodoxy (or otherwise) of Paulinism. The real trial of Paulinism as explicated by Breton is the simple question with which it faces us: are similarly dispossessing, value-inverting moments—in short, a radical and effective critique of ideology—possible? Can the catastrophic wreck of liberatory hopes be subsumed by a fierce enthusiasm in which the very matrix of the play of identities is transformed, whether of the remaining or newly faithful, the named catastrophe, the divine, or that "world" in which all alike find their space of a no longer atomized encounter? Is there a reality, a hope for, irruptions of freedom as "nocturnal passion," sovereignly opaque because ungrounding the very ground of all judgements about them? In that respect (we could summarize self-consciously in a Bultmannian vein) the *krisis* that was Paul's own is no different from our own. Is there, for us (and that with or without this name of an apostle) the possibility that we can avail ourselves of the freedom of the unsurveilled? One is tempted to conclude with the lines of Jacob Taubes, that great defender of a Paulinist *skandalon*:

[35] Breton, *Saint Paul*, 113.

The horns of the dilemma cannot be escaped. Either messianism is nonsense, and dangerous nonsense at that, but the historic study of messianism is a scientific pursuit ... or messianism, and not only the historic research of the "messianic idea," is meaningful inasmuch as it discloses a significant facet of human experience [sic]."[36]

[36] Jacob Taubes, *From Cult to Culture: Fragments Toward a Critique of Historical Reason* (Stanford, CA: Stanford University Press, 2010), 5-6.

Strange Crossings
Commentary to Ward Blanton

HANS RUIN

I am grateful to Ward Blanton for having brought into our discussion around the sacred the question of a certain Pauline legacy, mediated through a reading of Stanislas Breton and Louis Althusser. Paul is the founder of a new community, the self-proclaimed leader of a suppressed minority within a larger minority within the Roman empire. He is a preacher, a writer, and a politician at once, but most importantly he is the first Christian theologian. Through his creative ability to transform loss and grief into strength he lays the intellectual foundation for the new religion, the still operative cultural horizon of "the West," as the inheritance from the Western part of the Roman Catholic Empire. More specifically, it is Paul who creates what we could call "the poeticization of the cross," transforming this instrument of brutal torture into the most sacred symbol for the new community in the making. For a philosophical meditation on sacrality, the cross provides an extraordinarily dense and perhaps even unsurpassable example.

Paul is also more directly connected to the overall theme of phenomenology and religion. Already in Husserl's philosophy of spirit one can hear the resonance of a Pauline tone. More obvious however is the importance of Paul and Pauline theology for Heidegger. With the publication of Heidegger's early Freiburg and Marburg lectures from the early 1920s it has become clear how important his early confrontation with Lutheranism in general and with Paul in particular was for his development of phenomenology. An important impetus for what we today speak of as "the phenomenological turn to religion" was in fact the attempt to come to terms with Heidegger's early lectures on Kierkegaard, Luther, Augustine and Paul. In size they are not very encompassing compared to the total volume of his work. But for the inner development of his thinking they are truly decisive. The themes of a kairological temporality, of historicity, and of a destruction of tradition are to some extent what we could call Pauline themes, partly developed by Heidegger in direct relation to a reading of the Pauline letters. In recent years this phenomenological relation to Paul has been contextualized in a larger preoccupation with Paul, through books by Agamben and Zizek and Badiou in particular, but also several others, including Ward Blanton himself.[1]

Through Blanton's contribution in the present volume we sense the deeper motivations behind the contemporary philosophical interest in Paul, especially as a political thinker, as a thinker of revolutionary affectivity. By combining Althusser's late thinking on the subject as "interpellation" and Breton's reading of Paul from 1988, he elicits a deeper resonance of Pauline revolutionary mysticism behind contemporary attempts to articulate a political Marxist thinking. Blanton's own explicit aim at the outset of the text is to understand how the "self-appointed 'apostle of Christ'" can become an inspiration for a contemporary "materialist" thought. But as the argument progresses it becomes clear that rather than a neo-materialist politics, the radicalism of Paul, when read through Breton, has to do rather with the way he thinks and articulates an existential sense of void and emptiness that challenges every sense of fullness, identity, and materiality, pointing toward a messianic sense of a passionate "nocturnal" freedom. At the center of this problematic Blanton locates with Breton the significance of the *cross*, a cross that "signifies the pale void that renders inoperative the fullness of any ensemble of cultural form, that is of all ideology *tout court*."

Through the specific lens of the lesser known Breton's work Blanton thus opens the discussion toward the vast territory of the subterranean relation between Pauline messianic and mystical thought and different philosophical attempts to forge a transformative politics and ethics beyond subject metaphysics. In my short remark here I will limit myself to a few reflections on the figure of Paul and the message and legacy of his letters, with particular attention to the issue of the secular and sacred as condensed in the very ambiguous symbol of the cross.

---

[1] For a brief overview of this literature and for a more sustained argument about Paul between Heidegger and Foucault, see my "Faith, Grace, and the Destruction of Tradition: A Hermeneutic-Genealogical Reading of the Pauline Letters" in *Journal for Cultural and Religious Theory* (Vol 11, 1, 2010), 16–34.

In the Gospels the cross is primarily mentioned as the "burden" for each and everyone to "carry," in solidarity with the suffering Christ, and thus as an ethical-existential prerogative. But it is in Paul that the experience of the cross is transformed from humiliation to triumph, by means of a transformative gesture in which Christ willingly *endures* the cross (cf. Heb 12:2). It is an enduring, and a self-sacrificing that can also be seen as an emptying of oneself, of letting one's own body become the site of a kind of negative positivity. Paul thus gives it its truly sacrificial meaning. Precisely through his interpretion of the crucified Christ, Paul could be said to shape the affective center of the Christian world experience. In this interpretation the most brutal tool used in the ancient world for punishment, murder, and humiliation is transformed into the most sacred and venerable symbol for the community in the making. It is transformed from marking only a horrific end of life, to becoming the birthplace of a new and different form of life. It is transformed from facticity to future, and from materiality to spirit. This is done by viewing it not as the site of a simple punishment, but as an exemplary sacrifice, a making-sacred, in the original meaning of *sacrificio*.

In Romans there is no talk of the cross as such. But it is in 1. Corinthians that he states that the very word of the cross is madness for those who perish (1:18), but the power of God for those who are saved, followed by the central doctrine of a crucified Christ. And it is in Galatians, that we find the more mysterious reflections on the cross and crucifixion, that it is through the crucifixion of Christ that also the world is crucified and dead, and also that I am dead for the world. Here the cross marks the passage from life to death, and then back to life again. For in the next sentence he says that it is all about a new creation (6:14f). And through the blood of Christ on the Cross a reconciliation is brought about and "peace is made" as he also says in the letter to Colossians (Col 1:20).

The central point in Breton's reading of Paul as discussed by Blanton is similar to Vattimo's thesis, that there is in Paul a thinking of the emptying, *kenosis*, of power itself. With Breton, Blanton speaks of it as "a dispossession at the heart of all possessive identity," something like a "founding rupture." This is a primordially revolutionary moment and in existential terms perhaps the most important dimension of Paul's letters. Through this transformative gesture, that displaces the entire order or power, they obtain a strange and paradoxical force, and one that has had enormous repercussion. For Breton, the will to domesticate and to secure betrays a kind of death instinct, in relation to which the emptying takes place in favor of life. I would even go further than this and say that we find in Paul an invention of a new kind of subjectivity, one that short-circuits the philosophical ethics of his time as primarily seeking to establish the subject as an autonomous center of force. In Paul one can sense a sacrificing of the self, so as to give way to a new self. It is through this trope that it also opens itself up for the Althusserian interpretation of it as an "interpellated" self.

As a symbol of transformation and redemption the cross nevertheless remains highly ambiguous. To say with Breton, that the cross signifies a "pale void," that renders inoperative all ideology, and to present the cross as a symbol of the empty opening of oneself to otherness and as a kind of sacred space of transmission of forces, brings out only one aspect of its multilayered meaning. It circumvents entirely its role as also the symbol of violence, of universal power, and as an endlessly renewable tool of submission. The inner logic of the Christian cross—supposing there is such a thing—gathers from the start horror and veneration. And its veneration is inextricably connected to its horror. As a sign of pain, suffering, and humiliation, it is precisely something that can be endured, as the most demanding endurance. Yet in its sacredness this violence does not cease or disappear, but it is taken up by a subject that somehow integrates this violence within itself.

The creative interpretation of the crucifixion, whereby it is transformed from a narrative of utter failure and humiliation into a narrative of triumph and power, is reflected back into the Christian subjectivity, as itself such an inner transformation, whereby each and everyone somehow is transformed from a figure of humiliation, to one of triumph, a triumph in humiliation. This is also the revolutionary moment, which shapes the Christian identity, a transformation of horror to sacredness, of pain to pleasure, and of submissiveness to freedom.

When Constantine has his vision of the cross in the sky as a sword turned upside down, as "a sign in which he will vanquish," he usurps and corrupts the Pauline vision, but he also makes use in a creative way of its inner complicity with sacrificial violence. Holding the cross as a weapon he produces an equally creative transformation of this ancient symbol into a sign of military and political unity and triumph. By this gesture the cross is politicized, and thus a sign of spiritual endurance, overcoming and re-demption, emerges as the principal symbol of a spiritualized ruthless military violence.

In view of this inner ambiguity, is it reasonable to hope that we can, as Blanton suggests with Breton, reclaim the sense of this cross, as an impetus for "a critique of ideology"? Could we breathe sacred meaning again into this symbol, as indicated here, when the void of the cross is presented as also a way to escape triumphant ecclesiasts? How could this most dense of all Western symbols again designate failure and emptiness? And yet this is the direction in which Blanton is pointing, to lead us to explore with Breton a negative route, the negativity of which should open itself up to that "nocturnal passion," to that strange freedom that issues from the gesture of letting go, indeed of sacrificing oneself, thus making oneself and one's body itself into something *sacer*, a sacred passionate body.

Whatever the possibilities are for such a creative, philosophical and aesthetic renewal of the complex symbol of the cross, the hermeneutic exploration of its possibility points not only toward profound levels of the affective-signifying comportment underlying the "Christian" experience, but also toward the hidden logic of an ethics and a politics of the sacred. For anyone seeking a deeper reflexive understanding of religion and of a life in faith this avenue is as essential as it is difficult.

Minimalist Faith, Embodied Messianism
The Ambiguity of the Sacred and the Holy

BETTINA BERGO

Deformalization ... beyond Husserl and Heidegger; For What?

Arguably, phenomenology deformalized approaches to experience that had become sedimented and abstract over the course of neo-Kantian debates in the 19th century. Arguably as well, Heidegger enriched the temporality and in-the-world experience described in Husserl's phenomenology of inner time consciousness. Recent French reception of phenomenology has moved toward experiences of sensuous and affective excess, to break through the mould of intentionality (i.e., consciousness of x) and to ask: why should all consciousness be "of something"?[1]

But why break this mould, and how could we do so without abandoning meaning itself? In the 1950s, Merleau-Ponty—still massively indebted to a then-unpublished Husserl (*Ideen II*)—Levinas, Marion, Granel, Nancy (the list is considerable), all pursue the project of a deformalization of linear temporalizing consciousness and, above all, a rigid distinction between sensibility, temporally retained but unthought, and sensibility fully conscious as pain, pleasure or affect. Why attempt such a thing? It is to argue for the possibility that "theophany" might be experientially mean-ingful, in the case of Jean-Luc Marion. Or it is to trace the conditions of possibility of a "Christian" faith without orthodoxy, in the case of Jean-Luc

---

[1] See Jocelyn Benoist, "Le soi sans l'intentionalité: Austin sur les sensations" and "Senset non-sens social, au-delà de l'intentionnel" in *Les limites de l'intentionalité: Recherches phénoménologiques et analytiques* (Paris: Vrin, 2005), respectively 196–197, 232, 239, for the difficulty of describing the intentionality of color-perception according to Austin, and the importance of social meaning in addition to individual intentional meanings.

Nancy. Or again, it is to explore conditions of possibility of "religion," where the term denotes an intersubjective "fraternity" that accounts for our undying concern with ethics, with being good toward our fellows, in the case of Emmanuel Levinas. All these projects are unique; they are interrelated, but they are not equivalent. And, while they rely on the work of the founder of phenomenology, they move past, perhaps frankly abandon, Husserl's epistemological concerns in favor of realms of experience that are extra- or pre-cognitive. Readers can make of this what they will; the claims are as curious as certain of Husserl's own, when he speaks, for example, of a phenomenology of the unconscious, while discussing the passive spontaneity of "association."[2]

I propose to examine here Nancy's first volume of his deconstruction of Christianity. I believe it so deformalizes the ideas of faith and the sacred that it could also be a deconstruction opening to *other* types of faith than the Christian. From Nancy, I will turn to what has been called "messianism." I propose to keep my focus on Jewish messianisms, because it is here that I see a difference from Christian faith and explicit attempts to consider history differently than, say, according to a redemptive or a nihilistic model. I am thinking of Walter Benjamin, Ernst Bloch, and Theodor Adorno's "histories." I set Levinas in that tradition, which he readily allows by his own words at the end of *Totality and Infinity*, speaking of the *"vigilance extrême de la conscience messianique."*[3] But the 1961 project of inscribing messianic hope into history *fails* for Levinas, and so he moves toward sensibility in the French manner of a phenomenology of sensibility as "perception," desire and affectivity. I will unfold this with one question in mind here: can we approach something like a principle of hope—one that is, hopefully, free of ideologies and perhaps even faith—without a correlation to a world, and above all, starting from a subject of affectivity that is embodied, but not explicitly *alive*? This question is not an easy one; we assume that Levinas's subject is alive. But what does it mean, notably for phenomenology, to be alive? How shall we approach the multiple layers on

---

[2] Edmund Husserl, *De la synthèse passive*, translation Bruce Bégout and Natalie Depraz (Grenoble: Jérome Millon, 1998), respectively, 221. For Husserl un-conscious means simply retained but largely irretrievable, except in fortuitous cases of spontaneous recollection.

[3] Emmanuel Levinas, *Totality and Infinity: An Essay on Exteriority*, translation Alphonso Lingis (Pittsburgh: Duquesne University Press 1969), 285 (in the French original, 271). Hereafter TI.

dimensions of living embodiment—notably from within the formal framework of phenomenology, whose descriptions concern *conscious* meaning, but not that which makes it possible? This is the question that has recently preoccupied the Merleau-Ponty scholar, Renaud Barbaras. His answer is that phenomenology, even Merleau-Ponty's, affords no real access to the subjective experience of embodiment as self-affectation *and* the constitution of other living beings.[4] My answer, inspired by his arguments, will be that philosophies approaching "life" are philosophies whose reception has often been a dangerous endeavor.

Gérard Granel and the First, Worldly Duality

I turn first to Jean-Luc Nancy, who relies heavily on the phenomenological deformalizations of the one-time Marxist Catholic, Gérard Granel. Thus, Granel, cited in Nancy's *La déclosion: déconstruction du christianisme* (2005). Here, we read a deformalized description of the birth of the sacred-profane distinction within the correlation, body-world.

> *Sub-stance* [...] is, in effect, nothing other than the thetic profanation of the most banal of evidences, that of the presence of the real. That upon which I open my shutters each morning, that in which I attend to the affairs of life, that in which I fall asleep without concerning myself with what holds *Hypnos* and *Thanatos* together [...] and, despite all that, that *of which* I am never aware.

> Save perhaps in the mode of a sort of halting [*mise en arrêt*], a tiny and silent recoil before the nothing of that primitive All—let us say, a sentiment of the World, or of existing (this is not an alternative, or even a difference). It is always a detail, and nothing but a detail in the immense population of things, that

---

[4] Renaud Barbara's *Introduction à une phénoménologie de la vie* (Paris: Vrin, 2008), 19: "contemporary ontology, in which phenomenology is inscribed, is an *ontology of death*. Certainly, this is a repression, never wholly completed, like all repression, and that is why, as we indicated [...] the vocabulary of life makes its appearance in a recurrent and unthematic way, at the heart of phenomenological descriptions. Indeed, how to characterize the existence of the subject of the correlation, of which we have pointed out, in a simply negative mode, that it commands the appearing of the world all the while belonging to it? The answer is simple: this existence must be defined as *living* [...] in a double sense...as though the action of living (living itself) [...] implied being affected by [an] other in feeling [*éprouver*], as though vital action always had, as its reverse side, the passivity of perceiving." Also see p. 36ff. My translation.

provokes this infinitesimal suspension: the cry of a harrier streaking across the grey sky; a sudden chill that sends me back inside my skin; on another day a warm wind caressing my hair. [...] A red sun that sinks vertically down the far side of things; the tracery of branches, not to be untangled in, that great tree, whose shadow repeats it on a white wall [...].

One will probably say that all this concerns the poetry of the World, and that philosophy is not poetry. For my part, I would say that there reigns here...nothing less than a logic of phenomenality, a fabric of unsuspected *a prioris* that readily put to shame the formula we used earlier ("the presence of the real"), just as much as the one metaphysics utilizes.[5]

In his post-Catholic, post-Marxist period, Gérard Granel was working out modalizations of existence that recall the work of the later Heidegger and of Merleau-Ponty, except that his experiment sought to deformalize existence into movements and masses dissolving. All this, without proceeding according to an ontological difference. Painterly, Granel worked with and through a critique of formalist space and totalizing logics. Thus, we may say "all" about "things," but never "the all." What stands before "me" (Granel writes *prae-ens*), "disappears the moment I distribute it into matter and form" (DDC 165). Moreover, spaces and objects given or lived through the senses "oblige us to conceive all form as an arrangement of sensations in space." But how, asks Granel, already deformalizing, "brought about in what way" (DDC 165)? What authorizes our supposing that space is the *a priori* form of external representation; that is, space as a form, but of *what*? If space were really a formal *a priori* of perception, then the thinking of this or these forms would "break up" the validity of the pair, form and matter. Pondering Kant's transcendental "exposition," Granel agrees that space certainly does not denote the universal *concept* for things and their relations. It is clear that, in experience, the sheer evidence of material things precedes the evidence of form, external to or determining them. So as a condition, something may well be an *a priori* form—where *a priori* means something like *logically*, but not temporally, prior. However, space,

---

[5] Gérard Granel, "Far from Substance, Whither and To What Point?" in Jean-Luc Nancy, *Dis-Enclosure: Deconstruction of Christianity*, translation Bettina Bergo, Gabriel Malenfant, and Michael B. Smith (New York: Fordham University Press, 2007), 164. Hereafter abbreviated as DDC.

understood as condition of possibility of our *representation* of the world, would then be the *a priori* form of *nothing*, of no thing. Granel writes:

> What we have just rediscovered, with the tediousness of an apprentice, is what the Kantian mastery asserts from the outset: "The presentation of space cannot be delivered from the experience of relations between external phenomena" / "Space is not…a universal concept for the relations of things in general." The *Critique* will thus have the audacity to declare "a priori" the spatial character of the experience [*l'épreuve*] we have of the World, and to consider that the "manifold" of this spatiality "rests…on limitations." (DDC 165)

But what are limits? Granel will argue cogently that "limits" is a concept "frontally opposed to [the concept] of 'parts,' in other words, to that of 'matter'…" (DDC 165). A limit is either a boundary, a frontier, a point of intersection of lines or a fixed value; in any event, it is artificially imposed or suggests itself spontaneously in the presence of variegating fields. Why then should limits be opposed "frontally" to parts or to matter? For Granel, limits imply relations and transitions—degrees of spacings; while parts may receive limits artificially, they constitute wholes and not firstly relations or fields. Similarly, matter denotes an abstraction: the *apeiron* or what is unlimited. "That this concept of limit is opposed to that of […] 'matter,'" he argues, "and that, in consequence, the notion of 'form' used to qualify space itself (as an "*a priori* form of sensibility") would then become totally enigmatic" (DDC 165). This is easy to grasp when we consider that the "manifold" that is space—if it denotes what is "outer," in, or as, "the world"—only rests on limitations if what is "outside" consists *not* of parts and wholes, matter and *form*, but rather of fields, relations and movement. "This is what Kant seems almost to want to smooth over," Granel insists, "by simply 'exposing' this novelty (in his "transcendental exposition of space and time") […] as though he feared having to expose *himself*, the thinker, to a novelty for which 'words are lacking us'" (DDC 165, emphasis added). The "form" of space is thus subverted by its very conception as a "manifold." If it is not a manifold, however, then what is space, and what, does the "*a priori* form" of space mean?

Attempting to think around or beneath these binaries of parts and wholes, form and matter, *a priori-a posteriori*, Granel argues in the phenomenological-hermeneutic he learned from Heidegger that we may allow that the *a priori* form of space designate the form of "the world" qua manifold. Yet we will thereupon have to admit that this world we are aiming at has, *itself,* no form.[6] The density and dynamism of "content" cannot be ordered into an encompassing containment, and "no sensation [of it] can come out of its absolute closure to initiate the rapport of sensations among themselves. In a word, the spatial of the perceived *is* formal, and *no form is the affair of a content"* (DDC 165, emphasis added).

To illustrate the perplexity of using form and content to determine the very conditions of our perception, Granel gathers examples that show dynamics, instants and haltings, of which we say: "everything" or "it does x; it is y'ing." Worlds unfold in modalities that escape even most phenomenological descriptions—atmospheric modalities, adverbial modes pointing to kinds of "how": "it grew gradually darker," "the heaviness hangs oppressively, all around [...]" Worlds unfold as finite fields around limits and boundaries which *we* impose. These are the little noted perceptions supposed to deploy "space" as indeterminate manifold *without form.*

Sedulous and hard to set to words, it is all too familiar. Imagine the shape of a university building, Granel proposes, which rises in reds, is underscored by a "trail of vegetative green," then ascends in height with "a kind of notching that thrusts forward" (DDC 168). If he were to paint the building, it would lose its function as pedagogical structure. When and if we speak of it, in its banality, we restore function, or employ it as a geographic marker, and certainly treat it as a whole. However, "what are we aiming at when we designate, as a perceptual 'whole,' something that owes nothing to the pragmatic notion of a building, much less to a transcendent concept of an 'object,' yet which unfailingly distinguishes itself from the other 'wholes' represented by the trees around it, the cars...the sky?" What are we aiming at? he asks. No doubt at aspects of Merleau-Ponty's "perceptual faith." No doubt we live by our metonymies, little aware of the role of grammar in all perception. And we take for granted the passive syntheses of association, in which glimmers the sedimentation of perceptual, un-remarked experiences over time. Recall Husserl's surprising example of lights arising from the Rhine Valley and evoking other, different yet related lights—all of which have set themselves off as affective wholes, in purely passive associations.[7]

---

[6] See Gérard Granel, *L'équivoque ontologique de Kant* (Paris: Gallimard, 1970; reprinted Mauvezin: Éditions TER, nd).

[7] In his discussion of the "thematic position and delimitation of a phenomenological doctrine of association" (Section III "Association," Chap. 1, § 26), Husserl marvels at the curiosity whereby associations are mediate *and* immediate; if an *a* recalls a *b,* "and the

All this is prologue to the response that Granel has conceived. Foreshortening, he turns to the difference, the limitation he knows as the simplest and the first, having argued that the approach to presence should be thought in light of the basic *reserve* of the world, or the way in which wholes vary amongst each other—and not just through our bodies' movement alone. Granel thus evokes the atmospheric "giving" of the sky and the mobile limiting of light and dusk: "it is true that the light of day,

latter thereupon recalls a *c*, but we do not remember *c* immediately, but only in passing by *b* (194). He adds that the final member of the associative chain "gives itself to us like an incident or afterthought (*Einfall*)"; it may be unanticipated and, as intuition, quite different from much if not all of the prior givens, a, b, etc. For example, a seaside image spontaneously 'crosses our mind' while we are in the midst of a conversation. This allows Husserl to pose a question whose analytic difficulty surpasses the conceptual wherewithal of phenomenological investigation (though it can be described): "How can the I become conscious of the fact that it has behind itself an *infinite field of past experiences* insofar as they are its own, that it has a unity of a past life in the form of time, and this has a life that is accessible to it through recollection and which, in principle, is everywhere accessible [...] as liable to be awakened anew in its proper being? [...] We recognize, then, [in asking these questions] that it is a matter of nothing less than this fundamental problem: *to elucidate the conditions of possibility of subjectivity itself*" (196, emphasis added). After considerable development of types of synthesis—by resemblance and covering over or by dissimilarity, etc.—Husserl mentions the curiously intertwined effectivity of association, recollection and affectivity: "That every affection may not arise through the awakening of another affection is, in itself, understandable. Each case of affection <born> through extreme and isolated contrast, like an explosion, shows this essential possibility. Yet we need not recur to such extreme cases. If, during a walk one evening along the Loretto heights, a trail of lights suddenly flashes in our horizon in the Rhine valley, then, at that very instant, this trail detaches affectively in its unity, without the excitation having to lead, necessarily, to a conversion of attention" (221). This affective eruption, accompanied by a partial detachment of the experience from its (utterly distinct) context, the Loretto Heights, poses genetic questions that the young Husserl would not have addressed. As he puts it, "It goes without saying that we could give to the entirety of the considerations that we just developed the vaunted title of 'the unconscious'. It is thus a matter of *a phenomenology of what we call the unconscious*." See Husserl, *De la synthèse passive*, respectively, 194, 196, 221. The unexpected *Einfall*, and significantly, its affective force, which can isolate it without occasioning a "conversion of attention," corresponds to Granel's limits and fields. It also evokes Levinas's examples of the Other-in-the-same. Nevertheless, Husserl still insists that "formally, time is a one-dimensional and continuous 'rectilinear' ('homogeneous') succession; while the visual field, still from a formal point of view, is a two-dimensional plurality, which must be apprehended as a dual, continual succession (a succession of successions)" (215). Thus the flow of consciousness, as "temporal," has to be distinguished, formally from the visual field. Yet it is difficult to see why the visual field is merely two-dimensional. Importantly, Husserl here allows for an almost infinite plurality of affective fields and a visual plurality, *in order to preserve his formal conception of time and temporalizing consciousness.*

gradually erupting out of nocturnal chaos, 'engenders' the first duality of the visible, according to which it 'divides itself' into the non-thing that is the Sky and an Earth-of-things" (DDC 169). Here, with the sky, is an open that needs no "way out"; an opening inaccessible and ungraspable—"for not being," he adds. This open, *this* clearing—we say, "*the* sky"—differentiates intransitively, as a whole and as "rightly original," *for not being*. It is one of those "wholes" that should not become a mere noun. As eternal beginning and as evidence of evidences, it takes on a divine quality—in several traditions. *Dius* and *divus*: the association between light, the bright, and the divine—*sub divo*—this belongs to theogonies and creation narratives. When these "belong" to philosophy as well, it is as informal *a prioris*, as non-things; in a sense, as *styles* (DDC 169). Eternally repeating, for not being.

The beauty of Granel's other examples risks obscuring the moment of concentration in light, which is more than an exercise in deformalization, and the transition from presence-absence dynamics to their *how*, familiar also to Husserl and Levinas. Insistence on the perceptual as visual leads Granel to argue that his adverbial moments point to the "ungraspability of Being," whose other pole is the body-that blind site that deploys positions around its own unseeing core, like a black rectangle on a background of white.

Before we conclude that Granel, the one-time Marxist then Catholic Heideggerian, is extending his teacher Heidegger in the all too French direction of aesthetics and sensibility, we should know that the godless, subjectless occurrences that Granel describes, like touches of color or light on a body—represent a *fundamental faith* for Jean-Luc Nancy. Nancy's recent *Dis-Enclosure: The Deconstruction of Christianity* aims less at unearthing the historic or cultural conditions of possibility of Christian faith, than at proposing the simplest ingredients of a faith without beings. To that end, Nancy also uses the Epistle of James "the minor," which Luther called an "Epistle of straw" (DDC, 48).[8] Together with the deformalization of presence in Granel, Nancy's project works out faith as a kenotic poetics—ways of circulating in a "world" emptied of objects and tools, where transcendence is neither precisely temporal (as "now" or "to-come"), nor simply "spatial" (as here, there), but comes to pass as *perception créatrice*."

[8] Jean-Luc Nancy, "The Judeo-Christian (On Faith)" in *Dis-Enclosure,* 42–60.

World, then, as the open from which there is no exit route, no "way out." In parallel, Nancy reads faith out of James's still Judaic epistle, devoid of Christology, in which God is conceived as a creator and engenderer of humans, engendering humans in his image as creators and creative. James's creator would be one that gives light; a creator that gives and abandons itself in its gift: kenotic poetics. The following remark summarizes what he has in mind for a *philosophical* approach to the rudiments of faith: "to give and to withhold…are not contradictories here and…to be and to appear would be identical, here: a phenomenology that is theological but *not* theophanic" (DDC 49, emphasis added). Faith, in short, as a way of perceiving that has little to do with a truth *believed*: "This faith, above all, does not *believe*," insists Nancy. *It is a faith not believed. It is a non-belief whose faith guarantees it as non-believable* (DDC 53, 54).

What really does it not believe? Dogmatics first, then any kind of theodicy, above all a political version. It believes neither in a god that becomes man, nor in the messiah who has come or will come again, having transformed temporality—"doubled it"—with a pneumatic time stretched between presence and return. Consequently, this faith does not believe in Christian justice, at least so far as justice is tied, in Luther's understanding, to justification by the resurrection of bodies and the return of the messiah: "For if we have been planted together in the likeness of his death, we shall be also in the likeness of his resurrection" (Romans 6:5 and DDC 54). This will be important when I turn to Levinas and philosophies of the body and of life.

Other than 'Faith'? Messianic Themes in Judaism

Granel and Nancy do provide us with two deformalizations opening toward a post-orthodox faith, which escapes the conundrums of Christian representations. It is therefore no accident that the faith in question concerns, for Nancy at least, the "Judeo-Christian" of which "James the minor" is said to be exemplary. We should ask from *whose* perspective a figure can be exemplary of the *hyphen* between "Jewish" and "Christian." In any case, Granel is closer to a mystical Christianity—even an archaic "paganism"—in which "the aesthetic" moves between a symbol and a mode of presencing.

In the wake of these poetic deformalizations in search of an immediate of living faith, my first concern is with contrast. I would like to set what is informally called "messianism" apart from the faiths adumbrated here. I want to pursue an intuition I have that, along with points of intersection, there are important differences between messianic thinking and "faith" as Nancy unfolds it. I propose to set out some of those differences. Following that, I will review what is striking about Levinas's version of messianic consciousness and how it passes through bodies conceived differently than Merleau-Ponty, differently than Granel, and in a way that returns almost to insights from philosophies of life—even as it forecloses the return of those *Lebensphilosophie*. This is an overview of faith versus messianic history and consciousness, whose informal "narrative" concerns the challenge, for phenomenology, of thinking transcendence, goodness, and a living subject, together. That there is a narrative to be sketched here is tied also to the repetitiveness with which thinking in the 20th century has pursued the concrete, the immediate, and deformalized experience down to a host of approaches to the question of what motivates us, whether we call this motivation "willing," "desiring," *machines désirantes*, even "drives," *Triebe*, "livingness."

Before proceeding, let me review what you may already be familiar with, which is Jewish messianism and Levinas's inflection of it toward sensibility and substitution.

Without ever claiming that other religions, notably Christianity and Islam, could not have messianic dimensions, Gershom Scholem's *The Messianic Idea in Judaism* set forth original and recurrent features in Jewish messianism—features we cannot overlook if we are to think through Levinas toward the dilemma of formalism versus the inchoate "experience" that concerns phenomenology today.[9]

At its most secularized and rarefied, Jewish messianism would correspond to a principle, or a ground, of hope. Hope is almost transitive here because it represents a hope of overcoming the sting of death that consists in a life's work broken off (Ernst Bloch).[10] Or again, a hope whose

---

[9] Gershom Scholem, *The Messianic Idea in Judaism and Other Essays on Jewish Spirituality* (New York: Schocken Books, 1971, 1995). Hereafter MIJ. I will not address the debate about messianism that unfolded after the publication of Scholem's decisive work.

[10] According to Levinas's concise reading of Bloch's secularized messianism: "Time is then neither a projection of being toward its end, as in Heidegger, nor a mobile image of

possibility is forged through a profound change in historical understanding, such that the past can be mourned unfetishistically *and* affirmed in its value for life. These two "rarefied" forms correspond to aspects of Bloch's and Benjamin's messianism. Adorno's messianic "imageless image of the possible"[11] appears still more sober—as an aesthetics that appears to unravel itself even as it opens dialectical possibilities for the striving of desire. The sobriety of messianic thought in the 20th century extends to Levinas, who expressed his humanistic Talmudic interpretations with Rabbi Nachman's musing: the messiah might be someone like myself, or again: the messiah might indeed be *me*.[12] I will return to this point shortly.

Secularized, messianism has important, often dialectical relations with historical circumstances. It is tensed between poles that rarely diverge integrally from each other. We find the apocalypticism of a vision of the end of the world *or* an apocalypticism of extreme suffering tied to rampant injustice. Against this, Maimonides brilliantly deployed a rationalist messianism where an age of peace stands as a free promise, an open assurance of better circumstances, although humans are fully capable of "mastering [their] duties and thereby mastering [their own] future" (MIJ 31). Together with apocalyptic and rationalist messianisms, the messianic age may be restorative or utopian. And both restoration and redemption, apocalypse and peace, concern law and justice. Restorative messianism promises that world and law shall be as they were before humanity lived "under the tree of

---

the immobile eternity, as in Plato. It is the time of fulfillment, a complete determination that is the actualization of all potentiality, of all the obscurity of the factual in which stands the subjectivity of man alienated in his technical activities. He is the actualization of the incomplete [...].Time is thus taken seriously. The drive toward the future is a relation with *utopia* and not a march toward a predetermined end of history in the present, which is obscure. *Time is pure hope.* It is even the birthplace of hope. This is hope for a completed world in which man and his labor shall not be merchandise [...].The possibility for man to get his identity from somewhere other than the perspective in his being, to which Heidegger accustomed us; that is, from elsewhere than this *conatus* where death strikes its blow to the highest of all attachments, the attachment to being. Here, on the contrary, man is not primarily preoccupied with his being." Levinas, "Another thinking of death: starting from Bloch" in *God, Death, and Time*, translation Bettina Bergo (Stanford, California: Stanford University Press, 2000), 95–96, 103.

[11] See his *Problems of Moral Philosophy*, translation Thomas Schroder and Rodney Livingston (Cambridge: Polity Press, 2000).

[12] Emmanuel Levinas, "Messianic Texts" in *Difficult Freedom: Essays on Judaism*, translation Seán Hand (Baltimore, Md.: Johns Hopkins University Press, 1990), 88–89. Hereafter DF.

the knowledge of good and evil." Not innocence so much as balance—and the return of the reign of the other tree—*of life*. Utopian messianism embodies hope in the possibility of a state of affairs radically different and *novel*. An event that comes out of nowhere—if formally. Utopia and restoration of course can and did coexist (MIJ 51). Above all, both restorative and utopian messianisms concern *public* events—whether within time or consciously outside of time, and both concern a *community*.

The Messiah is not God or a son of God, except perhaps in a mystical sense. Thus, messianic energy either focuses on history, law, or—in Levinas's case—an ethical concentrate of the law, the radical event, and an interruption of the drives and chaos of the world. Because the Messiah is neither "God" nor world, redemption concerns forms of *social* emancipation, which again ties it to questions of justice (MIJ 53), or emancipation from our human inability to understand the Torah—thereby opening an age of enlightenment whose importance lies in the association forged between life, community and writing. Yet the antinomianism winding through Jewish messianism does not promise a *new* law, or a *new* Torah. (MIJ 28-29).

That the Messiah is tied to no historical or mythical person allows Rabbi Nahman to speculate that the Messiah could be anyone. That it could be anyone suggests that one does not worship or pray to the Messiah, much less cultivate an interiority that would open to the Messiah: there is no interiority cultivated in messianic thought.

With no original emphasis on a spiritualist interiority; with a concern for renewal by a figure either heroic and mortal, or utopian but not divine in the Christian sense, Jewish messianism moves between a principle of hope for restoration of peace, emergence of understanding, or a higher resolution of oppressions (MIJ 31). Human actions neither cause the Messiah to come, nor lead to resurrection: justice is therefore human and justification is enigmatic—a promise whose essence is to stand without causal relation to human history. Of course, that has not kept it from being recast in Marxist or Marxist-mystical terms. Of the above-mentioned elements we find, in Levinas, less concern with political history and the past than in, say, Benjamin. Yet there is in Levinas's thought the rationalist conviction that messianism must point to something like the mortality and ineluctable failure of the Messiah against the world. Hence Levinas's 1961 remarks that the Messiah is the one, *any* one, who suffers for nothing—which later become part of his phenomenology of sensibility, itself.

Between these two eventualities (the Messiah is the leper scholar of the Rabbi school and the Messiah is Rabbi himself or Daniel, the most desired man), there is the remarkable text which we have not yet commented on: "R. Nahman said: If he [the Messiah] is of those living [today], it might be one like myself, as it is written, *And their nobles shall be of themselves, and their governors shall proceed from the midst of them* (Jeremiah 30:21)." (DF 88)

To summarize, as a principle of hope, messianism has specific relationships to law and justice. It cultivates no particular interiority and maintains no causal connection between human actions and God (until it comes into contact with medieval Christianity). Messianism thus offers no phenomenalization of what the new event, the new state of affairs intimated in utopian messianism would be: an imageless image of the possible. If this principle of hope is faith, then like Nancy's surprising recourse to the Epistle of James, it is a thin faith without spiritualist interiority. As a deformalization, it is differently aesthetic yet denser than Granel's *dius divus* birth of the sacred; finally, messianism has a different reflex toward the world and to being. Levinas will write, for example, "There must be a rupture of continuity, and continuation across this rupture. The essential in time consist in being a drama, a multiplicity of acts where the following act resolves the prior one. Being is no longer produced at one blow [...]. Resurrection constitutes the principal event of time. There is therefore no continuity in being. Time is discontinuous [...] In continuation the instant meets its death, and resuscitates [...] But such a formal structure pre-supposes the relation of the I with the Others [...]" (TI 284).

In Levinas, then, messianism is refracted through the many I's and Others. It is from this, as experiences, that the question of resurrection becomes meaningful and not the other way around.

Time is finite and it is discontinuous; there is never a here and now of "resurrection" because the I, and most likely everyone, is resurrected through his children. Or again, the interruption provoked by an Other is simply the liberation she allows me from my cyclical time of existence. Messianism for Levinas amounts to the consciousness that there is a time that breaks free of the temporal circle or perpetual return. This is a temporality open to a free future, and when messianism is not caught up in its un-symbols, it is the promise of an open future that takes the sting out of death. Such a structure is not found in our relationship to being alone. (TI 284).

My passage through Scholem was important because the later work of Levinas develops his 1961 innuendo that ethical responsibility concerned the "vigilance of messianic consciousness," notably as hope for justice and as discontinuous time. Rooted in intersubjective bonds, but worked out at the level of sensibility, Levinas unfolds the meaning of this messianic consciousness in time, *not* in Granel's Open that suggests the birth of transcendence in the world. That messianic sensibility represents the apogee of Levinas's investigations is understandable, since the phenomenology he worked out in the 1960s turned on a duality of exteriorities: the exteriority of world and the exteriority of ethical transcendence, where the transcendence of the face belonged to what Husserl called in the *Logical Investigations* a non-objectifying intentionality. This duality will be largely resolved after *Totality and Infinity*, but only through a hermeneutics of embodied affect and memory. In 1961, however, Levinas's transcendence (and hope) passes either through a "family narrative," in a micro-history, or it comes to pass as other-worldly, with the Other who faces. Being is necessarily plural and nothing occupies the transcendent position, however enigmatic, of Heidegger's Being. Yet "pluralist ontology" carries logical inconsistencies and the primacy of something like a transcendental kept insinuating itself as a condition beneath his dual exteriorities and histories. That threatened his project of ethics as "first philosophy."

Levinas's later work—and it bears repeating because it had a significant impact on the French reception of phenomenology, from Michel Henry to Marion, to the meditations of Didier Franck, Jocelyn Benoist and Renaud Barbaras[13]—proceeds from a different logic: that of the other-in-the-same. This logic is spatial in an epidermal sense, which follows the dual, inside-outside structure of the skin. It is sensuous, with sensation and affectivity intertwined and corporeal. The new effort, a rethinking of messianism as

[13] Respectively Michel Henry, *Genealogy of Psychoanalysis [The Lost Beginning]*, translation Douglas Brick (Stanford, California: Stanford University Press, 1993), hereafter GP; Jean-Luc Marion, *Being Given: Toward a Phenomenology of Givenness*, translation Jeffrey Kosky (Stanford, California: Stanford University Press, 2002); then Didier Franck, "Au-delà de la phénoménologie" and "La dramatique des phénomènes," both in his *Dramatique des phénomènes* (Paris: PUF-Épiméthée, 2001), 105–124; 125–162; hereafter DP. Jocelyn Benoist, "Intentionalité et pulsionalité" and "L'intentionalité et les valeurs," both in his *Les limites de l'intentionalité: Recherches phénoménologiques et analytiques* (Paris: Vrin, 2005), 131–150; 151–168. Finally, Renaud Barbaras, "Les domaines absolus du survol" in his *Introduction à une phénoménologie de la vie* (Paris: Vrin, 2008).

pre-conscious affectivity, requires above all a different deformalization of time and a return to Husserl's passive syntheses.

> The subjectivity as *the other in the same*, as an inspiration, is the putting into question of all affirmation for one-self, all egoism born again in this very recurrence [...] Subjectivity taken as intentionality is founded on auto-affection as an auto-revelation, source of an impersonal discourse. The recurrence of the self in responsibility for other could never mean altruistic will, instinct of "natural benevolence," or love. It is in the passivity of obsession, or incarnated passivity, that an identity individuates itself as unique, without recourse to any system of references, in the impossibility of evading the assignation of the other without blame. The re-presentation of self grasps it already in its trace.[14]

The Other-in-the-Same: Levinas Thinking an Embodied Sensibility that is Intersubjective ... and radically passive

What is synthesized through the so-called passive syntheses of incarnated passivity? And how many kinds of syntheses should we expect to find? To address this, let me sketch an overview of some of Levinas's remarks about bodies and what moves them. That will require a brief passage through some "philosophies of life," in which the meaning of incarnation is extensively developed. In 1934, a young Levinas decried the new thinking that returned to bodies in light of matter and forces. He spoke of the drama that Germany was living out with neo-Nietzschean thought. "Zarathustra is not content with his transfiguration; he comes down from his mountain bringing a gospel."[15] The "gospel" is supposed to pass through the re-thinking of the pneumatic Christian body, product of Saint Paul's trans-valuation, by Nietzsche's physiology. The new Nietzschean body outstrips identities and causalities to make and remake itself thanks to the omnipresence, at many levels, of force, which Nietzsche also calls "spirits" and "intelligences."[16] It may be that the jubilant reception of Nietzsche was

---

[14] Levinas, *Otherwise than Being, Or Beyond Essence,* translation Alphonso Lingis (Pittsburgh: Duquesne University Press, 2000), 111–112. Hereafter OBBE.

[15] Levinas, "Reflections on the Philosophy of Hitlerism," translation Seán Hand, in *Critical Inquiry* 17 (Autumn 1990), 63–71. In French "Quelques réflexions sur la philosophie de l'hitlérisme" in *Esprit,* XXVI (Novembre 1934). Hereafter RPH.

[16] Didier Franck, *Nietzsche et l'ombre de Dieu* (Paris: Presses Universitaires de France, 1998), hereafter NOD. As Didier Franck puts out, echoing Nietzsche: "[...] the death of God makes possible and necessary [...] a sur-resurrection in the sense in which

tied to the thirst for new thinking and, above all, worldly messianisms. Levinas was, in any event, well aware of the Nietzsche reception in the 1930s. Nietzsche's logic of forces, which had always served his critical Christianity and his poetics for the "last man," was sliding toward a *mechanism* of forces in expansion. As Levinas argues, "force is characterized by another type of propagation [than the spread of ideals] [...]. [force] is attached to the personality or the society that exerts it, it expands them by subordinating all the rest to them [...]. Nietzsche's will to power, which modern Germany finds again and glorifies [...] is an ideal that brings with it at the same time its own form of universalization: war" (RPH 6).

Although he was in ongoing debate with Nietzsche about the meaning of living embodiment, Levinas approached being, or existence, as force and conflict throughout his reflection on life and bodies. Thus, when confronted with the questions: What causes us to experience our immanence passively? What acts on us that we could speak of the radical passivity of our sensations? Levinas will urge that the active *something*, whether in our body or in the world, which is structured through the passive syntheses of time and association—i.e., through the transcendental ground of all consciousness—this something cannot itself be thematized. It cannot be thematized or represented because, when and however it has been thought, it has *suffered* from anthropomorphic or mechanistic metaphors; we speak of forces, drives, *Reiz*, irritations, excitations. Now, this language is not so much a fault as it is circumscribed by the technological universe to which it applies or has been drawn. For Levinas, it is never a matter of denying that passivity, *pathos*,

Nietzsche speaks of the overman [*surhomme*][...] To take the body as one's red thread, is thus firstly to devastate the *I* of this function and to hold the unity of consciousness...for an appearance of unity," Franck, 175–6; also see Nietzsche, *Kritische Studienausgabe*, Vol. 12, eds. G. Colli and M. Montinari (Berlin: Walter de Gruyter, 1988, 2nd edition), hereafter KSA, 5, 56: "*immer nur einen Anschein von Einheit*"). In each body, we find "a plurality of forces which are situated in a hierarchy [...] such that the ones are conditioned by the existence of the others [...] man as a plurality of 'wills to power': each one with a plurality of means of expression and forms" See Nietzsche, *Beyond Good and Evil: Prelude to a Philosophy of the Future*, translation and ed. Walter Kaufmann (New York: Vintage Books, 1966), §19, 25–6 for the discussion of the will as a complex of sensation and affects. Remarks about the plurality of forces, or spirits, intelligences, wills, or souls, are frequently found in Nietzsche's published and unpublished works. The ambiguity of their nomination is due to changes in perspective as well as the use of metaphor; even 'souls', in Nietzsche, are finite. But Nietzsche did not want to be either a simple mechanist or a mere vitalist.

supposes something that acts on it (Nietzsche himself urged that Will to power is firstly, itself, *pathos*). It is, rather, that the associations that accompany drives, as opposed to passivity, with their ethical and aesthetic implications, should concern us; notably, when they take the form of strong voluntarism, hyperbolic virility, or the exaltation of power.

By 1965, four years after publishing *Totality and Infinity*, Levinas explicitly pinpoints a—perhaps the—core difficulty of Husserl's genetic phenomenology: the co-originarity and interrelation of our proto-impressions (*Urimpression*) and the spontaneous structuring flow that is temporalization as Husserl's transcendental subjectivity. His essay "Intentionality and Sensation"[17] underscores the "tension" at the heart of "in-tentionality." The embodied sensuous "material," however evanescent it may be, that the formal flow of consciousness structures—preserving both its position in the flow while pushing it backwards—this "material" is originally contemporary with its intentionalization, its formation (in other words, form and matter belong together at this fundamental, embodied level). And yet, this material of or from the body—excitations, drives—must also *precede* the intentional flow that gives it form when it becomes full-blown consciousness. Why must it also precede the flow of consciousness? For Husserl, what we call our sensations become conscious only inten-tionally, only as intentionality, only through the stretching of the moment's retention as that which affects us self-modifies and is replaced almost immediately by a new, slightly different sensation. Awareness of this process, of our *becoming* aware of our unfolding sensation, is *pathos*. This *pathos* is only possible because of the property of flow intrinsic to consciousness as a formal and dynamic structure. But is the idea of a conscious "flow" just a metaphor? It is and it is not. It is not: consciousness really does flow—but evenly? Little suggests the consciousness flows along in an uninterrupted line. We should not confuse the specifics of temporal positions with the regularity of marks on a measuring tape. On the other hand, it is indeed a metaphor in the sense that, at the level of the birth of dynamic consciousness, we cannot speak of bodily matter *entering into* spiritual forms, much less of drive material receiving the imprint of

---

[17] Emmanue Levinas, *En découvrant l'existence avec Husserl et Heidegger* (Paris: Vrin, 1982), 145–163. Hereafter IS. For the English translation of the essays on Husserl, see *Discovering Existence with Husserl*, translation Richard A. Cohen and Michael B. Smith (Evanston, Ill.: Northwestern University Press, 1998), 135–151.

something like a formal intellect or awareness. Yet Husserl's phenomenology would have to open to arguments from philosophies of life if it began to speculate about what lies beneath intentional consciousness. That is, if it speculated about the bodily drives as matter that creates its own form, as one sensation stretches and self-modifies in the retentional dynamic of conscious life. This is not an option that Husserl took; it lay too far outside the phenomenological project of describing consciousness as intentional aiming. Therefore, instead of making a Nietzschean or Bergsonian move, Levinas follows Husserl in 1965, and give priority to the universal form—and formalism—of intentionality: consciousness is always conscious of something. Sensation happens *to* our consciousness, in passivity. That which "fuels" sensation from the body cannot be thematized or represented within phenomenology.

Indeed, in 1965, Levinas argues, much as Husserl himself would, "every distinction between perception and perceived—every idealizing intention—rests on time, on the putting out of phase between the intending and the intended. Only the proto-impression is pure of all ideality. It is [...] the now, for which the unity of sensation, identical in the flow, is constituted, through the interlocking of retentions and protensions." Here we have the point of intersection between Levinas's phenomenology of lived time and the "now" that will subsequently characterize his re-thinking of messianic consciousness.

> But the flow is only the modification of the proto-impression that stops coinciding with itself [...] the unity of sensation, which is always becoming, is older and younger than the instant of the proto-impression as itself [...] (IS 155, emphasis added).

Everything suggests that it is the sensuous proto-impression (which can also be an *affective* proto-impression when it "insists" like a painful memory) that dynamically forges the form of the flow of consciousness. Husserl had re-defined the very meaning of the moment, allowing it to be both point-like and arguing that the point also stretched along as embodied retention, with the result that nothing other than "time" itself connected the hypothetical building-blocks, the points, composing the present moments in time's flow. But Levinas is saying something more: it is sensation that stretches as it becomes conscious, providing an overarching *feeling* of form, and uniformity, to consciousness. This means that the unity of sensation itself is the result of two fundamental alterations: the passage from pre-consciousness into consciousness, and the still more curious upsurge of a sensation so plastic that it continuously modifies itself, giving rise to a new sensation (which is simultaneously the old sensation, stretched) and a sense of continuity *that feels like a homogeneous flow.* What we therefore call the *unity* of sensation is enabled by two things: the ongoing upsurge of proto-impressions and the semi- or pre-conscious quality of embodied sensations. In effect, an original sensation is always changing, and thus older, and maybe different than what "I" feel now—now that it has stretched and modified itself. Of course, it is younger than what I feel now, too, because I do not yet "know," in the sense of "cognitive experience," *what* precisely I am feeling now—not until a tiny lapse of time, or stretching, has occurred. Given this, given that Levinas has put his finger on the paradox of sensibility in Husserl, he nevertheless opts for Husserl's original answer: the primacy of *formal* intentional unity: the so-called unity of sensation over the surging, chaotic proto-impression; *morphè* must structure *hylè*, here, even though they are initially indistinguishable; even though *hylè* is what makes its own form and formation possible.

Why does Levinas remain with so classical a phenomenology? Certainly, in the 1960s, this is because, for phenomenology, embodied passivity is the locus of *meaning.* This means that meaning, or sense, depends on the ordering or structuring that embodied forces and corporeal events undergo. To put it differently, we only *notice* sensations (and affects) as they come into the process that is intentional consciousness. Unnoticed, we might argue that sensibility (e.g., pain, apprehension, cravings or desire) drives *us*, as William James and even Freud argued. However by 1974, Levinas would rethink this classical argument. In *Otherwise than Being*, extreme passivity is primordial; it unfolds thanks to the wager, as he puts it, that there is a pre-synthetic modality of passion, which is *intersubjective.* As inter-subjective passion, the later conception of extreme passivity is neither fully conscious nor does it correspond to conceptions of "natural" drives or instincts. That is, it depends less on imponderable events in the body than it does on the intersubjective make up of our skin, our flesh. Extending Husserl's formalist phenomenology of passive synthyesis thus allows Levinas to deconstruct monadic subjectivity and avoid vitalist philosophies that characterized the body as a collection of unconscious forces. Phenomenological "meaning" becomes meaning-in-formation; it becomes sensuous-affective and under-determined; as Levinas puts it, it becomes "for-the-other." The genealogical arguments of the 1970s work locate meaning-creation in a body that is as readily "social" (intersubjective) as it is "natural." Levinas writes:

> Rather than nature, earlier than nature, immediacy is this vulnerability, this maternity, this pre-birth or pre-nature in which sensibility belongs. This [intersubjective] proximity is narrower, more constrictive, than [spatial] proximity, older than every past present. The ego repudiates the past present; bent under the charge of an immemorial weight, the inflexible ego, [like] an indeclinable guarantee against any elimination [*indéclinable garanti contre toute rayure*], bears the other that it confronts because, in regard to [that other], it would have been committed to it or, through reminiscence, would have assumed, as something ancient and essential, engagements that it [the ego] would have made unbeknownst to itself [*à son insu*] [...]. Non-thematized proximity does not simply belong to the "horizon" of contact [...] sensibility [...] is not constituted out of some apperception putting consciousness into relationship with a body. *Incarnation is not a transcendental operation* of a subject that is situated in the midst of the world it represents to itself [...]. The sensible [...] binds the node of incarnation into a plot larger than the apperception of self. In this plot I am bound to others before being tied to my body. [...] Intentionality—the [aiming of] noēsis—that philosophy of consciousness [claims to] distinguish in *feeling* [*le sentir*] and which it would like to take up, through a regressive movement, as the origin of ascribed meaning— [i.e.,] sensible intuition—*is* already in the mode of apprehension and obsession [...] (OBBE 76-77, translation Modified and emphasis added)[18]

The extended analysis of pre-cognitive sociality allows Levinas to lodge messianic hope in the wager that the other-in-the-same invests us, even into our intentional consciousness. In the stretching of sensation typical to the interlock of retention and protension, the "now" moment affects me, unforeseen and unexpected. "Bound to others before being tied to my own body," the upsurge of sensibility-affectivity may carry a charge of conscience, a certain sting or distress. This is, for Levinas, "intelligibility *before the light*, before the present of initiative" (OBBE 78, emphasis added), and it invites us to consider that a body-social—a body multiplied amongst other flesh, rather than assembled or condensed as the "my own" quality of a transcendental ego presiding over *its* events—precedes and weaves into the subjectivity of cognition and everyday representation.

---

[18] Translation slightly modified for fidelity to the French.

In this way, Levinas ventures that "my" passive vulnerability to others carries sensuous *and* affective modes, and at the least, it troubles Husserl's passive *synthesis*. Nevertheless, as a repeating "moment" or body-temporality—which has already passed when "I" examine the X that it represents—the intersubjective "present" entwines with intentionality, much the way the *prae-ens* that Granel describes inhabits us in the dawning of light. Indeed, the Granel-Levinas comparison would be worth making, were it not for the difference between Granel's solitary perceptual faith and Levinas's messianic investiture, which insists that we are connected to one another before we are perceiving subjects who marvel at the *sub divo* illuminated world. Moreover, the Levinasian analytic demonstrates that sensuous-affective passivity *opens* the possibility of speech as spontaneous address, or speaking-to someone. Conversation arises only out of words *given*, and these are not firstly or exclusively motivated by willing or interests. If the flesh, if our skin can have the open, under-determined vulnerability of being-for another, then the possibility of messianic peace—as the brief halting of natural forces—lies therein.

The Levinasian "subject" thus recalls the figure of the messiah who, in Jewish lore, redeems nothing but was nevertheless *there*, in the catastrophe. With the poignancy of a suffering that is "for nothing," Levinas pulls messianism away from history, away from futurity, and may even avoid the utopianism of Adorno's "imageless image of the possible." Levinas also develops a non-spiritualistic interiority, where messianic sensibility is both "now" and "is" *not*. In saying "is not," I mean simply that the conscious-ness-preconscious dynamic is too complex and too multiform to be defined as the difference between an event and objects in the world. The concept of "not-being," for Levinas, has to do with what is *not synthesized* spontan-eously and passively; it is, as Granel argued, *against the grain of predication*, in the way that the sky self-differentiates as justly original, "for not being." Although their inspirations are very different, Granel's ontology is close to Levinas's wager about sensibility. What we are able to think, of existence, or of Being, is what we—perhaps with great difficulty—can ultimately thematize, if fleetingly. Levinas's elaboration of pre-conscious sensibility, conjoined to affectivity, is a wager because we can hardly "think" what is not (yet) conscious. Yet accepting the wager has the result of enlarging the hermeneutics of modes through which we "are" in the world or with others. To be sure, the implications of Levinas's intersubjective, sensuous "modes" are very different from those explored by Heidegger and Granel. I would contend, in closing, that the difference lies precisely in this: the last, and unsurprisingly paradoxical, attempt at messianic hope in the 20th century depends on a sensibility, which proceeds from Husserl's formalism even as it rehabilitates a pre-conscious, embodied "inter-subjective" instant that stretches itself in retention and loses itself as it takes form as cognition. Perhaps the question is whether this is the only site from which to unfold a meditation on hope; indeed, a meditation that *would be* hope itself.

By Way of Conclusion

At the risk of simplification, let me attempt to summarize. Levinas deformalizes Jewish messianism as intersubjective ties. These come to pass on a daily basis as the *in*-sistence of bodily memory taking the "form" of recurring affects or passions. This can only be the affair of living body, in which sensation—whether endogenous or exogenous—is effective, that is, under way *before* it has become the full consciousness of an object or the awareness of a milieu. Like Granel's pre-intentional, sacred world of light, Levinas's deformalization works with and against Husserl's and Heidegger's phenomenologies—*even* though Heidegger's is already a phenomenology that interprets being-in-the-world. True to certain *leitmotifs* of Jewish messianism, Levinas privileges the moment of intersubjective election over the worldly sacred, which has important consequences for questions of justice as what is due another person. I have alluded to a kind of ancient "paganism" in Granel. This is to underscore the universality of Granel's *sub divo* "sacred." Levinas's inspiration lies elsewhere. He would argue starting from the ethical *élan* of the Hebrew prophet or *nabi*, who is not a seer, a "*mantis*," so much as one who speaks ethical words that he neither chose nor initiated. The prophet's words are exhortations to repentance and just acts. Unlike the Greek "seer," prophetic "future seeing" is ultimately for the sake of avoiding it, as the terrible outcome of human injustice. Levinas's intertwining of sincerity, the "Saying," and discourse, or the "Said"; his presentation of the other-in-the-same, deformalize Hebrew prophetism with a view to reaching its conditions of possibility in pre-cognitive experience; that means the experience, essentially, of anyone, and not simply the prophet. The profound intersubjective passivity that Levinas wagers lies at the root of the prophetic call to ethical responsibility to others. It is as different from Husserl's passive *syntheses* as it is from the surplus of meaning that Heidegger finds in the address of the poet.[19] Above all, the differences between Greek seer and Hebrew prophet, German poet and Hebrew prophet, faith as meaning and messianic unrest, cannot be sublimated. There is neither a higher third term, nor a synthetic "result" available to raise and preserve both world and Other.[20] Hence, ethics and ontology cannot be conflated at the level of their first coming into cognitive awareness or intentional consciousness.

Despite this, passivity lies at the heart of all these approaches: our pre-intentional connections to world and other are inescapably passive, perception is firstly corporeal and fleshly, pre-thetic and pre-representational. It has been argued that such passivity necessarily assumes a kind of ability or power to *be affected-by*—world or Other. Certainly, Levinas alludes in 1974 to the non-sense of chaotic sensations intruding into a structure that is intentional and in-forming, like a capacity or power. But to go beyond that and to attempt, from within phenomenology, to thematize the dynamics of our embodied life would require revisiting philosophies of life or vitalisms that speak of forces, drives, etc.—all of them unconscious and forming our *primary* evaluations. Is there no place, then, for such "values" in a messianic reflection—especially when it dares to start from inter-subjective embodiment? Recently phenomenologists, notably Renaud Barbaras, have argued that the formalist Husserlian heritage leaves "life" out of conceptualization, with the distressing consequence that phenomenology remains idealistic, and worse, dualist (i.e., divided between an subject that experiences its embodied immanence passively *versus* other living beings that must be "constituted" in consciousness). Classical phenomenology would thus unfold from a formalistic ontology, which Barbaras polemically calls an ontology of death.[21] Without evaluating the provocation intended by this claim, I nevertheless wonder whether a "new thinking"—or a new, "new thinking"—could really unfold a minimalist faith, much less

---

[19] See Heidegger, *Erläuterungen zu Hölderlins Dichtung*; Gesamtausgabe 4 (Frankfurt am Main: Klostermann, 1975–), 66; in English, *Elucidations of Hölderlin's Poetry*, translation Keith Hoeller (Amherst, NY: Humanity Books, 2000), 51–65. The distinction between the Greek seer or "*mantis*" and the Hebrew prophet or "*nabi*" is discussed in Marlène Zarader, *The Unthought Debt: Heidegger and the Hebraic Heritage*, translation Bettina Bergo (Stanford: Stanford University Press, 2006), 53–57.
[20] Although this appears precisely to have been Merleau-Ponty's project in light of the extension of passivity into sleep, the unconscious, and intersubjective perception.
[21] See above, note 4.

embodied messianic hope, while wholly avoiding the consequences of philosophies of life and will. Hopefully, what it can avoid is the aestheticization of force that we find in the Nietzsche reception of the 1930s. In short, the activity of a living body opens an abyss of activity, feeding passive sensibility when we venture "behind" passive synthesis and conscious meaning. This is a danger Levinas understood, and confronted; it is why he refused to thematize immanent forces, arguing instead for a wager about the possibility of ethical meaning whose locus lay between "my" body and that of the Other.

Life as Limit-drawing Event
Comments on Bergo's Discussion of Formalism vs. Vitalism

JONNA BORNEMARK

In her paper Bettina Bergo wants to find a principle of life beyond formalism, a messianic principle of hope, body and life that does not run the risk of being locked up in interiority which she points out always haunts Christian faith. But she also asks herself whether there is a philosophy of life that does not imply all the dangers of fascism, as did the 1930s and 1940s reception of different kinds of vitalism and Nietzsche.

Bergo draws our attention to Granel's attempt to think beyond a binary division of parts and wholes, form and matter, etc. He understands that a first divide between sky and earth is at the root of such binary thinking: the earth of objects and the sky as a "way out," between beings and non-being. The sky is not a non-being in general but rather *the* sky and thus "'rightly original,' *for not being*," as Bergo cites him in the previous chapter. And this is, of course, also the division between earth and the divine. Granel argues against an understanding of limits as something that creates self-sufficient parts, and instead argues that limits imply relations and transitions. Limits thus do not create wholes that are what they are in themselves, they rather create the tension that separates through relating.

I think that a development of Granel's understanding of limits could also help us find a way between vitalism and formalism. Instead of understanding the limit as already established, we could focus on the limit-drawing event. An event where separation is created but not yet established. Such a limit-drawing event would be the separation between earth and sky, and between beings and non-being. It is an event beyond form, but where form is born. Maybe it could even be understood as the movement of life itself. With a concept from a totally different context, namely the Indian, it could be called *Pratitya-samutpada*—"emergence in mutual dependence." Such limit-drawing would not mean the birth of a self-sufficient transcendence or interiority, but would be truly intersubjective in the sense of "in need of another."

But how do we access an event such as limit-drawing? If it is a pheno-menological idea, it would need a place where it could be experienced and would be related to a willing and experiencing self. Bergo proposes the idea of "the other-in-same," drawn from Levinas. And I agree that this denotes the place in phenomenology where these questions have to be discussed, i.e. the place where we experience our immanence passively (even though not necessarily with a starting point in Levinas). Where we are experiencing ourselves as receiving ourselves, and not in control of ourselves. A place that provides us with a radical passivity of sensation, i.e. not only that the "object" is out of our control and received, but also that the means and forms through which the "object" is given, are themselves given to us. There is thus a double-sidedness of passivity: both the stream of proto-impres-sions, and the receiving of intentionality. Already in the passive reception of oneself there is a split, and a limit is immediately drawn between what is received as proto-impression and what is received as the structure of intentionality. These two, however, also need one another and cannot be thought of in isolation. And beyond this, they also have in common that they cannot be fully thematized without losing something essential. The phenomenological analysis has shown that neither of them can be fully visible: A proto-impression loses its "now" and is formalized through passive synthesis. In a similar way intentionality always partly escapes its own thematizing eye, as was first shown in Husserl's analysis of inner time consciousness.[1] The paradox of sensibility is thus also the paradox of intentionality and thematization. Intentionality is thus not pure form, but is, dare I say... alive.

I do not think we should understand unformed life and constitution as two separate moments in experience. What I find interesting is instead to think their interconnection, and maybe even their common birth *as* separated. That is, to think the *limit* between life and constitution, the place

---

[1] This analysis runs through several of Husserl's works with start in *Zur Phänomenologie des inneren Zeitbewusstseins* (Hua X, ed. Rudolf Boehm, Haag: Martinus Nijhoff, 1966).

where they are separated from each other. Or rather the event of limit-drawing in which they become two; two that are both received passively and creating the possibility of activity.

Levinas is aware of this double passivity, but does he use it fully? Thus, when Husserl privileges form—and formalism—of intentionality (as Bergo says), he also privileges one passivity and reception over another, i.e. the reception of intentionality above the reception of the world, one side of a movement at the cost of the other. And I do agree that *such* an emphasis exists in phenomenology. But there is a reason for this: phenomenological analysis has shown that there is a mutual interdependence between the reception of these two passivities, although there is above all an interdependence that is asymmetrical. The world is only given through the *means and forms* of intentionality, since intentionality is what gives. But even then, I would argue that this does not result in a pure interiority, but precisely in an asymmetrical interdependence. Only through abstraction can we separate them. Their relation is structured in the same way as the body that is both felt and feeling. Maybe we could even say that their relation *is* the body: as something that we passively receive in its double-sidedness, and through which our activity is possible.

The task to try to make these passivities (and not only what can be felt and seen) visible in language, and the will to discuss a *pure* passivity that loses every connection to activity, have been topics for discussion in phenomenology, especially in the so called turn to religion.[2] This is a problem connected to the problem of naming and of metaphors. Since Husserl's analysis of inner time consciousness, phenomenology has tried to make this double passivity visible. And thus it has also tried to make visible that which escapes objectifying intentionality, that which we cannot make into an object. For example, Aron Gurwitsch examines this in *Marginal Consciousness*, but maybe the philosopher who has pushed this the furthest is Michel Henry, who even claims that objectifying intentionality is unreal in relation to an immanent intentionality.[3]

---

[2] See Dominique Janicaud, *Phenomenology and the "Theological turn": the French debate* (New York: Fordham University Press, 2000) and Hent de Vries, *Philosophy and the Turn to Religion* (Baltimore: Johns Hopkins University Press, 1999).

[3] Aron Gurwitsch, *Marginal Consciousness* (Ohio: Ohio University Press, 1985). Michel Henry explicitly argues for the unreality of the objectifying intentionality in *I am the Truth* (Stanford California: Stanford University Press, 2003).

I do think that the need to make the experience of a passive reception visible is one reason why human beings throughout history have formed different concepts of "Gods," of the "Holy," etc. But it is precisely this will to render apparent that withdraws from experience and visibility, at the same time that it makes them possible, is of course a paradox and places us in front of a dilemma: either we must name that which cannot properly have a name, *or* reduce experience to that which can show itself as an object. Through naming, concepts (for example "God," "nunc stans," or, as here, "Life") are formed and endowed with power, they enter the human world of language as something of which some "chosen ones" have a more refined knowledge, with which they are in touch. And from here the whole power structure can grow forth. These authorities have different names in different contexts: "religious leaders," "philosophers," or "scientists."

The alternative would be to avoid naming and bringing these issues to language. But this would mean that we became blind to a whole field of experiences, and phenomenology could even be understood as a rebellion against such blindness, in its constant attempts to formulate the passively received possibilities for experience. To deny the possibility of bringing this to language would mean that only what can be measured and objectified is understood as real.

These two alternative ways of dealing with this paradox also have political consequences. I would suggest that totalitarian societies, religious or non-religious, can be understood as radical consequences of the first alternative, of bringing the passivity of human activity to language and making it into a foundation for a world-view. Some words ("God," "Race," "Life" etc.) are capitalized and made absolute. On the other hand, liberal and scientist societies could be understood as a consequence of the second alternative. In avoiding a language for this passivity they take only that which can be measured as real into account. And measurements of different kinds are often transformed into financial and economical measurements.

If phenomenology could be seen as a protest against a scientistic society, it is also true that a similar debate, and an equally problematic relation to this paradox have been present in phenomenology itself. Starting from Husserl's concept of *nunc stans* (then developed by Klaus Held)[4],

[4] Klaus Held, *Lebendige Gegenwart—Die Frage nach der Seinsweise des transzendentalen Ich bei Edmund Husserl, entwickelt am Leitfaden der Zeitproblematik* (Den Haag: Martinus Nijhoff, 1966).

phenomenology has repeatedly tried to object to the reduction of knowledge to object-knowledge, and emphasized passivity, affectivity, and the
non-given in the given. But, and this is important, phenomenology has also
time after time returned to a criticism of these concepts to the extent that
they have grown too predominant—i.e. when they have been recognised as
"Names." This dilemma is one way of understanding "The Ambiguity of the
Sacred," within which the sacred is understood in terms of those passivities
that escape naming.

As I have argued, limits do not necessarily have to be understood as
borders between two fields, but rather as a place of birth: an event where
form and matter are separated and where life comes forth. Life is thus not a
"Something," or a harmonious experience, one in itself and before reflection. Life could rather be understood as the separation between one and
the other, between experiencing and experienced, a split that is inherent in
all living. And this split does not have to leave one side behind, as
thematized objectivity, as well as unformed life, has tended to be left behind
in a phenomenology that has given priority to thematizing and transcendental intentionality. Focusing on the event of limit-drawing means that
thematized and thematizing can never be isolated from each other, and that
form and matter appear together as departing from each other and thus as
both dependent upon each other and as separate parts. Their birth means
that they are seperated and move away from each other, becoming more
and more independent, or seemingly independent; since they are forever
bound together in their original emergence in mutual dependence.

"Life" would then not mean will to power, having, as Levinas says on one
occasion, only one way to become universal: war. Instead, "life" would
mean limit-drawing, and as such differentiation and conflict, it would mean
eroticism (that demands separation in order to attract) as well as war, it
would mean "world." It would definitely not mean one harmonious Being,
Will, or solution, and as soon as it becomes fixed as a concept of power or
fundation it needs to be deconstructed, once again finding the place where
it is born, and form and content are separated. As such, the concept of life
has an advantage since it is connected to the proto-impression as well as to
the movement of intentionality. In such a focus on the event of limit-
drawing there is neither a transcendent world of forms or gods, nor any
pure, unformed matter or a pure, non-constituted life. The forms could
never leave the world or the body, but only over and over again formulate
their birth. In my understanding faith is a name for such a movement, a will

to relate to the withdrawn that does not have to be connected only to a transcendent beyond, but rather to a movement of giving birth, maybe a movement of hope?

Bergo's question was whether we could approach messianism as a principle of hope in correlation to a world and a subjectivity of affectivity that are embodied but not explicitly alive. And furthermore, can we do this through a return to a philosophy of life that would be able to save phenomenology from formalism and idealism, but without falling into the dangers of fascism, as did the reception of Nietzsche?

Maybe the concept of limit-drawing could be helpful in such a task, as a fruitful "in-between," between the dangers of philosophy of life and phenomenology? Maybe it would mean a phenomenology of birth.

An Unresolved Ambiguity
Politics, Religion, Passion in Hobbes and Spinoza

FREDRIKA SPINDLER

"The mob has no ruler more potent than
superstition."[1]

To claim that Spinoza has a problem with religion would be somewhat of an understatement. His excommunication from the Jewish community at the age of 24, stated in the harshest possible words in the Herem of 1656 is well known, as are the numerous accusations of atheism (against which Spinoza, however, would repeatedly defend himself)[2] made by both his contemporaries and his later readers. As one of Spinoza's only two books published during his lifetime, the *Theologico-Political Treatise* would be received as a scandalous work undermining the Holy text itself; the *Ethics*, with its claim that God be understood as Nature and as submitted to necessity—thus denying both God's transcendence and his free will—would not be met more favourably. Indeed, for Spinoza who, in what appears to be a rare outburst of frustration, considers the notion of God's will to be "the sanctuary of ignorance"[3] and devotes all his efforts to dismantling the affectivity underlying any religious fervour as sadness and ignorance, religion as such appears to be nothing but an illustration of man's tendency to fight "as bravely for slavery as for safety."[4] Nevertheless, these observations, however

---

[1] Spinoza, *A Theologico-Political Treatise*, preface, translation R. H. Elwes (New York: Dover Publications, Inc, 1951), 5. Spinoza refers his quotation to Curtius, lib iv, chap. 10.
[2] See for instance the exchange with Oldenburg in letters 73–78.
[3] Spinoza, *Ethics*, I, app., translation E. Curley (London: Penguin Books 1996), 29.
[4] *A Theologico-Political Treatise*, 5.

accurate, do not suffice to clarify the philosophical point of religion being a *problem* to Spinoza. If, on the one hand, religion, both understood as vulgar superstition and as a more enlightened form of piety is indeed, throughout the work of Spinoza, submitted to a devastating analysis showing its profound anchorage in inadequacy, religion is on the other hand not only considered as an inevitable part of social, thus political, life, but furthermore, must even be used as a tool enforcing the possibilities of a sustainable political society—the same political society in which Spinoza wishes to abolish any religious authority as a structure of political power. How are we then to understand this apparent contradiction? It appears that we are dealing with a problem that can be understood on at least two levels: one related to the epistemological question of adequate knowledge, the other related to the larger context of the political, where religiosity, understood as an inevitable passion, not only has to be dealt with but furthermore will prove to play a crucial role, be it of a negative or positive kind.

This problem, however, also seems analogous to the one expressed in one of Spinoza's predecessors—Hobbes—main works. Like Spinoza, Hobbes—also accused of atheism—, in *Leviathan*, understands religion chiefly as the result of human ignorance, while, at the same time, he claims its necessity in a functioning political science. Both argue, in a similar way, concerning the position of religion in regard to the political context: Hobbes, by claiming that it is necessary that religious authority in practice be subordinated to the political authority; Spinoza asking that there be a radical line of separation between the two, but furthermore, that it is crucial to disarm the religious authority as a structure of political power—that is, in short, advocating a political control over religion. But where Hobbes in fact ends up reducing the role of religion to issues of dominion, Spinoza appears to leave open a space for profound reflection concerning not only how religiosity plays a role in the political, but also its possible potential regarding knowledge. In both, we thus find a substantial ambiguity concerning the status, the signification and the implication of religion—in relation to the political, but also in a wider sense—that requires further exploration. This is why an investigation where the different levels—the epistemological, the affective and the political, but also the ontological and anthropological—are interrelated and interwoven, is called for.[5]

Religion and anthropology:
origin and occurrence in Hobbes and Spinoza

In both Hobbes and Spinoza, we find two fundamental theses concerning religion as a phenomenon, and concerning the connection between politics and religion. The first one is that religion—and religiosity, no matter in what form—is a human phenomenon and nothing else, that is, has fundamentally nothing to do with any transcendent reality. The second one is that religion has an exclusively political function, and that this function may be of a positive or negative kind—that is beneficial for the state, or harmful.

To start, let us see how the first one of these theses is formulated in Hobbes. A schematic analysis of Hobbes' basic anthropology starts out from a certain materialism: there are, in Hobbes' understanding, nothing but bodies, to the degree that the very concept of an immaterial substance is in itself a contradiction.[6] Even God, as it were, must be understood as corporeal. The human being is a body among others, and, like any other body, is primarily motivated by self-preservation.[7] However what distinguishes the human being from other beings, animals in particular, is that she possesses an ability of language (in itself, a mechanical phenom-enon): she emits and makes use of certain sounds and signs that are deeply

---

[5] The relation between Hobbes and Spinoza on a level bringing together not only their political philosophies as such, but on one that would confront them also from an ontological, anthropological, epistemological and affective perspective, remains yet, in contemporary philosophy, largely to be examined. Such an analysis, parting from on the one hand, their joint terminology and themes—the theologico-political analysis, corporeality, materiality and the notion of self-preservation—; and on the other hand, from their constitutive divergencies concerning key concepts such as *conatus*, *potentia* and *potestas*, natural and civil rights and forms of government, would prove to be fruitful not only for situating Hobbes and Spinoza with and against each other in a philosophical-historical manner. More importantly, it also appears that such an analysis would open towards the possibility of thinking the Spinozian political philosophy as a forceful alternative to the Hobbesian legacy in contemporary political philosophy and theory.

[6] Hobbes, *Leviathan*, I, ch. 4 (London: Penguin Books, 1968), 108.

[7] Ibid. ch. 6, 118–119.

transforming or making evolve her being. By associating certain things with specific sounds and signs, and by remembering them she thus enters a temporality that does not only involve the present but also the past and the future; rather, she acquires the capacity of projecting the past towards a future time. To Hobbes, it is precisely the capacity of projection towards an indefinite future that characterizes human identity.[8] However it is also thereby that human being's great tragic event occurs: by projecting herself into the future, she becomes aware of her own finitude, whereby death becomes her main focus. Thus, it is from the experience of a radical uncertainty—or lack of security—and awaiting an always untimely and threatening death that the human being realizes her need of controlling and rendering as secure as possible her future life. The human being will thus from now on, in all possible ways, accumulate and capitalize all she can in order to guarantee her future lie, that is, in clear, obtaining sufficient power, while all at the same time, she realizes that ultimately, no power will be sufficient in order to keep death away forever.[9] In other words, we find ourselves in a vicious circle, where the accumulation of capital in order to render life safe must itself be protected, which demands yet further accumulation that must be protected and so on, all this with the result that the fundamental anguish will never diminish or disappear.[10] To Hobbes, it is from here on obvious how religion originates, deeply anchoring itself in human's psyche: in fact, religion has the same origin as science, since it is the fear of the future that motivates us to seek for the reason and causes of things and events.[11] The knowledge of causes actually constitutes a very forceful means of power, since this knowledge makes it possible for us not only to explain how things have appeared, but more importantly, how they are likely to appear and occur in the future, thus giving us the possibility of preventive actions. In order to deal with our fear of death we thus need to

[8] Ibid, ch. 11–12, 160–172.
[9] "So that man, which looks too far before him, in the care of future time, hath his heart all day long, gnawed on by feare of death, poverty, or other calamity, and has no repose, nor pause of his anxiety, but in sleep." (Ibid. ch. 12, 169.)
[10] "So that in the first place, I put for a general inclination of all mankind, a perpetual and restless desire of Power after power, that ceaseth only in Death. And the cause of this, is not always that a man hopes for a more intensive delight, than he has already attained to; or that he cannot be content with a moderate power: but because he cannot assure the power and means to live well, which he hath present, without the acquisition of more." (Ibid, ch. 11, 161.)
[11] Ibid., 164–165.

find the causes of things, in order to, in turn, be able to act ourselves upon these causes.

This state of affairs may have two consequences: either we manage to have knowledge of causality in general, thus being able at least in part to act upon them; or we do not manage to acquire any knowledge. Interestingly enough, for Hobbes, both these possibilities will lead to religious belief.

In the first case, which is rather rare and concerns only a small number of persons, as philosophers or true scientists, we manage to find causes, and regress indefinitely in causality to the point where we must, necessarily, stipulate a first cause or force.[12] In fact, we will find no other ontological proof of God in Hobbes, and there is also very little that we can know of God as a first cause. What we can know is that he exists and that he is omnipotent (since he produces all things); possibly also that he must be corporeal since only bodies exist.[13] However we know strictly nothing of his nature other than the above mentioned facts: in other words, this lack of knowledge results in the fact that there is nothing in principle that would contradict the possibility of God performing miracles, or communicating with specific and chosen persons, such as prophets, ordering them to per-form certain acts, and so forth. Contrary to Spinoza, as we will see, it is thus completely possible for Hobbes that God manifest himself in accordance with the different ways described in the Bible, precisely because we cannot have more than a minimal knowledge of him in the first place. And if that were the case—that is God wanting, desiring or ordering us to do one thing or another, we cannot do anything but obey his will: this is a completely reasonable conclusion since there is absolutely no way in which we could resist an omnipotent will. So God exists, and he is omnipotent; we must obey him: this is the origin and result of religion in the first case.

In the second case, which is far more common, we actually do not succeed in figuring out causality in a satisfying way. In order to conjure our fear of death, we will thus imagine invisible powers that we will call god or gods, that we will try to render favourable to us in order to protect and preserve us. In this case, we will act accordingly to how we would act towards very powerful humans: we will worship them, we will sacrifice to

---

[12] Ibid., ch. 12, 170.
[13] Ibid., 170–171.

them, perform certain cults and rites according to what we believe would cause them joy and contentment.[14]

To summarize and conclude: the origins of religion must thus be understood from the point of view of human's fundamental conditions as finite and self-preserving. Religion may have a rational ground, that is, be founded in real knowledge of causality, or it may have an irrational ground; however the main question will still, to Hobbes, be what effects it will have in society rather than what origin it actually has. To Hobbes, there is certainly a difference between false and true religion, that is, whether it is a product of imagination or succeeding from true revelation; however, as soon as it gets into the circuits of transmission, its consequences will be altogether human. In fact, no matter what its origins, there are in reality no absolute proofs for true religion as such: since faith in any case is fundamentally grounded in the combination of the instinct of self-preservation and the fear of death—*timor mortis*—this means that it is in itself a forceful vector of conflicts that the state must deal with and regulate. Thus, for Hobbes, the main question concerning religion will be how it is put to use in human interactivity. And the answer to this is: dominion, since, as previously established, all human quest is for power—which in turn necessarily calls for a political regulation.

Spinoza's point of departure appears to be quite similar to Hobbes'. Like his predecessor, Spinoza claims that human being strives to persevere in her being—*in suo esse perseverare*.[15] However, and this is crucial, Spinoza's notion of *conatus* does not mean that human beings strive in order to maintain her biological existence at all costs, but rather that it is about actualizing the consequences of her individual essence,[16] that is, doing absolutely all that her nature determines her to do. The nuance is decisive: naturally, Spinoza's conatus also implies a self-preservation in the classical sense, that is resisting death, however this is rather a consequence of her effort to develop and increase her power than a primary motivation, which also means that the main focus, in an individual, will not in the same way as in Hobbes be on accumulating the largest possible amount of preserving and protective things, but rather on the things or contexts that in various ways have a favourable effect on our vital power. In accordance with the

[14] Ibid., 170.
[15] Spinoza, *Ethics*, III, pr 6.
[16] Ibid., pr 7.

analysis in the *Ethics*, this also leads to a multiple variety concerning human interaction: human has a natural inclination to wish to rejoice in the same things that her fellow humans rejoice in, but this can be done in many different ways. Either, she can do so by diminishing anything that is hurtful or bad to the other, or she can strive to give something to the other that, to him, is associated with joy. Yet again, she can do so by trying to make the other cherish the same things she cherishes herself, or even taking away that which only benefits the other and not herself.[17] It is thus clear that the interhuman relationship, for Spinoza just as for Hobbes, *can* indeed result in the need of dominion, however this is not primarily what characterizes it: interhuman relationship or coexistence is highly dependent on a large number of conditions and circumstances, which is why we can see at a very early stage why the political context is going to be so decisive. Having outlined these preliminary conditions, Spinoza sets up two possible scenarii. In the first one, we would have sufficiently good knowledge of ourselves as well as of our fellow humans in order to act accordingly to this knowledge. In the second scenario, we would have little or no knowledge neither of ourselves nor of our fellow humans, and would thus to a very large extent be determined by external causes that we do not understand. In the first case, it is impossible for religion, in a traditional sense to occur at all, since the adequate knowledge of ourselves and of the world excludes any desire for or need for any transcendent notions of God, and instead implies a comprehension of God as the substance, *natura naturans* producing all things with the same necessity that it produces itself:[18] knowledge, in the Spinozist sense, is nothing but the knowledge of this fact, which makes us see and understand things either in their respective and necessary relation to each other (knowledge of the second degree, through common notions), or in relationship to how their singular essence expresses a specific degree of power within the substance or God (knowledge of the third degree or intuitive knowledge). The second case—where we would largely or entirely lack this knowledge, will necessarily give rise to one form or another of religious belief. We can talk of these two scenarii in other words: in the first case, most of our actions would be active, explained by our own capacity of thinking and acting—we would thus act accordingly to reasonable ideas; in

---

[17] See ibid., pr 27–32 et sq.
[18] See the whole of *Ethics*, I. For a summary, see *Ethics*, I, app.

the other case, we would mostly be determined by our passions and inadequate ideas.

However, discussing these two possible scenarii is, in truth, for the sake of formality. In reality, Spinoza notes that it is very unusual for humans to be led by adequate knowledge and reasonable ideas: the fact is that most of us, to the largest extent, have inadequate knowledge both of ourselves and the world, that we are thrown between different passions, and are ignorant both of what really benefits our conatus and what is harmful to it. In other terms, we do experience and feel joy and sorrow in different ways, and we are also conscious of doing so, however we cannot, mostly, explain what happens to and in us other than in a defective, truncated way. For religion to appear is therefore for Spinoza inevitable, and he gives a detailed explanation of this process in the appendix of the first book of the *Ethics*. As Hobbes, Spinoza notes that humans seek to find causes for things and events—however not primarily in order to ascertain her future, but because she is characterized by a will to know in order to obtain favourable affects. But since she is primarily conscious of her affects without having any real knowledge of where they come from, she naturally makes the mistake of reading nature as such—all things—exclusively from her own perspective. Being conscious of doing things herself in order to obtain a certain result, she thereby concludes that nature acts in the same way: as she also mistakenly thinks she has a freedom of willing, desiring, thinking and acting, she thereby concludes that it is the same for nature. The result of this is a dramatic confusion between cause and final cause, where the question "why?" or "how come?" is immediately transformed into "to what end?"; a confusion that increases exponentially when she systematically includes the whole of nature—and its supposed creator—into her own inadequate understanding of herself. From an inadequate knowledge of ourselves, we are thus led to an anthropomorphic view on nature, and further yet to an anthropomorphic projection concerning the notion of God: since all in nature appear as being at the service of humans, she concludes that nature must have been created to this end, and that it must have been created by a will that can only belong to one or several anthropomorphic divinities. In turn, these divinities are ascribed further human characters since we immediately assume that they, in order to continue being friendly towards us, should be honoured, worshipped and obeyed. This is how religious belief occurs and is anchored within human mind: the linking between passion, that is external determination, inadequate ideas, that is ignorance, and religious belief is given from the very start, as an inverted mirror of nature where, in a most mistaken way, human figures herself to be the measure of everything.[19]

This however constitutes only the first step in Spinoza's analysis of religion, where, like Hobbes, he concludes that it is indeed an altogether human affair, but where Spinoza appears to be more radical than his predecessor since he expressedly points out how religion is anchored within inadequacy—the basic and altogether natural phenomenon of ignorance, leading to a contorted view of self and other, nature and God, and, furthermore, to a life ruled by passion more than by action. But this far, religion has only been analysed in terms of inaccurate epistemology, which as such does not necessarily imply any anomalies on the social or political level. Basic religiosity can in fact be limited to an anonymous relation, to divinities whose aims are unknown to us, but that, in return, do not necessarily appear to demand too much of us in terms of worship or sacrifices: as long as no catastrophic events occur and as long as we find ourselves in a functioning society, there are no particular reasons for an exaggerated religiosity. But things take another turn in times of need or crisis. When socio-economic circumstances suddenly are such that we live in insecurity, oppression or misery, our uncertainty and ignorance re-garding the future makes us desperately look for something within the order of things to grab a hold of. From an uncomplicated notion of God, that we so far have been contented to love and respect, we come to the idea that this hitherto un-interested God is now communicating with us through signs and signals that we must interpret in order to be assured of further benevolence and protection. Spinoza's image of human is perhaps more nuanced than Hobbes': where the latter saw fear as the primary motivation also in religious belief, Spinoza on the contrary sees human as continuously inclined to alter between fear and hope according to how external circumstances present themselves and to how she is influenced by them.[20] Nonetheless, a difficult situation, that may have arisen both by natural causes and bad politics, will lead to the feeling of impotence and despair: in desperation, we seek signs to interpret and obey—and since we, in ac-

---

[19] An important contribution to the analysis of the relation between religion and the particular aspect of inadequate ideas produced by imagination is made by Henri Laux in *Imagination et religion chez Spinoza* (Paris: Vrin, 1993).
[20] *A Theologico-Political Treatise*, preface.

cordance with the theory of affects as presented in the *Ethics*, are always inclined to interpret nature according to our own preferences, the risk of interhuman conflicts is very big, just as is the risk of various authorities and structures of power trying to use our vulnerability to their own ends. This analysis, undertaken by Spinoza in the foreword of the *Theologico-Political Treatise*, shows the real danger of a natural religiosity that in times of need and hardship develops into superstitions; superstitions that in turn lead to intolerance, conflict and possibly in the end, to the devastation of the state.

Here we also see how the real question concerning religion to Spinoza is necessarily connected to the political: if on the one hand it is obvious that the occurrence of superstition, with its associated forms of oppression and insecurity, is intimately linked to historical and social circumstances, it is on the other hand just as obvious that it is only possible to prevent superstition and ignorance by acting upon the social and political context.

Religion and politics: distribution, links and structures of power in Hobbes and Spinoza

How are we then to understand the political function of religion in Hobbes and Spinoza?

To Hobbes, the question of religion is in a certain sense logical, and at least theoretically quite uncomplicated. Since religion appears inevitable—and it can have many shapes, but is always grounded in the idea of self-preservation at any cost on the one hand, and an inevitable fear of death and the future on the other—religion, understood as human belief and creation of sense, becomes a forceful social vector that can give rise to a strong community just as it can create strong dissension within it. Without going into the details of the analysis conducted in *Leviathan*, we can note that it appears as literally necessary that the sovereign, in order to maintain a durable and peaceful state, take control over whatever religion there happens to be—religion that by the way must also be one and not several. Since religion expresses what is good and evil, what is desirable and what is not, its commandments must be the same as the state's in order not to generate conflicts. There can thus be no freedom of religion, for the same reasons that there is no real freedom of opinion in Hobbes ideal state.[21] In the name of the covenant, where the citizen has handed over all his natural right to the sovereign in order to acquire civil right, the sovereign has an unlimited right and duty to rule, perhaps not in fact regarding the actual belief or faith of the subject (since this is quite impossible) but over his actions. Subsequently the sovereign rules in an absolute sense over what opinions and doctrines that may be divulged in the public. If religion both in practice and in theory appears as inevitable, it is also necessarily subordinated to the political—in the positive sense, when used for the sake of society and contributing to obedience to the law and, thereby, to security; in the negative sense when perverted and having acquired an authority that opposes or is in concurrence with the sovereign, and thereby as an alternative political structure threatens the state peace.[22] It appears thus permitted to conclude that Hobbes' stand on religion is mainly pragmatic, with religion as a necessary political tool aiming at obedience. Philosophically speaking however, the question is more problematic: while on the one hand, religion, as in there existing a true religion, is taken for granted, it appears on the other hand that Hobbes is unable to state what epistemological foundation this truth—the true revelation—may hold.[23] In the end, what counts is nothing but the conviction—that is opinion—of the sovereign.

Spinoza, in turn, agrees completely with Hobbes concerning the view on religion as a strong social force, and goes even further concerning the extensive analysis of its different ways of expression. Also like Hobbes, he claims that political authority necessarily must use this ideological material for its own benefit, that is of course in order to create good conditions for a peaceful and durable state of which the ultimate aim is nothing but the freedom of the citizens[24]—a freedom, thus for Spinoza, that is synonymous to the possibility of adequate knowledge. This is also why the political authority must rule over the religious insofar as the latter must not be allowed to define any fundamental values concerning good or evil, permitted or forbidden, in concurrence with civil law. But Spinoza's

---

[21] Hobbes, *Leviathan*, ch. 18.
[22] Matheron rightly claims that Hobbes, in this respect, can be seen as a pedagogical utopist: the conditions of realization of the optimal state rests upon the sovereign's full knowledge not only of his own absolute rights but also of the citizen's rights and duties—that is, complete knowledge of all that is included in the covenant (Alexandre Matheron, *Le Christ et le salut des ignorants chez Spinoza* (Paris: Aubier, 1971), 136).
[23] Hobbes, *Leviathan,* ch. 32.
[24] Spinoza, *A Theologico-Political Treatise*, preface.

analysis here is yet more complex. Against Hobbes, he claims that it is, in fact, impossible for the state to rule over opinions and convictions: since fear of death (or punishment) does not necessarily constitute the strongest motive or affect, and since affectivity is a play between hope and fear, joy and sorrow it is useless or even contra-productive to legislate over opinion.[25] Also, the legitimacy of any government for Spinoza is valid only for as long as it can actually be enforced—in short, any legislation countering with too much violence the desires of the multitude will be overthrown and thus invalidated.[26] Consequently, any acceptable and durable political regime always implies a handling of, as well as a forming of the desires (or conatus) of the multitude, that is favouring positive affects. Social balance is thus always about a putting together of, or an equilibration of, common de-nominators: hence, the political authority must determine, and endow responsibility for, which religious conviction or convictions that are the most consistent with the fundamental aims of the state, and that serve them. What, then, is to be found in the Bible—the text, according to Spinoza, by far the most influential in any modern western society, thereby highly important to anyone trying to understand the desires of the multitude, to this end? The critical exegetic reading of the Old and New Testament undertaken in Spinoza's *Theologico-Political Treatise* shows that in fact, once all contextual, linguistic and historic circumstances have been brought to light—and its internal contradictions have been eliminated[27]— their teachings can be reduced to two fundamental commands: justice (that is obedience to the law) and charity (that is the creating of a positive affectivity).[28] In these commands, the objectives of both the political and the religious would be achieved: for both, law-abiding is the corner stone of peace; for both, so is also a good social context. In short, justice and charity would serve the joint function of maintaining both emotional and juridical order, with no harm done either to the multitude's inevitable penchant for religious belief or the necessity of it being controlled. And the conditions, for these commands to be followed, are, according to Spinoza, happily few: a total of seven principles, simple and universal enough to find acceptance by any sensible religious—and political—authority that would admit to

[25] Ibid., ch. 18.
[26] Ibid., ch. 17
[27] Ibid., ch. 2.
[28] Ibid., ch. 13.

them expressing the core of the Holy Text. Totalling the number of seven, these principles—or basic credos, common denominators for all, are outlined in the *Theologico-Political Treatise*'s chapter 14: God exists, He is unique, omnipresent, omnipotent, He is honoured through the practice of justice and charity, He saves those who follow this rule of life, and He forgives those who repent. As *minima* and *maxima* at the same time, it is clear how these seven basic credos conform to Spinoza's vision of society, both from a philosophical and a political point of view: a close reading of the *Ethics* will see no contradiction to Spinoza's ontological and episte-mological claims[29]—at least as long as no further question concerning the meaning of the notion of God is asked; a joint comprehension of Spinoza's theory of affectivity and his claims of a peaceful society where the quest for knowledge—that is philosophy—can be pursued undisturbed is in perfect coherence with the credos as well. Whether they would satisfy repre-sentatives of official religiosity—in Spinoza's time or any other—is, of course, a different question. What, in fact, are we left with, concerning the position—and the value—of religion in the political?

A close analysis reveals that Spinoza entwines three questions in a complex way; questions of which the two first may be seen as purely practical and concern the actual relationship—that is distribution of power—between religion and politics. The point of departure is in fact that of the common ground: both the religious and the political are grounded in human's inevitable, and natural passionality, that is a) her being as desiring; in other terms, her essence being conatus; b) her being necessarily deter-mined to a large extent by external factors and c) her being mainly ignorant of her own nature as well as of others.' As we can see, there appears to be, between the religious and the political, a curious double bind where not only both originate from the same state of nature, but also, where both are necessary as institutions co-determining each other.[30] The first practical

---

[29] The two last credos, given their highly anthropomorphic formulation, are obviously the two most difficult to conciliate with Spinoza's philosophy. For an enlightening discussion of this, see Matheron, op. cit.

[30] In the same way thus, that there would actually be no need for any political government in a society that would altogether be led by reasonable ideas (that is, where the multitude would acquire a constant adequate knowledge), there would not either be any religiosity at all in that kind of society: however, it is evident that this is not the case, nor can it be, in reality: this is why all political reflection must start in the knowledge of the passions of the multitude.

question—to which the analysis in the *Theologico-Political Treatise* constitutes the answer—thus concerns the necessary hierarchy of the religious and the political, where despite their codetermination, the political must have precedence. If on the one hand, it appears impossible to abolish religiosity, but moreover, the maintenance of a certain number of beliefs prove to be necessary for the upholding of the state, it is on the other hand only within the political that the possibility of pursuing rational research can be guaranteed. However, needless to say, this guarantee is itself wholly dependent on what kind of political regime we have in mind—this question would be more closely developed by Spinoza in the *Political Treatise*.

Unfolding itself from the double-bind and the necessary hierarchy between the religious and the political, the second question has a both essential and a speculative aspect: what particular ends are aimed by the political, that religion can contribute to? The essential aspect here is largely also given in the *Treatise*: religion—as far as by this, we understand it solely as expressed in the seven common denominators—has a favourable effect on social obedience, thus on peace; just as it enhances the notion of mutual respect and generosity, thus favouring a social climate where differences can coexist.[31] The speculative aspect is about how to organize religiosity in order for it to contain and favour as much joyful passions as possible: that is, politically speaking, how to avoid superstition by what could be called social engineering.[32] The status of religion, here, would appear to have a larger potential—that of actually actively contributing to creating joyous passions—than in the previous, utterly pragmatic lines of reasoning, but still remains linked to inadequate thinking as such. However useful, religion still appears to be seen by Spinoza as a crutch, a palliative against the lack of real adequate knowledge, necessary simply because all, according to Spinoza, do not have the same capacity for real knowledge.[33] And yet, at no point in Spinoza's texts, the practical analysis is separated from the all-encompassing question concerning the possibility of adequate knowledge, the theory of which the *Ethics* is entirely devoted, but that clearly is what is ultimately at

---

[31] For two interesting discussions concerning Spinoza's resolute preference of the notion of "generosity" over that (far more common) of "tolerance" as a social virtue, see Alain Billecoq, *Spinoza: Questions politiques* (Paris: L'Harmattan, 2009) and Zeev Levy, *From Spinoza to Levinas* (New York: Peter Lang Publishing Inc, 2009).

[32] On the function of norms in Spinozian politics, see Jacqueline Lagrée, "Spinoza et la subversion des normes religieuses" in *Spinoza et la politique* (Paris: L'Harmattan, 1997).

[33] Spinoza, *A Theologico-Political Treatise*, ch. 13.

stake also in the theologico-political analyses. Indeed, the political challenge is and remains how to create a peaceful society where the citizens have the largest possible freedom, that is, where there are a maximum of conditions for adequate knowledge. But this cannot be separated from what is also at stake in religion, if at least it has the potential, under good political supervision, to contribute in developing joyful passions—those precisely, that in the *Ethics* constitute the very possibility of the second degree of knowledge, which in turn can, however not always do, lead to the third degree of knowledge—would it not thus be possible to speak, in Spinoza, of religion as emancipatory in the strong sense? Such an opening appears to be sketched out by Spinoza himself in the fourth chapter of the *Theologico-Political Treatise*, where he argues for the compatibility of reason and what he calls "real" or true religion—this question obviously being at stake since the preface. If, on the one hand, it is clear that adequate knowledge, that is reasonable ideas, as much as true religion embrace the two principles of justice and charity, it is also clear, on the other hand, that things also work the other way. The very large definition of religion given in the *Ethics* indeed connects it to "whatever we desire and do [...] insofar as we have the idea of God":[34] insofar as this idea is adequately constituted, this means that our essence, adequately understood, implies a desire for knowledge;[35] that our inclination to concur with others, adequately understood, implies a desire to share this knowledge—the knowledge in question being that of the identity of God and Nature and its implications.[36] In order for this knowledge to spread, a well-functioning society is necessary: reason commands us thus to contribute to this by endorsing the principles of justice and charity grounded in the love for God,[37] by which the further propagation of adequate knowledge is made possible. Indeed, thus, the link between adequation and religion exists—but only insofar as we understand that to Spinoza, religion in this sense is radically different to what is commonly called so.[38] Steering clear of any notion of faith, Spinoza's notion of real religion points to a renewed investigation of the different notions of

---

[34] *Ethics*, IV, pr 37, schol.1, 134.
[35] Ibid., pr 26.
[36] Ibid., pr 28; V, pr 24.
[37] Spinoza, *A Political Treatise*, II, 23.
[38] This fact is painfully obvious to Spinoza's readers also in his own time: see the exchange with Oldenburg in letters 73–75.

truth in the three different degrees of knowledge: as such, this investigation is what constitutes philosophy—or spinozism—as such.[39]

---

[39] For a very thorough discussion of this last point, see Alexandre Matheron, "Politique et religion chez Hobbes et Spinoza" in *Anthropologie et politique au XVIIe siècle* (Paris: Vrin, 1986).

Religion and a Critique of the Concept of Materialism
A Commentary to Fredrika Spindler's Paper on the Ambiguity of Religion in Spinoza

KAROLINA ENQUIST KÄLLGREN

It is a most interesting theme—that of an unresolved ambiguity concerning religion in Spinoza—which Fredrika Spindler takes as a point of departure for her analyses. Understanding that it is in the political where epistemology, ontology, metaphysics and ethics coincide in both Hobbes and Spinoza, Spindler analyzes religion and its relationship to politics as explained by both philosophers.

In her analyse Spindler begins with a defining description of what is religion in Spinoza and Hobbes. She claims that in both Hobbes and Spinoza two basic ideas about religion and politics can be found. Firstly, that religion is a purely human affair, and that it cannot be understood in relation to any transcendental reality. And secondly, that religion has an exclusive political function, either positive or negative from the point of view of the up-holding of the state.[1] I will in the following suggest that these two primary definitions are in fact what causes the ambiguity—or unresolved problem—in the interpretation of Spinoza. I will do so by counterposing the interpretation made by Spindler with two other interpretations of the properties and function of religion in Spinoza. Both these interpretations, by spanish philosophers María Zambrano and Vidal Peña García, could possibly be understood as pertaining to a Spanish reception of Spinoza, and they lay the ground for somewhat different conclusions on the political, based in Spinoza.

---

[1] Fredrika Spindler, see above.

María Zambrano started her philosophical and academic career working on a thesis on Spinoza, which she unfortunately was forced to abandon, interrupted by the Spanish Civil War and her subsequent flight into exile.[2] Even so, Spinoza is considered one of the most important influences on Zambrano, obvious in her main works, such as *El hombre y lo divino*.[3] Zambrano also published an article on Spinoza in 1936 that could be seen as an outline of the doctoral thesis she intended to realize.[4] Vidal Peña García is one of the most renowned translators of Spinoza into Spanish, and has written a doctoral thesis on the concept of materialism in Spinoza.[5] Both base their interpretations mainly on the *Ethics*, but in a way that I would suggest has consequences for the understanding of the political in Spinoza. Their commonalities imply a fruitful discussion on Spinoza somewhat at the side of the mainly French discussion that has reached Sweden.

In her article "La salvación del individuo en Espinosa" Zambrano focuses on the question of identity and individuality in the *Ethics*. She concludes that the individual as traditionally understood, does not exist in Spinoza. He is a paradoxical non-being submerged in nature and renounces every essential character, only preserving his being. But, at the same time, he has

---

[2] María Zambrano (1904-1991) is one of the most recognized 20th century spanish philosophers and her main contribution is the notion of "poetical reason." From the beginning a pupil of Ortega y Gasset she developed her reasoning influenced by and in discussion with philosophers like Heidegger, Scheler, Spinoza and Plotinus. She took a great interest in both christian, arabic and "oriental" mysticism, the knowledge of which she procured from Spanish and French orientalists such as Miguel Asín Palacios and Louis Massignon. Her philosophical work mainly deals with the grounds of knowledge, the possibilities of the subject and a critique of the ethical and political grounds of modernity. Although often accused of developing a phenomenology of religion she never agreed with the description, critizising among others Heidegger and Husserl of being heirs of "idealism." She spent over forty years in exile after the Spanish Civil war, because of her open contribution to the republic cause. She lived, among other places, on Cuba, in Puerto Rico, France and Rome.

[3] María Zambrano, *El hombre y lo divino*, 1953. Jesus Moreno Sanz concludes at the end of *Book IV* of his four volume synthesis of the works of María Zambrano that what Zambrano tries throughout her entire production is to investigate the third kind of knowledge as presented in Spinoza. Even if one does not need to agree with such a statement in all its implications, it is reasonable to agree that Spinoza is a very important source for Zambrano all throughout her career. Moreno Sanz, Jesús, *El logos oscuro: tragedia, mística y filosofía en María Zambrano* (Madrid: Verbum, 2008), 147.

[4] Zambrano, María, "La salvación del individuo en Espinosa," in *Cuadernos de la facultad de filosofía y letras* (1936:3, Universidad Complutense de Madrid), 7–20.

[5] See, Vidal Peña García, *El materialismo de Spinoza. Ensayo sobre la ontología spinozista* (Madrid: Revista de Occidente, 1974).

the ability to think. He has a way of arriving at knowledge about nature and, it must be added, nature is here understood also as God. Furthermore, this knowledge of the nature-God means self-consciousness for the individual, because he is only in so far as he is in and through the infinite and plural nature-God, and with the nature-God as his necessary cause. Zambrano argues that between the only and infinite—and therefore plural—substance of nature-god and the finite life of the individual there is a gap, which suggests that the individual is separated, fallen, from his unity with nature-God. There is, though, a way for the individual to get "salvation," according to Zambrano, and that is to, thinking and using the ability to reason freely, gain adequate knowledge about nature-God and so be part of God's self-love. The goal: To become conscious of one's dependence and insufficiency so as to better preserve one's being.[6]

Identity seems to take on two different meanings in this article. Zambrano separates them with a language-game not possible in English: substance as the identity that is essentially equals the Spanish verb *ser* and identity as temporary and thus exposed to change equals *estar*. For Zambrano the two verbs suppose two different planes of being. Surprisingly enough it is precisely because the substance (or nature-God) is defined as identity (rather than one absolute whole) that it can be understood as infinite plurality, and consequently, from the perspective of the temporary individual (estar), the cause of all possible change. In this line of thought, even if not explicitly expressed by Zambrano, inadequate knowledge becomes the inescapable condition of human life, since exhaustive knowledge is never possible.

---

[6] Zambrano does not mention the "complex individual" of which Spinoza sometimes speaks in the Ethics, probably because of direct influences from the interpretation Hegel made of Spinoza. Hegel's main critique on Spinoza was that he did not conceive of the dialectical movement from which something individual is separated from the general and then, becoming its own sufficient cause, converts into generality in itself. See, for example Hegel's *Lecciones sobre historia de la filosofía*. Her reasoning around the individual (at the level of bodies that can be affected) tends to treat the concept as a pre-given, where individual stands for a free whole, which of course is precisely what Spinoza critiques, and, thus, she sometimes seems to discuss an ambivalence in Spinoza that she herself has created understanding the concept of individual in a way that is not necessarily his. Influences from Hegel can also be seen when she states that the substance understood as *causa sui* "Signals a fundamental identity, in which all nature's plurality is inserted." Zambrano, "La salvación del individuo," 8.

Vidal Peña in his *El materialismo de Spinoza. Ensayo sobre la ontología spinozista* treats the question of materialism in Spinoza from a perspective he calls "philosophical materialism" and which has somewhat phenomenological resounding outsets.[7] Philosophical materialism criticizes Marxist material-ism for being corporealism, meaning that it concedes existence only to bodies that can be the object of rational experience and investigation. Vidal Peña argues that the same critique is valid also for, for example, Negri in his understanding of several of the Spinozian concepts.[8] Vidal Peña instead proposes an understanding of Spinoza based in different categories of materialism, which can be thought as radically different but not understood as transcendent to each other or owning "spiritual" non-corporeal existence. The different categories can then be used to point out the radical separation of the one, infinite and plural, substance and material particularities (complex bodies, modus, affects). What is material in Spinoza, according to Vidal Peña, are not only bodies, but all human activity, including thinking. And since thinking can only be thinking in the infinite substance this necessarily also needs to affect our understanding of the concept of materialism, which can be perceived through rational thinking, as bodies in a rational order but never reduced—because it is infinite—to that same order.[9]

This, much too short, recompilation of Zambrano's and Vidal Peña's views serves the purpose of bringing to light the four things they seem to have in common (and around which one could try to reconstruct a Spanish discussion on Spinoza). First of all, the insistence that the idea of one only and infinite substance becomes highly problematic when looked upon in the light of finite bodies. Secondly, that a corporeal materialism, reducing materialism to bodies bound by natural law, cannot explain this problem and tends to reduce thinking and reason to complying with natural law. Thirdly, that this overlooks what in Zambrano is understood as salvation,

---

[7] The concept was first introduced by Spanish philosopher Gustavo Bueno in *Ensayos materialistas* (1972). Its base concept is "life" which can then be articulated in different categories of matter, the general ontological matter and the specific ontological matter. Both of them are completely material, but include as material also for example the products of man's thinking, both illusions and truths. Here it suffices to point out that this has several coincidences with Ortega's *razón vital* and also with the way that Zambrano uses her own concept of "vida."

[8] Vidal Peña García, "Introducción" in *Ética,* by Baruch Spinoza (Alianza Editorial, 2009), 18

[9] Vidal Peña García, *Materialismo de Spinoza,* ch. 2 and 3.

and in Vidal Peña as a creative and positive power in recuperating the capacity to think in the substance. Fourthly, they both underline the plurality implied in the idea of an infinite substance, making it the necessary base for the creative movement with which all preserving in ones being is possible at all. And this movement—which is not to be understood as the movement of the individual towards the substance as individual, or as the relationship between one materialism and the other—must be considered transcendent in so far as it is the movement of the substance as such, with its particularities and individualities, as rational thinking or, with the words of Zambrano, in salvation.

Rather than underlining for example desire, they both understand thinking—irrational rather than rational in the sense that no rationality can exhaust the plurality of the infinite substance—as the way to best "preserve in being." This is where questions of religion, thinking and materialism coincide. Both Zambrano and Peña agree, as do Spindler, that for Spinoza it is in the state that free thinking can be guaranteed, and that it is only through man's equals that he can find the mutual help which best allows him to preserve in his being. But the problematic of religion in the state, following Peña and Zambrano, emerges when one supposes a corporeal materialism that does not allow for any other creation or movement than those of the natural order or law and where immanent ontology is considered the only basis for political conclusions. Assuming such a materialism means that Spinoza's universal religion, with its seven principles, cannot be understood in any other way than as a hypothetical question, religion becomes an ambiguity. But what if we would turn the order around, interpreting the political, the state and its way of governance, as a means to recuperating metaphysics in a rationalist world? Religion, with its double function, in Spinoza, of maintaining community in spite of the inadequate knowledge that is the condition of man's existence and of being a road to a more just and reasonable life, becomes one (but not the only) of the important, and paradoxically enough, best defined ways to bridge-over that gap between infinity and particularity, making the true religion and its dependence on the political what constitutes the being of the substance as such.

Understood in this way, religion and politics becomes the two-sided sword with which Spinoza tried to cut what we could call the *Descartian knot*, the question of the relationship between an infinite substance and a natural and finite order. It does not mean a repudiation from politics nor from religion but rather the resurgence of metaphysics or religion in politics, as an ethical demand. The third kind of knowledge in Spinoza does thus become a kind of mediating knowledge between natural law and the substance (between finitude and infinity) which, according to this interpretation, constitutes a transcendent being per se and which corresponds to the notion of true religion in Spinoza. This connection between religion and politics, as the mediations of the substance into particularity, constitutes a space or society in which man *must* act ethically to be a part of politics or society (and thus have the possibility of the third kind of knowledge). Interpreted like this Spinoza's entire project becomes religion, and the ambiguity—if we still can call it that—between religion and politics becomes an answer to another maybe more pressing question: The function of transcendence in a society based on the individual, and immanent materialism.

Nominalistic Mysticism, Philosophy and Literature[1]

PÄIVI MEHTONEN

Art, mysticism and science are the three languages that must help each other. (Mauthner, *Wörterbuch der Philosophie*)

The Middle Ages, having exhausted the contents of eternity, gave us the right to love transitory things. (Cioran, *Tears and Saints*)

I. A Linguistic Turn and Mysticism

The *avant-garde* aesthetics and poetics of the early 19th century—the "Age of Abstraction"—is based on the lost outer object: "object" in the sense of a positivist fact or realistic verisimilitude, and "lost" in the sense of an intentional gradual process rather than an abrupt halt. The story of the experimental anti-realism in the *avant-garde* arts has often been rehearsed and yet the question remains: from where did the process of "loss" and the subsequent boom in new ways of perception enter the theoretical scene—a process captured, for instance, by abstractionist Wassily Kandinsky's simple question *Was soll den Gegenstand ersetzen?* (What will replace the object?), before he went on to suggest literary and pictorial solutions to the problem?

The turn of the 20th century witnessed an emergence of language philosophies that engaged in articulating such a loss and inspired contemporary writers to experimentation with new forms of expression. One of

[1] This article is part of my larger study *A Quest for Abstract Literature. Medievalism and Mysticism*, funded by the Academy of Finland (project 125257).

the earliest of these philosophies was the modern scepticism and radical empiricism of Fritz Mauthner (1849–1923), the father of the term *Sprachkritik*. Medieval mysticism was one of his recurring sources, one he treated with an engaging mixture of admiration and opposition— admiration when it comes to the mystical apophatic realization of the limits of language and thought, and yet opposition to the metaphysical closure that had gone along with the tradition of Christian mysticism. Modern philosophy, art and science no longer required, according to Mauthner, metaphysical objects but a new *Geistesfreiheit* in order to resist the inheritance of the previous century—the allegedly mechanistic and realistic world view of the 19th century—with empirical and inner experiential sensitivity of the linguistic conditions of human knowledge.

These themes became a persistent current in 20th century thought. The connections in later phenomenology and philosophy between mysticism and philosophies of (post)modernism are well known, thanks to the best known "atheological mystics" and apophatic philosophical writers such as Bataille, Blanchot, Foucault, Heidegger, Lacan and Derrida. These names have become a strong canon whose attitudes to the tradition of medieval negative theology have been debated over the years.[2] Recently, Bruce Holsinger studied what he calls "theoretical medievalism': the return of French critical theory from Bataille to Lacan, and from Barthes to Derrida to medieval models of thought—in the ways these "found in the Middle Ages a constant source of revisionist engagement with tradition."[3] Holsinger thus mainly concerns himself with post-war French philosophy, and in his brief references to the German tradition merely reiterate the received opinion that medievalism in German philosophy "has fertile roots in the work of Martin Heidegger" (6). One may take this useful notion of theoretical medievalism—one that is able to capture a broad and significant cultural *topos* in the dialogues between philosophy and literature—and

---

[2] See Jürgen Habermas, *Der philosophische Diskurs der Moderne: Zwölf Vorlesungen* (Third edition, Frankfurt am Main: Suhrkamp Verlag, 1986), 214–18 *et passim*; see also the Bibliography for Budick & Iser 1996; Heimonet 1996, 69; Wolosky 1995; Caputo & Scanlon 1999; Cunningham 2002. For a useful anthology of texts and critical essays by the editor, see William Franke, (ed.), *On What Cannot be Said. Apophatic Discourses in Philosophy, Religion, Literature, and the Arts*. 2 volume (Notre Dame: University of Notre Dame Press, 2007).

[3] Bruce Holsinger, *The Premodern Condition: Medievalism and the Meaning of Theory* (Chicago: University of Chicago Press, 2005), 3.

nevertheless extend its beginnings further back in 20th century thought. I will attempt to look beyond this eminent canon in search of earlier, characteristically linguistic means of exploring and comparing the discourses of the secular and the sacred in the early 19th century.

The opening years of the century preceded the categories that now tend to be taken for granted—say, analytic and continental philosophy;[4] in later histories of philosophy Mauthner frequently makes brief appearances in the studies of the early Wittgenstein's critique of language and analytic philosophy.[5] Yet the problems of skepticism preoccupying Mauthner between the years 1900 and 1910 were not unlike the transcendences and immanences that concerned Edmund Husserl in his early attempts to formulate the phenomenological method.

> If all knowledge is questionable, then the phenomenon "knowledge" is the only thing given, and before I permit one particular kind of knowledge as valid, I perform my research in a purely intuiting (as if it were aesthetic) fashion: what validity in general means, i.e., what knowledge as such means, with and in its "known objectivity." [6]

In what follows I will first look at the role of medieval mysticism in Mauthner's sceptical and atheistic critique of language and, second, proceed to speculate on the possibilities of a philosophical language in the process of its de-ontologization and divorce from metaphysical concerns. What replaced the loss of the (realistic) object?

---

[4] Without any black-and-white paradigmatic constraints one is even tempted to ask: could there be analytic phenomenology? Or phenomenological positivism?

[5] The early reception of Mauthner in literary criticism ranged from admiration to ambiguous mystification. Leo Spitzer's early study on Morgenstern contains an illuminating appendix on the linguistic and stylistic parallels between Mauthner and Morgenstern: Leo Spitzer "Die groteske Gestaltungs- und Sprachkunst Christian Morgensterns," *Motiv und Wort. Studien zur Literatur- und Sprachpsychologie* (Leipzig: O. R. Reisland, 1918), 53–123; whereas according to (otherwise perceptive) Wolfgang Kayser, Mauthner's *Kritik der Sprache* "surpassed every critique of language previously furnished by poets, mystics and philosophers" and his aim was "to destroy language altogether"; Wolfgang Kayser, *The Grotesque in Art and Literature* (New York: Columbia University Press, 1957/1981), 155.

[6] Husserl's letter to Hofmannsthal 12.1.1907. Edmund Husserl, *Husserliana Dokumente: Briefwechsel*. Vol. 7: Wissenschaftlerkorrespondenz (Dordrecht: Kluwer, 1994), 133–36, translation Sven-Olov Wallenstein in *Site* 26-27, 2009, 2 (See also section IV of this paper.) I am indebted and grateful to Marcia Sá Cavalcante Schuback who brought this exchange to my attention.

II. The Unholy Union of Nominalism and Mysticism

In the beginning there is a word, although a feeble one. In the entry "Mystik," Mauthner reveals the linguistic tactics not only of his philosophical dictionary, but also of his language critical philosophy in general. This tactics is *a nominalistic, sceptical mysticism*: the attempt to go on "speaking the unspeakable" (*wieder einmal das Unsagbare zu sagen*)—or, in Martin Buber's later words, to cherish *das Sagenwollen des Unsagbaren* (the will to say the unsayable)[7]—even after the realization that language cannot be transcended. According to Mauthner, to assume a reality outside language is to give in to word-realism, *Wortrealismus*, the unwarranted shift from language to some sort of trans-linguistic reality. Thus the value of the (medieval) tradition of nominalism was in its attack against realism and the idea that words and concepts do not concern reality but human judgment, *Urteil*. Mauthner does not deny that there are realities beyond the language-shaped one and human mind—but they just cannot be easily imagined or grasped from *this* side of language. The entry "Mystik" as well as other related entries such as "Nominalismus" appeared in Mauthner's popular, witty and somewhat apophatic dictionary *Das Wörterbuch der Philosophie. Neue Beiträge zu einer Kritik der Sprache* (1910, Dictionary of Philosophy. New Contributions to Critique of Language; hereafter W) where the author makes it his task to transmit to a wider audience his major language philosophical work *Beiträge zu einer Kritik der Sprache* (1901–02, Contributions to Critique of Language). Mauthner also contributed a small booklet *Sprache* (1906, Language) to the series of pamphlets called *Die Gesellschaft*, edited by Martin Buber; the other volumes included for instance *Die Religion* (1906) by Georg Simmel and *Die Revolution* (1907) by Gustav Landauer, Mauthner's younger colleague and anarchist friend. Later in his career Mauthner also compiled a voluminous history of atheism, *Der Atheismus und seine Geschichte im Abendlande* (1920, Atheism and Its History in the Occident).

In his language philosophy, Mauthner criticises modern science, philosophy and politics for their word-realism, which is a relic of the religious *Weltanschauung*; it typically perceives the relationship of language and reality as a naïve unproblematised reference. This was an error of even the

---

[7] Martin Buber, (ed.), *Ekstatische Konfessionen* (Leipzig: Insel, 1909/1921), 5.

finest critics of language such as Meister Eckhart (*ca.* 1260–1328) as he filled the primary nothingness of language and God with the "reality" of divinity, thus becoming a word-realist. Modern atheism therefore needs a new understanding of the world and language—one which takes seriously the linguistic trap of human perception and experience. In his writing between the years 1901 and 1910, Mauthner formulates his language-critical stance, claiming that the human condition is to be inescapably bound to language; thinking and language are one and the same.

It is thus gradually becoming clear what medieval mysticism and nominalist language philosophy, flavoured with radical empiricism, might have in common. A literally oriented philosopher might find in both a distrust of language that, paradoxically, leads to a heightened awareness of the linguistic means of thought and expression. Mauthner transports his *Sprachkritik* into the tradition of medieval nominalism, Kant, the British empiricists, Schopenhauer, Nietzsche and Ernst Mach; although no single - *ismus* can ultimately solve the problem of language as a mere *Schein*, nominalistic mysticism, according to Mauthner, is a good tactic in resisting the dogmatising efforts of word-realism. There can be no reform or method to make language more capable of the precise expression of reality. The task of the critic is to *point* to the limits, and explore the contingent (particular, historical) instances of language in the communities of language users.[8]

It has been plausibly suggested by Katherine Arens that the reason why Mauthner was so well received by the big Central European (German-speaking) audience and yet dismissed by the academic circles of his time, was not his theory of language as such but the aspect of *linguistic mysticism* therein.[9] It was something completely new and, one may add, something completely streetwise in terms of the evolving literary *avant-garde* movements around the year 1910. Mauthner was well versed in different styles of language; having worked as an author and theatre critic before his major philosophical works, he never seemed to accept the conventional scholarly mode of written expression. He repeatedly articulated his distaste

---

[8] For an elaboration of Mauther's discussion of realism and nominalism, see Päivi Mehtonen, "Encyclopaedic Nichts: Mauthner, Mysticism and the *Avant-garde.*" *Nothing Left to Say: Nothingness in Philosophy, Theology, and Literature*, eds. Antti Salminen and Sami Sjöberg (forthcoming).

[9] Katherine Arens, "Mach und Mauthner: Der Fall eines Paradigmenwechsels" in *Fritz Mauthner: Das Werk eines kritischen Denkers*, eds. Elisabeth Leinfellner and Hubert Schleichert (Wien, Köln, Weimar: Böhlau Verlag, 1995), 105.

for "the superfluous jargon of the Learned" (*eines überflussigen Gelehrtenjargons*) that was indeed alien to his own witty and language-critical style.[10] His philosophy inspired contemporary vanguard literature and politics, not least due to its self-questioning style and anti-academic as well as anti-institutional approach. Thus his *Sprachkritik*, first published in 1901–1902, seemed to aspire in philosophy to what *avant-garde* poetics somewhat later would manifest in literature and revolutionary socialism and anarchism in society (Landauer). Authors and philosophers sought a heightened sense of spirituality that would not exclude societal action and community, and the new century was to become "the century of the Inner"[11]—an inner orientation against the positivism and realism of the previous century.

This anti-institutional inner orientation also made the early (non-Cartesian) forms of spirituality, such as medieval Christian mysticism, a source of inspiration for the radical *Sprachkritik* and the literary quests for new "transrational" languages. In this secular reception, the God-seeking progress of a religious mystic towards the imageless realization of a sort of immanent transcendence could inspire a sceptic's realization of the perceptual as a route towards the inner. This modern mystical impulse was so strong that philosophers from different backgrounds—from Mauthner to Russell, from Steiner to Buber to Wittgenstein—took part in commenting on it.[12] In the dictionary entry "Mystik" Mauthner proposes that the history of mysticism—one yet to be written—reveals a pattern; a mystical period always follows an epoch of a scientific bankruptcy and a hyperbolic human *hubris* regarding the possibilities of science. However, each mystical period also produces its foul windbags and hypocrites (*ganz ekelhafte Schwätzer und Heuchler*; W II, 116) and it is here that Mauthner

---

[10] Fritz Mauthner, *Fritz Mauthner – Sprache und Leben: Ausgewählte Texte aus dem philosophischen Werk*, ed. Gershon Weiler (Salzburg, Wien: Residenz Verlag, 1986), 190. All translations from Mauthner by Päivi Mehtonen. None of his major works have been translated into English.

[11] Sixten Ringbom, *The Sounding Cosmos: A Study in the Spiritualism of Kandinsky and the Genesis of Abstract Painting* (Åbo: Åbo Akademi, 1970), 29.

[12] See, for instance, William James, *The Varieties of Religious Experience* (1902), Rudolf Steiner, *Die Mystik im Aufgang des neuzeitlichen Geisteslebens und ihr Verhältnis zur modernen Weltanschauung* (1901), Martin Buber (ed.), *Ekstatische Konfessionen* (1909/1921), Bertrand Russell, *Mysticism and Logic and Other Essays* (1917). In the Nordic countries, William James inspired, among others, Hans Ruin's insightful *Poesiens mystik* (1935).

once again confesses his admiration of *great* mystics (Eckhart, Angelus Silesius, Gerson, etc.) as well as his rejection of such pseudo-mysticisms as occultism and spiritualism.[13]

III. Empiricist *Sprachkritik*: The Pictures of the World

The division of the three worlds according to the most important parts of speech in grammar must naturally be understood only *cum grano salis*. (W II, 528)

Now it is becoming clear why I thought that thinking and language were the same. For thinking is a kind of language. (Wittgenstein 12.9.1916 / 1961, 82e)

How can, then, the modern critic avoid the word-realistic automatics of consciousness, automatics that shows in the ways that language, in the course of its long use and history, has been abstracted further and further away from experience and perception? Whenever one tries to express a feeling of some true presence or cosmic magnificence—today an exemplary discourse would concern, for instance, the value of nature experience—religious interpretation and discourse is near, regardless of whether or not the speakers consider themselves religious. A religious contemporary of Mauthner's, Rudolf Otto, argues in *Das Heilige* (1917, *The Idea of the Holy*) that all attempts to describe the *overplus of meaning*—such as the aesthetic and psychological concepts of the sublime, the beautiful, the numinous, *stupor* (blank wonder), or fascination—bear some resemblance to the non-rational aspects of the "holy."[14] Thus Otto, unlike Mauthner years earlier, defended a cause that was traditionally religious; the secular dimensions of the surplus of meaning are but a pale reflection of the possibility of a new

---

[13] Also theosophy belonged to these "pseudo-mysticisms." For Mauthner's comment on Rudolf Steiner as a "new Cagliostro" (an 18th century occultist, alchemist and—in this context—charlatan), see Mauthner, *Der Atheismus*, vol. IV, 402. For Steiner's refutation of Mauthner's notions of chance and necessity, see *Chance, Providence, and Necessity: eight lectures held in Dornach between August 23 and September 6, 1915*, translation Marjorie Spock (Hudson: Anthroposophic Press, 1988). Both Mauthner and Steiner were interested in the concept of the three worlds; for discussion of Steiner's notion of the physical, psychical and spiritual worlds, see Ringbom, *The Sounding Cosmos* 74.

[14] Rudolf Otto, *The Idea of the Holy: An Inquiry into the Non-Rational Factor in the Idea of the Divine and its Relation to the Rational*, translation John W. Harvey (London, Oxford, New York: Oxford University Press, 1958), 5, 19, 41–49.

numinous transcendence—something that is "perfectly *sui generis*": "like every absolutely primary and elementary datum, while it admits of being discussed, it cannot be strictly defined" (7). Yet Otto's discussion of this unsayable always returns to the primacy of the religious.[15] Otto's thesis is an interesting contrast to Mauthner's who had likewise acknowledged the mutual attraction between the secular and religious discourses but had seen it to be the task of the modern philosopher to resist the metaphysical attraction and the "word-realist" conclusion. A realist rapidly abstracts the elements of perception to mean something else, something presumably "real," yet this real is merely our linguistic picture of the world, already structured by our mind. Even if one turned to the good old apophasis of "speaking the unspeakable" but nevertheless postulated a transcendence beyond the nothingness of apophasis—for Otto, for instance, the realization of the numinous cannot be taught but only awakened in the mind "as everything that comes 'of the spirit' must be awakened" (7)—one would in Mauthner's view become a word-realist.

In order to describe the workings of the inescapably linguistic human perception, Mauthner proposes a theory of the three pictures of the world that should not be torn apart. On the contrary, "the world is there only once," *die Welt ist nur einmal da* and "art, mysticism and science are the three languages that must help each other" (W II, 529, 531).

Adjectival world	Substantival world	Verbal world
Empfindung	*Sein, "die Dinge an sich"*	*Werden, Bewegung*
Kunst	*Mystik*	*Wissenschaft*
Welt der Erfahrung	*Raum*	*Zeit*

The adjectival world (*adjektivische Welt*) is a sensual world—the only world one experiences immediately. "What a thing is, we know by its qualities

---

[15] Almost hermetically so, one could add, as Otto addresses the reader and invites him to direct his mind to a moment of profound religious experience: "Whoever cannot do this, whoever knows no such moments in his experience, is requested to read no farther; for it is not easy to discuss questions of religious psychology with one who can recollect the emotions of his adolescence, the discomforts of indigestion, or, say, social feelings, but cannot recall any intrinsically religious feelings," Otto, *The Idea of the Holy*, 8.

[*seine Eigenschaften*]; what else it is but these qualities, is a metaphysical question" (W I, 12). All sense data and sensations are adjectival—without any unity or wholeness. The adjectival picture of the world is also related to the immediate value judgements we make, for instance, right or beautiful. This world is the most real as it has not yet been organised into unities or abstract substantives; it is "the lowest form of articulation but is has also the highest reality-content."[16] The substantival world (*substantivische Welt*) is the "unreal" world of being. The oldest superstition of the human being is the belief in the reality of the things in space (W II, 531). The third picture of the world is the verbal world (*verbale Welt*), the world of becoming and movement. The verbal world neither "believes in" the substantival nor is it satisfied with the adjectival world. It is the world of relations and change— the qualities interrelated in time in daily life as well as in science; this picture may be processed into a describable shape (*Die verbale Welt läßt sich beschreiben*).[17]

If dealt with as separate pictures, these languages would lead to the untenable conclusions of (adjectival) sensualism, (substantival) idealism or (verbal) theory of the flux of all things. None of these pictures is enough alone—even the great Meister Eckhart was too obsessed by the substantival world despite the fact that he paved the way to modern *Sprachkritik*. "For Meister Eckhart, the substantival world was truer than the adjectival, [...] the ideal reality truer than the material/bodily reality" so that eventually this "purest mysticism" becomes *a hidden rationalism.*[18] Thus, according to Mauthner, the overt rationalism of modern science is not far from the covert rationalism of religion.

---

[16] See Gershon Weiler, *Mauthner's Critique of Language* (Cambridge: Cambridge University Press, 1970), 283. Cf. Gilles Deleuze on Bergson in *Bergsonism*, trans. Hugh Tomlinson and Barbara Habberjam (New York: Zone Books, 1991), 24–25: "perception is not the object *plus* something, but the object *minus* something, minus everything that does not interest us."

[17] S.v. "adjektivische Welt." "substantivische Welt" and "verbale Welt." in W I, 12–14; W II, 464–468 and W II, 526–531. See also Weiler, *Mauthner's Critique of Language* 282–88 and Mauthner, *Fritz Mauthner* 20–27.

[18] "[...] für Meister Eckhart war die substantivische Welt wahrer als die adjektivische – wenn er das auch nicht so aussprach, die ideelle Wirklichkeit wahrer als die gemeine körperliche Wirklichkeit, die Erkenntnis das wahre Sein, so daß – ich glaube nicht mit dem Worte zu spielen – selbst diese reinste Mystik ein heimlicher Rationalismus war" Mauthner, *Fritz Mauthner*, 197.

Mauthner's solution to overcome the earlier dominating epistemologies seems two-fold. Both ways rely on the co-existence of the three pictures of the world. One is that of literature, in the way it faces the adjectival world and the challenge of "the most sayable" and "the most unsayable" (*das Sagbarste, das Unsagbarste*)—the superlatives adding a Mauthnerian ironical language-critical twist, as if one could even grasp the unsayable *an sich*. By acknowledging the special role of literary language to the conditions of human language, Mauthner's theory has a strong poetic aura in emphasising the inescapably linguistic (ap)perception of the world. This aura emerges from Mauthner's conception of literature and poetry that is connected to the possibility of philosophical language, too—that is, *language that would not operate under the overt or covert laws of mechanical rationality and word-realism*. A writer works with "inadequate tools" (*mit unzureichenden Mitteln*)—that is, language that is a historical and social convention. Here literary language, the language of art, becomes important since it is furthest away from the whirlpool of word-realism; "language, precisely due to the uncertainty of its word-sketches, is an excellent handmaiden [*Werkzeug*] of literary work or poetry."[19] Thus literature—good literature—reminds the reader of the limits of language.

The other, related way to resist realism in language and epistemology, is philosophical *Sprachkritik* and a stylistic awareness, the latter point being something implicit in Mauthner's own style rather than overtly argued by him. The language critic's task is an exploration of the instances of words in ordinary language use and the endless historical shifts of linguistic meanings (*Bedeutungswandel*). The *how* and *what* of Mauthner's thought is neatly captured by the dictionary entry *"sogenannt"* ("so-called") where he responds to the critics who had castigated his earlier *Beiträge* for the vicious circle of using philosophical language in order to criticise philosophical language. Mauthner repeats that language exists in present communities of human beings and as a historical convention, and *only* there.

---

[19] Fritz Mauthner, *Die Sprache* (Frankfurt: Literarische Anstalt Rütten & Loening, 1906), 19–20.

I could have remained silent or could have placed 'so-called' before almost every word [...]. But my so-called 'I' wanted to share, so to say, my so-called ideas with the so-called human beings.[20]

Sensitive to the ambiguous aspects of communication, Mauthner's nominalist mysticism is thus a sort of negative theology introduced into the context of modern secular language philosophy and linguistics. In the light of this modern nominalistic and atheistic mysticism, the later famous debates concerning the relationship of, for instance, Derrida and negative theology— whether or not he was *really* inclined to mysticism[21]—seem to miss something relevant in ignoring the early discussions on post-secular thought.

Mauthner summarises the possibility of philosophy: the critique of language must teach liberation from language as the highest aim of self-liberation. Thus the crucial question also concerns any *me*, the ego, who may not even be able to experience him-/herself. Mauthner denies (in the Humean sense) that the ego may be experienced as an entity; it is a collection of adjectival and verbal experiences while the substantival world remains elusive. Moreover, Mauthner's language-historical view includes a profound sense of an old world view that needs a change. Unlike Heidegger years later, showing classicist and even conservative preferences in his literary taste,[22] Mauthner discussed recent literature and grounded the need for a new philosophy in a radical shift in the notion of poetry. The end of the old Christian world view and the beginning of modern atheism marks a new era and a new notion of poetry (W II, 250–66). Likewise, the words of the old *Kultursprachen* have become a mere play with marbles; "it is time to learn again to remain silent" (*Es ware Zeit, wieder schweigen zu lernen*; 1923, 230)—*in* language, that is. This task to revitalise the tired languages of the mechanical world view was shouldered by the contemporary poets.

---

[20] Ich hätte schweigen können oder ich hätte vor fast jedes Wort sogenannt setzen können [...]. Aber mein sogenanntes Ich wollte sozusagen meine sogenannten Ideen den sogenannten Menschen sozusagen mitteilen. (W II, 412)

[21] See footnote 137 above.

[22] Jürgen Habermas, *Der philosophische Diskurs der Moderne*, 98.

IV. The *Avant-garde* Revolution of the Adjectival World?

The urge towards the mystical comes of the non-satisfaction of our wishes by science. We *feel* that if all *possible* scientific questions are answered *our problem is still not touched at all*. Of course in that case there are no questions any more; and that is the answer. (Wittgenstein 25.5.1915 / 1961, 51)

A lost object—or a *new* object in the sense of the processual adjectival know-how? And what sort of language at all would satisfy the language-critical desire of a nominalist language and new signs devoid of any reminiscences of the old religious world view? Mauthner's *Sprachkritik* only required an artistic or political application in order to serve as a manifesto of new ruthlessly linguistic literature.

A political meaning of mysticism was introduced by Mauthner's assistant and friend Gustav Landauer (1870–1919). In his *Skepsis und Mystik. Versuche im Anschluss an Mauthners Sprachkritik* (1903; Scepticism and Mysticism: Essays in Connection with Mauthner's Critique of Language) Landauer proclaimed the vanguard implications of Mauthner's critical philosophy—a step towards political action that a sceptical Mauthner never took. Landauer claims that just as Kant's *Kritik der reinen Vernunft* was a philosophical impulse behind many 19th century revolutionary movements, so for the new century Mauthner's critique of language is a guide towards new mysticism and new strong action.[23] In collaboration with Mauthner, Landauer also compiled the first modern German translation of Meister Eckhart's works (see Landauer 1903/1991). Thus medieval mysticism did not merely provide pre-war intellectuals and culture bohemians with an ideal mystical-social rebellion but also—through Mauthner's contribution—a critical philosophy of language that explores the linguistic identities and suspensions.

The idea of a medieval mystic as a "proto-language-critic" and "proto-rebel" against prevailing *mores* was thus an important element in the early 20th century dialogues between the religious and the secular. An indubitably persuasive element in Mauthner's philosophy was that it assumed the "plot"

---

[23] Gustav Landauer, *Skepsis und Mystik: Versuche im Anschluß an Mauthners Sprachkritik* (second revised edition, Köln: Marcan Block, 1903/1923). See also Bertrand Russell for comments on mysticism and anarchism: "Mysticism and Logic" (1914); *Roads to Freedom. Socialism, Anarchism and Syndicalism* (1918); "Mysticism" (1961).

of a change of an era—"our time" having grown tired of the "mechanical world view" (W II, 529). One of the earliest literary reactions to Mauthner's *Sprachkritik*, Hugo von Hofmannsthal's famous "Lord Chandos Letter" (1902), formulated this dilemma in the words—addressed to Francis Bacon—of the aristocrat and poet Lord Chandos.

> [...] the language in which I might be able not only to write but to think is neither Latin nor English, neither Italian nor Spanish, but a language in which dumb inanimate things speak to me and wherein I may one day in my grave have to justify myself before an unknown judge.[24]

Hofmannsthal—whose fictional letter was considered by Mauthner a "poetic echo" of his own *Sprachkritik*[25]—was one of the writers who years later made Husserl see a connection between his phenomenological method and artistic perception.

> The enigma [i.e. the abyssal depths of the possibility of a knowledge enacted in subjective experiences, yet containing objectivity] can only be solved if we place ourselves on its own ground and treat *all knowledge* as questionable, and accept no existence as pre-given. This means that all science and all reality (including the reality of one's own I) have become mere "phenomena." Only one thing remains: to clarify, in a pure intuiting (in a pure intuiting analysis and abstraction), the meaning which is immanent in the *pure phenomena*, without ever going beyond them, i.e. without presupposing any transcendent existences that are intended in them.[26]

In the "Lord Chandos Letter" the protagonist's modal expression "I might be able" points towards an unknown language although as for now everything takes place in a well-organized language that has not yet gone through the shock of the Mauthnerian three pictures of the world. More radical experiments with sounds and poetic "vernaculars" were to follow, from the German expressionism and dada to authors often found under the rubric of

---

[24] Hugo von Hofmannsthal, *Ein Brief* (Brief des Lord Chandos an Francis Bacon), Projekt Gutenberg, 24 April 2010
<http://gutenberg.spiegel.de/?id=5&xid=1247&kapitel=1#gb_found>
[25] Mauthner's letter to Hofmannsthal 22.10.1902, see Joachim Kühn, *Gescheiterte Sprachkritik: Fritz Mauthners Leben und Werk* (Berlin, New York: Walter de Gruyter, 1975), 27.
[26] Husserl's letter to Hofmannsthal, 12.1.1907.

"philosophical writers": Wassily Kandinsky, Hugo Ball, Robert Musil, Jorge Luis Borges, James Joyce, Samuel Beckett and so forth.[27]

The nominalistic critique of naïve word-realism paved the way for an experimental language focusing on the radical immanence of the perception—that is, artistic attempts to *suspend* the immanence of the perception before it is born away by the verbal or substantival world. In discussing the possibility of an adjectival language of the adjectival world, at times Mauthner uses "picture" in the very visual sense of the word.

> ...the language of the [adjectival or sensual] world should also be adjectival. One could by and large compare it to the richness of form of the impressionistic painting of the pointillists: points, nothing but points, points in all colours, but also points as signs for an instant (visual) impression of other senses (*als Zeichen für Augenblickseindrücke der andere Sinne*).[28]

In 1910 Mauthner could not foresee the next phase of *avant-garde* art that would criticize impressionism as the last vestige of naturalistic representation and strive towards even purer abstraction. Yet the idea of an adjectival language, as a sort of proto-abstraction, allows one to imagine the key devices of a new literary language—devices that follow from the emphasis on perception, or the hiatus between the perception and the realization of a perception. Although for a sceptic, the sense-data of the adjectival world are not yet a picture, we nevertheless tend to think of it as if it were one. "The very concept of an adjectival picture of the world already presupposes that we have transcended it."[29]

What happened to the nominalistic mysticism in the discourses of philosophy and the arts? At least the term lived on in a poeticized form among the avant-gardists of the 1910s and 1920s. Christian Morgenstern positioned his own language critical poetry in the tradition of medieval nominalism. The surrealist Louis Aragon was characterised by a contemporary as a "nominalist mystic"; the same contemporary—Eugene Jolas, the first publisher of Joyce's *Finnegans Wake* and Beckett's early texts—once revealed his "nominalist fiction" of a new poetic imagination he called

---

[27] For Morgenstern and Mauthner, see Spitzer, "Die groteske Gestaltungs- und Sprachkunst Christian Morgensterns" 108–23; on Kandinsky's "Poems without Words" (1904), Ringbom, *The Sounding Cosmos*, 30.

[28] Mauthner, *Fritz Mauthner*, 193–94; cf. W I, 13.

[29] See Weiler, *Mauthner's Critique of Language*, 283.

"language of night": inspired by mystics such as John of the Cross and Angelus Silesius, this new imagination would be able to create the new narrative or paramyth, Kafka-like grotesque, fantastic fairytale.[30] Even earlier, Marcel Duchamp (1887–1968) wrote in his notebooks of the "nominalism of each thing," toying with the idea of poetry that would erase the link required by conventional poetry that established likenesses between objects. "Could we erase the "*memory* imprint," he asks, "forcing the reader/viewer to focus on the *thisness*, the nominalism of each thing?"[31] Duchamp writes further in his notebooks:

> Conditions of language: The search for "*prime words*" (divisible only by themselves and by unity). Take a Larousse dict. and copy all the so-called "abstract" words, i.e. those which have no concrete reference [...] (91)

> *Nominalism* [literal] = No more generic specific numeric distinction between words (tables is not the plural of table, ate has nothing in common with eat). No more physical adaptation of concrete words; no more conceptual value of abstract words. The word also loses its musical value. It is only readable (due to being made up of consonants and vowels), it is readable by eye and little by little takes on a form of plastic significance.[32]

This transitory thisness of words and perceptions becomes what Duchamp calls *infra-thin*: the minutest of intervals or the slightest of differences— "delays to be perceived." This "empiricist" language of the infra-thin is able to catch perceptions in the overwhelming sensuality and materiality of

---

[30] Eugene Jolas, *Man from Babel*, eds. Andreas Kramer and Rainer Rumold (New Haven, London: Yale University Press, 1998), 94, 107, 155; Eugene Jolas, "Workshop," *Imagining Language: An Anthology*, eds Jed Rasula and Steve McCaffery (Cambridge, MASS., London: The MIT Press, 2001), 43. For Jolas's reminiscence of himself reading "Mauthner's German volume on language" to almost blind James Joyce, see Jolas, *Man from Babel* 166. Jolas was part of the literary group activity—with Hans Arp, Carl Einstein, Samuel Beckett, and others—that produced such post-expressionist manifestos as "The Revolution of the Word" (1928) and "Poetry is Vertical" (1941). See Mary Ann Caws (ed.), *Manifesto: A Century of Isms* (Lincoln, London: University of Nebraska Press, 2001), 529–31.
[31] Duchamp, cit. Marjorie Perloff, *21st-Century Modernism: The "New"Poetics* (Malden, Oxford: Blackwell, 2002), 91.
[32] Duchamp 1914, cit. Thierry De Duve, *Pictorial Nominalism: On Marcel Duchamp's Passage from Painting to the Readymade*, trans. Dana Polan (Minneapolis: University of Minnesota Press, 1991), 126.

reality: "The warmth of a seat (which has just been left) is infra-thin."[33] How to reproduce this effect or moment in language?

Although these examples of a nominalist poetics are scattered and arbitrary, there is still much to do with the (likewise thin and unproven) thesis of de Duve that "the nominalistic dialectic ... drives the history of the avant-garde" (1991, 128, in the context of Duchamp studies and without references to the philosophical tradition of nominalism). While the history of theology has discussed the legacies of nominalistic mysticism—a pair of terms that apparently reconciles two ends that seem to belong to competing paradigms of philosophy, but only *seem to*[34]—the secular significance of nominalistic mysticism remains to be explored more thoroughly. At least in the early 20th century it emerged, for a while, as a refreshing alternative to the temporary inflation of realism.

Such nominalistic mysticism was also characteristic of the generation of philosophers that followed and overshadowed Mauthner's—Buber, Benjamin, Wittgenstein, Heidegger and after them an unbroken chain of 20th century reflection. If nominalist mysticism as a style of philosophical writing could somehow be defined, it would come close to Susan Sonntag's picture of Walter Benjamin's language, one that does not produce an obvious line of reasoning. On the contrary (I quote Sonntag on Benjamin), "each sentence had to say everything, before the inward gaze of total concentration dissolved the subject before his eyes"; [...] "his major essays seem to end just in time, before they self-destruct."[35]

The Mauthnerian practice and theory of language philosophy seems almost a manifesto of such later writing—one that is not afraid of sublime themes but, nevertheless, keeps the language almost frustratingly near the elusive godless presence of the adjectival world. It is according to these principles that Mauthner also positions his favorite mystic, Eckhart, in the history of ideas: Eckhart is owned neither by philosophy nor theology; he becomes "own"—and that is for *us*—only in his language.[36]

---

[33] Cit. Perloff, *21st-Century Modernism* 115, 116.

[34] See for instance the chapter "Nominalist Mysticism" in Heiko Obermann, *The Harvest of Medieval Theology: Gabriel Biel and Late Medieval Nominalism* (3. edition, Durham, NC: The Labyrinth Press, 1983).

[35] Susan Sontag, "Under the Sign of Saturn" in *Under the Sign of Saturn* (New York, Picador, 1980), 129.

[36] The entry "Mystik," W II, 126: Ein Eigener ist er also weder in Philosophie, noch in Theologie; ein Eigener ist er, und ist er uns, nur durch seine Sprache.

Radical Ambiguity
The Dilemma of Progressive Politics and the Reification of Language

JON WITTROCK

I. On the Contemporary Relevance of Fritz Mauthner

Päivi Mehtonen, in her illuminating essay, *Nominalistic Mysticism, Philosophy and Literature*, sets out to describe the radical linguistic criticism of Fritz Mauthner, a crucial but, at times, today, somewhat marginalized figure. Mauthner, Mehtonen argues, anticipated key themes of the subsequent development of 20th century philosophy and its core feature of a critique of language—and I think that she shows this beyond any doubt. This, however, does not necessarily render Mauthner an important thinker in his own right. For that to hold true, it is not enough to merely note Mauthner's influence, neither is it sufficient to focus on the parallels between his critical attempts and similar notions in later writers, whether these latter were directly influenced by Mauthner or not. For Mauthner to matter today—for him to matter, not only as a historical figure, but as a relevant *contemporary thinker*—it has to be shown why, and in which sense, he matters.

As for the parallels between Mauthner's critique of language and later developments of 20th century philosophy, these are indeed striking—there are similarities between Mauthner's notions and Wittgenstein's early logical atomism, as well as his later philosophy of language games. And the radical conclusions reached later on by Heidegger and Adorno seem anticipated by Mauthner as well, in his "conception of literature and poetry that is connected to the possibility of philosophical language, too [...]." Such parallels, however, can do little more than, at best, secure Mauthner a place in intellectual history; they do not of themselves render him a great or even important thinker.

If Mehtonen's aim is only to argue in favour of Mauthner's place as an important figure in intellectual history, she has surely succeeded. But there are hints in her essay, suggesting that there is also something else going on; something pertaining to the eventual *political* relevance of Mauthner's thought: "His philosophy inspired contemporary vanguard literature and politics [...] Thus his *Sprachkritik* [...] seemed to aspire in philosophy to what avant-garde poetics somewhat later would manifest in literature and revolutionary socialism and anarchism in society [...]" And it is here we find, I believe, the signs pointing towards a crucial nexus which I would like to comment on. Firstly, then, in the following, I will attempt to retrieve the core of the matter, the tension between the possibilities of progressive politics, on the one hand, and a radical critique of reification or instrumentality in thought and language, on the other. Thereafter, we shall seek to ascertain whether and to what an extent Mauthner may remain relevant in this regard. Rather than concluding decisively, one way or the other, I shall seek to outline one of the possible conditions for his continued relevance.

II. Progressive Politics and the Reification of Language

The radical is often thought of as an uprooting—the old and decayed is destroyed, and replaced with the new. A radical politics, however, cannot merely be a matter of uprooting. It must itself, to avoid becoming an exclusively destructive exercise, be rooted in something. Let us, then, return to the roots of radical politics. The very term "radical," indeed, stems from the Latin word *radix*, meaning exactly "root." In what, then, is radical politics rooted? Without attempting a final and all-encompassing de-finition, we may still observe a pervasive tendency for radical politics to be profoundly rooted in an ideal of *utility*. It thus tends to become—and the expression is still used today by some, as a sign of something desirable and sought after—"progressive."[1] The word progress derives from the Latin *pro* and *gradus*; the original meaning is "to step forth," "to walk forward."

That radical politics should often turn "progressive" is not difficult to perceive: it is progressive because it is allied with progress, understood both as a march forward in time, towards some desirable ideal state of affairs, if only vaguely imagined, or conceived of in the forms of negations, and as the continuous creation, in the present, of a better world, through instrumental means. And both of these seem to presuppose some notion of utility—if we are to create a better world, or at least improve the one we have already got, we need some means of doing so. We need instruments to be used in the pursuit of our aims. Hence, one may easily conclude that as long as our aims are the right ones, the means will be more or less neutral. However, the notion of utility is itself a problematic one, and a powerful polemic against its pervasive influence, even within the deepest layers of the human psyche, within thought and language, arose and spread widely within German-speaking intellectual culture in the generations succeeding Mauthner's, and became a powerful theme all over the political and ideological spectrum of the Weimar period and beyond.[2]

---

[1] An interesting contemporary example, and a case in point, is Chantal Mouffe's usage of the term "progressive" in her influential treatise *On the Political* (London: Routledge, 2005), e.g. "The events of 1989 should have provided the time for a redefinition of the left, now liberated of the weight previously represented by the communist system. There was a real chance for a deepening of the democratic project because traditional political frontiers, having been shattered, could have been redrawn in a more progressive way." (31)

[2] To follow the web of influences in the recurring formulations of a critique of instrumental rationality and the threats of its attendant processes of technological transformation into and out of the Weimar period is to simultaneously move between widely distinct ideological positions and shifting political allegiances. For example, Max Weber and Georg Lukács influenced Carl Schmitt, whose friend, author Ernst Jünger, similarly sought to characterize the contemporary world in terms of the domination of a certain kind of instrumental rationality tied to technology, and whom was read extensively by Martin Heidegger, who was also influenced, of course, by similar critical notions in the works of Edmund Husserl. For a review of the influences on Schmitt, see e.g. John P. McCormick, *Carl Schmitt's Critique of Liberalism: Against Politics as Technology* (Cambridge: Cambridge University Press, 1997). Ernst Jünger's influence on Heidegger is well known and is apparent from the recently published nineteeth volume of the *Gesamtausgabe* (Frankfurt am Main: Vittorio Klostermann, 2004). On the left side of the political spectrum, thinkers associated with the Frankfurt School of critical theory pursued similar trains of thought, with partly parallel influences, a type of critique which was carried on by Herbert Marcuse, who exercised a great influence as an inspirational figure for the radical student protests of the 1960's. Marcuse is also interesting, however,

It is against this very briefly sketched background that I would like to bring up two of the crucial thinkers of the generation following after Mauthner: Martin Heidegger and Theodor W. Adorno. Both of these thinkers, while divided politically and ideologically, came to actualize the problem of an unrestricted instrumental rationality, and in so doing, indicate an underlying dilemma of contemporary political thought.[3]

because he, being a student of Heidegger's, transmitted this shared concern of right- and left-wing thinkers of the Weimar era into the post-war period, as did Hannah Arendt. Cf. Richard Wolin, *Heidegger's Children: Hannah Arendt, Karl Löwith, Hans Jonas, and Herbert Marcuse* (Princeton: Princeton University Press, 2001).

[3] There are of course significant differences between the two thinkers, but the overlap seems to me much more striking, especially given their opposed political and ideological stances. This overlap, however, is hardly wholly incidental: not only were Heidegger and Adorno, despite their different backgrounds, arguably part of the same wider cultural and intellectual context, they also shared more specific formative influences in a confrontation with Husserl's phenomenological project as well as being crucially involved in the transformation and reinterpretation of religious themes that was a key element of their respective critical attempts—indeed, what Walter Benjamin said of his own work in *The Arcades Project* (Cambridge: The Belknap Press of Harvard University Press), could equally well be applied to them: "My thinking is related to theology as a blotting pad is related to ink. It is saturated with it." (471) The same thing, however, could arguably be said of contemporary critical reflection as a whole. Indeed, in the end, it is extremely difficult to distinguish clearly between versions of a Judeo-Christian Messianic heritage along ideological lines. Both Adorno (cf. e.g. Arnold Künzli, "Irrationalism of the Left" in Judith Marcus and Zoltán Tar, eds., *Foundations of the Frankfurt School of Social Research* [New Brunswick: Transaction Books, 1984]) and Heidegger (cf. e.g. Herman Philipse, *Heidegger's Philosophy of Being: a Critical Interpretation* [Princeton: Princeton University Press, 1998]) have been severely criticized on these very grounds. However, such polemics must be careful not to lapse into conceptually dubious arguments, at the very moment that they seek to restore conceptual rigor or defend a historically grounded interpretation of reason; when Philipse, for example, suggests that Heidegger tried, in his later writings, to develop "an authentic German religion" (382) he conveniently forgets that the very notion of "religion" is much too ambiguous for such sweeping statements, making it difficult to judge whether this statement is justified or not, and which its implications would be. Similarly, when Habermas, in *Religion and Rationality: Essays on Reason, God, and Modernity* (Cambridge: Polity Press, 2002) distinguishes (157) between a "dialectical" and a "mystical line of thought" within (primarily German) intellectual history, one is somewhat astounded to find Jakob Böhme within the former, and not only Heidegger but also "perhaps Wittgenstein" within the latter. The notion that one could, in such a manner, distinguish between "mysticism." on the one hand, and "dialectical thinking." on the other, must appear compromised at best when applied historically in order to divide thinkers neatly into one category or the other. While it is certainly legitimate to point out the ways in which distinct thinkers in different works interpret and reinterpret a Jewish or Judeo-Christian heritage, one should probably abstain from drawing too sweeping inferences from the fact in terms of set conceptual categories.

While many theorists are concerned, mostly or even exclusively, with how to decide between individual and collective rights and interests—a problem which keeps resurfacing, in the discussion concerning "positive" and "negative" freedom, in debates surrounding "multiculturalism," in the dilemmas of humanitarian intervention, in the attempts at formulating a "communitarian" critique of liberalism, or of resurrecting a tradition of "republicanism" or "civic virtues," and so on—Adorno and Heidegger explored a distinct dilemma, inherent to instrumental thinking. One way of expressing this dilemma would be to say that the future *captures* the present, but this is of course not entirely true. Rather, *an image* of the future captures *the moment*. For that is the only way to be secure in the enjoyment of what has yet to come, what remains, in the present, blurred shapes, indistinct shadow figures, which appear to approach the self, slowly; and then only speak—become, at least for a fleeting moment, *real*—in exchange for a sacrifice of blood.

In *Dialectic of Enlightenment*, Horkheimer and Adorno use the metaphor of Odysseus binding himself to the mast of his ship, in order to listen to the song of the Sirens, while not being forced by it to change his steadfast, disciplined course; and earlier on, in the same work, they suggest that "The distance between subject and object, a presupposition of abstraction, is grounded in the distance from the thing itself which the master achieved through the mastered."[4] Whether this is historically true or not, its implications, even as a mere analogy, are in themselves quite revolutionary, at least as far as radical thinking is concerned: for what Horkheimer and Adorno are claiming is that the very division into subject and object presupposes a *violent mastery*. And since it concerns, not only the interrelations between human beings—which is most often the subject of the various formulations of human rights or justice within the confines of a universalizing ethics or morality—but also the interrelations between humanity and its surrounding world, in full, it becomes a kind of *ontological mastery*. A mastery, not only of human over human; a mastery which transcends the division into life and death, and those conceptualizations of a universalistic ethics which usually pervade "radical" or "progressive" politics, in one shape or another.

---

[4] Adorno, Theodor W. and Horkheimer, Max, *Dialectic of Enlightenment* (London: Verso, 2008), 59, 13.

And Heidegger agrees: the division into subject and object, where both come to be increasingly understood within the parameters of a mathematically conceived, spatiotemporal grid, "banishes man into that kind of revealing which is an ordering. Where this ordering holds sway, it drives out every other possibility of revealing.[5]" This "revealing" even constitutes, in analogy to what was declared by Horkheimer and Adorno above, a kind of "violence" which, Heidegger claims, "makes an assault upon" things.[6] And this is where we enter our dead end, our final *cul-de-sac*.

III. *Cul-de-Sac*: Does Mauthner Matter?

The problem is that the two dilemmas alluded to above appear to coexist in a state of tension: when we reduce the world according to set conceptual schemes, in order to secure a future gain—a presupposition of much radical, "progressive" politics—we simultaneously appear to exercise violence over the present, the moment. Of course we may hope for a new language that does not reify and for an experience of wonder in the moment, which is bereft of any connection to the institutional hierarchies that we associate with the churches. But which are the minimal requirements of entering something similar to, as Mehtonen formulates it, "the God-seeking progress of a religious mystic towards the imageless realization of a sort of immanent transcendence"? Set free, what do such experiences tell us, and what do they presuppose? They tell us that any "reified" understanding of the world and of existence as a whole is reductive. But in the latter case, many "mystics" have been clear on one thing: they demand a reigning in of desire.[7] So if radical politics desires to

---

[5] Heidegger, Martin, *The Question Concerning Technology and Other Essays* (New York: Harper & Row, 1977), 27.

[6] Heidegger, Martin, *Basic Writings: from Being and Time* (1927) to *The Task of Thinking* (1964) (London: Routledge, 2002), 150–151.

[7] The complexities of defining the concept of "mysticism" cannot be dealt with at length here; however, the attempts at pursuing or inviting intense experiences by means of asceticism may surely be said to be a prominent feature of what we today commonly call "mysticism." even if the meanings of that concept itself has changed historically. John Cassian, the founder of Western monasticism, certainly does not hide the aim of his *Institutes* (Mahwah, New Jersey: The Paulist Press, 1997): "When desire has died all the vices wither away." (102) Cassian is not primarily a theoretical thinker in this respect; rather, he provides us with the whole "language-game" of the ascetic life, telling us how

reduce reification away, it must also be prepared to assume the heaviest burden: to reign in desire.

The dilemma, then, is this: in so far that we merely seek to distribute resources within a given political community, there is no guarantee against the instrumentalization of even the deepest layers of language and thinking—it may go on unchecked and unaddressed. And if we take this critique seriously, the question then arises as to its implications for political thought and praxis: not only do we need to mitigate between distinct individual and collective desires—there is also the question of assuming responsibility for desire as such. This, however, naturally, does not entail a mere repetition of early Christian asceticism; rather, it needs to be conceived of in relation to our respective conceptualizations of the specific questions surrounding the flows of desire pervading the contemporary world.

This, then, to conclude, constitutes perhaps the final frontier of radical politics: the possibilities of a renewed asceticism, situated in a present context, with its perceived problems, meet the claims of a progressivism which, as one of its most eloquent contemporary defenders puts it, aims "to radicalize the liberal democratic regime and to extend the democratic revolution to an increasing number of social relations."[8] In so far as Mauthner can aid us in thinking this dilemma anew, he remains a supremely relevant thinker.

---

much to eat, work, sleep, and pray. But the point that should be emphasized here is that this is not merely a matter of a negative reducing away, but also of opening ourselves up to that which is otherwise hidden away, or forced away, by the flows of desire: to those intense experiences of an unfathomable, divine presence which Cassian describes so poetically.

[8] Chantal Mouffe, "Politics and the Limits of Liberalism" in *The Return of the Political* (London: Verso), 152–153.

Appearing in Fragility, the Fragility of Appearing

MARCIA SÁ CAVALCANTE SCHUBACK

> There is in all beauty a forbiddance to touch,
> From which emanates I don't know what of sacred
> That stops the movement and puts the man
> On the point of acting in fear of himself.

Paul Valéry, The blank sheet[1]

What is the meaning of looking *today* for a meaning of the "sacred"? What is the place of this question in our today? These questions attempt to address problems that arise from our today based on theoretical perspectives we already have or are on the quest for. We could start asking if we today need such a question, if it is merely a scholarly question or a question of theoretical curiosity or occupation.

We have inherited a certain theoretical discourse about the sacred. The sacred has also a history of its naming. The name of the sacred is a poetical gesture and shares with poetry the secretedness of its offspring. A beautiful testimony of it can be read in an Elegy attributed to Xenophanes, edited by Diels and Kranz as the first fragment.[2] The sacred has been named as the place and the time in which abyssal differences and identities appear. Its

---

[1] "En vérité, une feuille blanche/Nous déclare par le vide/Qu'il n'est rien de si beau/Que ce qui n'existe pas./Sur le miroir magique de sa blanche étendue,/L'âme voit devant elle le lieu des miracles/Que l'on ferait naître avec des signes et des lignes./Cette présence d'absence surexcite/Et paralyse à la fois l'acte sans retour de la plume./Il y a dans toute beauté une interdiction de toucher,/Il en émane je ne sais quoi de sacré/Qui suspend le geste, et fait l'homme/Sur le point d'agir se craindre soi-même." Paul Valéry ur *"La feuille blanche."*

[2] Hermann Diels, *Die Fragmente der Vorsokratiker*, Bd 1 (Zürich-Hildesheim: WEidmann, 1989), 126–127.

archaic and historical way of being named, invoked, situates the sacred as the place and time where the difference and identity between life and death appear.

We know about sacred places—places that cannot be occupied, into which one shall not enter. St. Augustin talks about the sacred in terms of the ambiguous feeling of both feeling horror and fascination. "*Et inhorresco, et inardesco.*"[3] He explains it as the awareness of both the absolute difference and the absolute identity between the divine and the human. Rudolf Otto in his famous book *Das Heilige,*[4] (The Sacred) will also insist in this ambiguity of *tremendum* and *fascinans,* tremendous and fascinating. In this way of naming the sacred for the sake of defining it, the sacred appears not only related to the cult and the abyssal realm of death but also to the mysterious dimension of birth. The sacred appears as abyss and mystery.

In this vocabulary that expresses awareness about the sacred, the contrary of the sacred is the profane, *profanus.* The word "sacred," comes from *sacer,* that beholds the ambiguity of both sacred and sorcery, good and evil, *s-acer,* separated from the *acer,* the field of the common. Profane is in its turn a strange word, thus it does not deny the sacred. It denotes a direction and a position, *pro-fanus,* beside the *fanus,* the temple. Profane means in the near of, beside and hence outside the sacred but necessarily in relation to the sacred. The profane is thus profoundly connected to the sacred rather than the other way around. Summarizing anthropological, historical, theological views for the sake of finding a concept of the sacred, Roger Caillois, in his book from 1949, *L'homme et le sacré,* defined it as: The sacred is what gives life and gives vivacity to life, it is the source from where life emerges, the place in which it vanishes, "*le sacré est ce qui donne de la vie et la ravit, c'est la source d'où elle coule, l'estuaire où elle se perd.*"[5] He follows meanings intrinsic to the Latin semantic of the "sacred" and the "profane," affirming that common life, the usual, everydayness is related to the sacred. He follows the view that institutional life, the life of the city and the singular was organized in primitive and ancient societies from the point of view of the sacred, experienced fundamentally as the abyssal and

[3] Augustine, *The Confessions,* book 11, translation Henry Chadwick (Oxford: Oxford University Press, 1991).
[4] Rudolf Otto, *Das Heilige: Über das Irrationale in der Idee des Göttlichen und sein Verhältnis zum Rationalen* (Munich: Verlag C. H. Beck, 1931).
[5] Roger Caillois, *L'homme et le sacré* (Paris: Gallimard, 1950), 184.

mysterious difference and identity of life *and* death. The threat of the sacred does not lie only in the separation of life and death but above all in their union. Although the ancient vocabulary of the sacred underlines the sacred as the place of an abyssal difference, as birth of hierarchies, of separation between the pure and the impure, the belonging and the non-belonging, the divine and the human, the threat lies in the danger of contamination, of fusion and con-fusion of life and death. This threat is so strong that the images of the sacred present it rather as absolute "other" than as fragile "sameness." The sacred presents the "fragile sameness" of life and death, sameness that is fragile insofar as it only appears in its differentiation.

In this heritage of names and practices, and of anthropological, theological and philosophical descriptions of the sacred, we recognize the prevailing discourse on the difference between the sacred and the profane,[6] between the uncommon and the common, between the uncanny and the familiar, between transcendence and immanence, between death and life. What falls into the shadows in this heritage or "memory" of the sacred is the fragile sameness of life and death—the threat, the tremendous mystery of this contamination. This shadow of "fragile sameness" of life and death is however what might show us the difficulty of addressing the question of the "meaning" of the sacred. Indeed the meaning of the sacred undermines the sacred and the sacred undermines its own meaning.

Listening to and reading of narratives about sacred practices we can talk about forms of consecrating and even of desecrating places and events. It seems that it is something we humans can do or not do. But if the sacred is a name for the abyssal and mysterious difference and identity of life and death, we would have to admit that the sacred cannot be chosen because we are already in it. And we are in such a way already in it that we can neither step into it nor step out of it. The dual relation between life and death, abyssal difference, tremendous identity, is given. It appears in this situation a "no way in and no way out." The sacred cannot be chosen. It cannot be a need. It cannot be something to be wanted or rejected, thus the sacred is nothing, being a non-thing. George Bataille has shown how the sacred, as source for religious sensibility, is fundamentally anchored in the experience of viewing not the nothingness of life but the non-

---

[6] Mircea Eliade, *The Sacred and the Profane, the nature of religion* (New York: Harper and Brothers, 1961).

thingness of life *and* death.[7] In this sense, the sacred is profound ambiguity, *Zweideutigkeit*, the expression of a double meaning, life *and* death. The ambiguity of the sacred appears in this "and," that separates and unites at the same time and at once.

The topology and chronology of the sacred—its "religious aesthetics" so to speak—the places and times of the sacred seem to demark very clear and hard separations. They ground hierarchies. But these separations are demarked in such a manner that what most appears is the difficulty of stepping into and stepping out of these places and times. The difficulty points towards this strange no-way-in-no-way-out from the "fragile sameness" of life and death. Rather than building separated places for the sacred, the landscapes and architecture of the sacred show the impossibility of getting into and getting out of the sacred, thus we are already in it. Places and times of the sacred reveal—in the photographic meaning of the term— this no way in and no way out of the sacred. We can interpret therefore rites of initiation, of consecration and even of desecration as rites of initiating and consecrating this no way in and no way out of the sacred, in the sense that the gift of life *and* death—within which we are always already immersed—has still to be received. That can perhaps explain why consecration implies desecration. No way in, no way out of the sacred—this is a way of describing the way the sacred is given. It is given as a gift that is always already given, but that has still to be received. To be received here means—to be discovered as a gift. The word sacred is therefore intimately related to sacrifice, the gesture of offering, giving what has always already been given—the abyssal and mysterious difference and identity of life and death—the sacred. In this sense, it would be possible to say that we—the people of today—have never lost the sacred. We are today completely lost in the sacred. We are today completely lost in this no way in, no way out of the sacred difference and identity of life and death.

No way in, no way out is indeed the way we feel about our today as a whole. It is the way we feel today the whole as the global, the planetary: no way in, no way out, nihilism and boredom, absolute immanence and messianisms without future. But the no way in, no way out shows how the today appears sensible, sensitively and sensuously for us. Beyond possible meanings and values we can give to it, the no way in, no way out shows an

[7] Georges Bataille, *Théorie de la religion* (Paris: Tel Gallimard, 1973).

appearing. It does not indicate how things appear but how the appearing from which things appear appears itself to us. We cannot "see" the appearing as we see things, entities, and "realities." The appearing withdraws in what appears. There is not first the appearing and then what appears. There is therefore no sequential logic of time. Time does not go by for the appearing appears in its own dis-appearing. The appearing as such is not a space, but the impossibility of escaping from it. If there is space it is a space of perplexity.

No way in, no way out—describes not when and where things appear but the overwhelming of an appearing. The appearing as such overwhelms insofar as it shows itself as an *event*. As event it is what is happening and not what has happened or would happen. Different phenomenological names for it, "apodictic evidence," "self-donation," "self-affection," "Ur-impression," "*Es gibt*," "il y a," "radical immanence," despite their different degrees of stringency and perspectives, they are all trying to name this "is-being" of the appearing that eludes temporal and spatial determination of things. The appearing appears as such as meanwhile, as in-between. (In my native language, Portuguese, we use a different present participle of the verb to be than *ente* (ens, étant). We use above all the poetical *sendo*, in the sense of being meanwhile, being in-between). No way in, no way out describes sensibly, sensitively and sensuously the in-between and meanwhile of the appearing. The appearing as such is already appearing in everything that appears, but it appears withdrawing itself in what appears. The appearing as such cannot be seen but it can grasp us, can take us with the same intensity that we cannot grasp or seize it.

What kind of sensibility enables us to be grasped by what has always already grasped us? What kind of perplexity is demanded in order to seize what has already seized us, the appearing as such? Ferdinand Solger, the forgotten romantic philosopher, author of Erwin, or four dialogues about the beautiful and art, spoke about the "*Hinfälligkeit des Schönen*," the fragility of beauty, to indicate the way the appearing as such appears in its own dis-appearing.[8] The fragility of appearing is beauty. Beauty here has

---

[8] K. W. F. Solger, *Erwin. Vier Gespräche über das Schöne und die Kunst* (München: Wilhelm Fink Verlag, 1950). Oskar Becker, the phenomenologist, wrote about this concept of Solger in the aim of developing a phenomenological ontology from out but beyond Husserl and Heidegger at the basis of aesthetical experience. See "Von der Hinfälligkeit des Schönen und der Abenteuerlichkeit des Künstlers. Eine ontologische

nothing to do with harmonious or pacifying forms. Beauty means here unconcealment of the fragile sameness of life *and* death, revelation of the fragility of life as life's most intense strength. Solger described it in the image of someone at the top of a mountain from where one can see the whole at the same time as one can fall down in the most profound abyss. The top is a *Spitze*, a peak, the needle point of uttermost fragility thus whatever tiny step can lead into death. At the top of the mountain, in this *Spitzeheit*, all and nothingness, life and death touch each other showing their fragile sameness. Solger's Erwin describes this solitary view of the encounter between all and nothingness at the top of the mountain as the vision of an appearing as such—a vision of the fragility of beauty. It has nothing to do with alienation from the world insofar as the top of the mountain and its distance grows from profound depths of the common ground. Solitude and immensity, heights and depths, the unique and the common, sky and earth show their fragile sameness, all and nothing, life and death at once. Romantic views, we may say. Word realisms, we could also say. But in this vision of beauty as the fragility of the appearing, Solger touches on the sense of perplexity in which the appearing appears as such. Beauty means here to break down the thinghood of things, giving back to things their value of enigma, as Paul Valéry once said. Beauty means here the breaking through of wonder, silence rather than words.

"Fragility of beauty," *wonder* is the feeling or better the attunement in Heidegger's sense in which the appearing as such appears, in which the already being grasped grasps us. The wonder is the feeling for the sacred, thus the sacred perhaps is nothing but the appearing of the appearing. Wonder breaks down the contingency or everydayness in which "we make our griefs and afflictions the measure of things."[9] Wonder breaks down modern man's "intoxication with lived experiences"[10] because it gives us the "*Es gibt*," the "Il y a." In Bataille's terms, this means that wonder destroys

Untersuchung im ästhetischen Phänomenbereich" (Pfullingen, Neske 1963). Maurice Boucher wrote a book about Solger to situate him as a proto-phenomenologist of presence. See K. W. F. Solger, *Esthétique et Philosophie de la presence* (Paris: Stock, 1934). See also the study of Manfred Franck on Solger in *Das Problem "Zeit" in der deutschen Romantik: Zeitbewusstsein und Bewusstsein von Zeitlichkeit in der frühromantischen Philosophie und in Tiecks Dichtung* (München, Winkler verlag 1972).
[9] Martin Heidegger, *Grundfragen der Philosophie: Ausgewählte Problem der Logik*, GA 45 (Frankfurt am Main: Vittorio Klostermann, 1984).
[10] Ibid.

the thinghood in things. It destroys different levels of reification that structures theoretical and practical life, the life of everybody and every "body." Wonder attunes us with the appearing as such, with the fragile sameness of life and death. Wonder attunes us with the sacred. The sacred appears. That is why the terms *hierophany, epiphany* and *theophany* are so central in the vocabulary of the sacred.[11] The appearing as such is pure fragility, insofar as it shows itself in its own withdrawal.

Wonder is however also how the Greeks defined the breaking through of this strange life, called Philosophy, the strange life of a questioning, that questions insofar as the fragile sameness of life and death questions and compels the one who asks these kinds of questions. In lectures held 1937-38, titled *Grundfragen der Philosophie: Ausgewählte "Probleme" der "Logik,"* Heidegger discussed in several sessions philosophical wonder. He made here a phenomenology of wonder as the attunement in which philosophical inquiry breaks through. He begins by making a distinction between admiration, astonishment and wonder and thereafter proposes thirteen different dimensions of wonder. He defines admiration as relation to what appears as outstanding, admirable, remarkable, exciting. Admiration is connected to amazement, incapacity to explain, as being taken by the inexplicable, a displacement from the ordinary and familiar. Admiration is also understood from the perspective of the one who admires, showing this act as self-referential and an act of taking position, insofar as the one who admires feels him/herself capable to judge and even as superior in relation to that which is being judged. Admiration is defined by who admires and what is admired. It is in these senses that the dichotomy between the sacred and the profane, the religious and the secular, is usually discussed.

Heidegger then describes astonishment as suspension of position taking, a separation between the usual and the unusual. Astonishment is astonishment with or in relation to something, being an unconcealment of something. Something new appears in astonishment.

As the attunement that "compels us into necessity of primordial thinking" wonder is in its turn never related to something in particular. Wonder is never attached to something. Wonder opens the whole in everything. Wonder breaks down precisely the order of things in the middle

---

[11] See here Walter Otto, *Theophania Der Geist der altgriechischen Religion*, second edition (Hamburg: Rowholt, 1956).

of things. If we follow Heidegger here, we could say that unlike admiration and astonishment that are always related to a subject and an object, wonder is the attunement where the appearing as such appears, insofar as it opens the whole and all in and within everything—and not beyond things. Heidegger insists that wonder differs from admiration and astonishment precisely because it does not separate the common from the uncommon, the usual from the unusual, the visible from the invisible. Wonder is the discovery of the extraordinary within the ordinary, the unusual within the usual, the uncommon and uncanny in the common. We could say then the sacred within the profane, life in death, death in life.

Wonder, *thaumazein*, is the attunement in which the sacred and the philosophical inquiry of beginnings touch each other. The relation between philosophy and the sacred could be understood as another sense in which the sacred and the profane touch each other, showing their affinity. At stake in the relation between the sacred and the profane is the overwhelming experience of, on the one hand, the abyssal difference and mysterious identity of life and death and, on the other, the gift of the whole in everything. Both experiences: fragile sameness of life and death and the all in everything, are related and even correlated in ways that are still to be deepened and discussed. The affinity between sacred and profane philosophy appears in the everyday relation and correlation between the sacred and what we could call tentatively "cosmoaesthetics," the feeling of world's immensity. I am using the term "cosmoaesthetic" to sum up the being grasped and touched by world's immensity in which the "world" appears not only in an existential-phenomenological perspective but even in a cosmic dimension.

Talking about the sacred—from mystical African-Brazilian experiences of the sacred to the extreme rationalism of Spinoza, from animism to rational cosmology, in these most discrepant discourses about the sacred, the sacred is recurrently pronounced in relation to the power of "nature," of world's immensity, of the all. I am not denying crucial differences here but just pointing out how naïve both everyday representations of the sacred and theoretical accounts are. They both articulate the sacred through the "cosmic," that is, with a sense of the world that exceeds the innerwordly togetherness of man and things, and exceeds intersubjective relations. Something in the vague and diffuse ideas and representations about the sacred articulates it as cosmic nature, to the play of forces between day and night, heaven and earth, the elemental, etc. What the articulation between the sacred and the cosmic shows is perhaps something other than a possible relation to magic powers, irrational forces, unconscious energies. At stake here is a certain sense of togetherness that can show why the question of the sacred—as source for something like religion in both senses of *religare* and *relegere*—seems to address the question of how to live with others.

The connection between the sacred and the cosmic all, and world's immensity[12] indicates another sense of togetherness, of living with otherness that departs from an experience of existence as being in itself beyond and out of itself. This corresponds to a certain extent to the ek-static meaning of human existence described by Heidegger in *Being and Time* and later works. The experience of the sacred as connected to the experience of the "cosmic" expands however the ek-static meaning of existence insofar as it seems to bind human existence to the whole of cosmos. The philosopher that tried to develop this expanded meaning of being-in-the-world was Eugen Fink.[13] In Fink, Husserl's notion of the earth[14] complement Heidegger's notion of the play of world and earth. Here the play of day and night, of diurnal and nocturnal, heaven and earth, sleeping and awakeness, Eros and Thanathos, feminine and masculine, are seen as "existential," that is, fundamental structures of human life. The sense of togetherness is not the one of being-with others, with otherness or even with the Other. As I would like to formulate it; togetherness appears here as *being-other-within* the self, in the sense that existence is nothing that is and further is in relation to other things. Existence, being, is relatedness as such, in-betweenness. Existence is con-fusion.

Understood as the abyssal difference and mysterious identity between life *and* death and, in this sense, as the "place" and "time" we already are and from which we cannot step out, the "sacred" can be seen as source for religion and philosophy, but also for secularization. In most part of contemprary discussions about secularization, post metaphysics, religion, etc. a question is still missing. Religion, the sacred, etc. used to be considered as the presence of a past—a past that we can see either as

---

[12] See my article "On Immensity" in *Phenomenology and Religion: New Frontiers*, eds. Jonna Bornemark and Hans Ruin (Stockholm: Södertörn Philosophical Studies, 2010).
[13] See Eugen Fink, *Existenz und Coexistenz* (Würzburg: Königshausen and Neumann, 1987).
[14] See Edmund Husserl, "Grundlegende Untersuchungen zum phänomenologishcen Ursprung der Räumlichkeit der Natur" in *Philosophical Essays in Memory of Edmund Husserl*, ed. Marvin Farber (New York: Greenwood Press, 1968).

something we need to keep and develop or as something we do not need at all, but anyway as presence of the past in our today. In this sense, religion is usually related to institutions, to forms of common life, to cultural and traditional heritages, etc. Secularization means in everyday discussions modernity, an inexplicable moment or event in history where a separation from the sacred, from the religious, (rather than from religion) happened, the cutting of the bound with tradition, disenchanted autonomy, etc. But what would happen if we did not read history in this historiographical meaning, in terms of episodes in successive or linear time, but as an appearing in history of how the sacred and the profane relate to each other? The sacred and the profane could then be seen as "historical names" for the abyssal difference and mysterious identity of life and death, and for the whole in everything. In this sense, we could say that secularization, the desecrating of the sacred belongs to the sacred. This cut from the whole of life—I mean the cut or treat from the whole of nature that we call modernity, the discontinuity that modernity seems to have installed in the course of history, would appear no longer as the opposite to historical continuity but as the way life lives continuously. This would also mean to discover how the opposition between continuity and discontinuity is too metaphysical, too logically oppositional in order to clarify the relation between the sacred and the profane. Bataille's way of describing what Aristotle already saw very clearly, in his works *On the parts of Animals* and other "biological" writings, is very inspiring since he showed how individual existence—of a singular or of a historical moment—is the discontinuous continuity of the whole of life. In other words: if the sacred indicates the ambiguity of life itself—life as birth and death—the in-betweeness after death and before birth, the presence of the dead and of the unborn in present life, and therefore the existential peak where logic of oppositions, dual systems break down (we call this irrationality), then what would happen with the oppositions we are dealing with here if we were to see these experiences from the point of view of their ambiguities?

But today, why should we discuss those things? What is our today? Is it not a situation of historical no way out thus how could we go back and how could we step out of it? How do we experience our today? The today is an experience of a no way out. The no way out of a today is experienced today as loss of grounds and roots, as a *no longer belonging* to earth and nature, and neither to history nor to man. It appears as a no longer belonging without, however, arriving to another ground or heaven. The *historical sensation* is the one of having departed without return but also without arrival. The historical sensation is the one of a historical exile in the in-between. Our today is such that an existence in exile is not only an individual or collective experience but also an epochal one, something like an age or era of exile.

A life in exile is a life in exile from life, choosing not to live for the sake of not dying (as Seneca formulated in his dialogue *On Consolation*). It is a life in continuous estrangement, a life where one becomes a stranger in one's own home and never feels at home in strangeness. It is a life living as illegal in the disquiet of the in-between. It is a loss without return but also without arrival insofar as the natural identity with the self is broken and the identity with the other can never become natural. A life in exile has in fact no time and space because it exists in a space- and time-between. It is a life in which one experiences at once a suspension and an intensification of proximity and distance in time and space. A person in exile is never here nor there, being always here and there, in the presence of the no longer and of the not yet. In the exile of the today, we are with and without the past and the future. In English, we can simply say we are *with-out*. We are with-out the past and the future as we are with-out our deads and unborns. Assuming the exilic nature of the today, it becomes possible to assume another sense of community that is not solely restricted to the living beings, but includes our deads and unborns, dimensions of an after death and a before birth. Here another meaning of difference emerges, the meaning of difference as non-otherness. In the exile of the today, overwhelmed by the no way out, we experience primordially the fragility of the singular. A life in exile is a life exposed to its own fragility, to its being with-out a home and a beyond both at home and beyond. In our today, we experience in different levels of existence the fragility of the life of the singular in the middle of the gigantism of the exploration of our world. We experience further the fragility of life in nature and in history. In these experiences where the fragility of the life in nature, in history, in human existence becomes exposed we experience the fragility of the today. In it, we discover how fragility is the point where nothing and everything coincides.

Exile is life in the fragility of being with-out the self and the other, the familiar and the strange, suffering and joy, life and death. It obliges a strange learning. Rather than learning new commandments, it demands to "learn to dis-learn" as the Portuguese poet Fernando Pessoa phrased it. Life in exile asks for what could be called a *negative pedagogy*, a learning to dislearn, showing what kind of distance is at stake in the thinking-feeling of a today. Philosophy is commonly defined as critical and self-critical thinking. By critique is meant on the one hand *reflection*, i.e., moving back thoughts to their ground and presuppositions, and, on the other, *separation* from given states of facts and statements in order to see their limits and contradictions. Today, this sense of self-critical critique may be necessary but it is not enough. We live in a moment where there are too many words, thoughts, references, information, activities, ambition, productivity, where knowledge, critique, reflection, feelings, ethics and politics are consumed as merchandises. Urgent is to learn to dis-learn in the sense of placing philosophical inquiry in the risky point of today's fragility, in which we abandon what is our own, dare to remain in this point where we no longer have something but neither have something else. If our today is experienced as the today in which, paraphrasing some verses of T. S. Eliot, "the lost word is lost, [...] the spent word is spent, the unheard, unspoken word is unspoken, unheard; still is the unspoken word, the Word unheard, The World Without a Word, the Word within the World and for the world." Still is the fragile existence of life *and* death in nature, in history, in the human. The task today is to think carefully and to care thoughtfully for this fragile sacred "still" of *life and death* in our today as the place and time of the sacred, as the sacred place of life and death.

Bibliography

Adorno, Theodor W., *Problems of Moral Philosophy*, translation Thomas Schroder and Rodney Livingston, Cambridge: Polity Press, 2000

Adorno, Theodor W. and Horkheimer, Max, *Dialectic of Enlightenment*, London: Verso, 2008

Agamben, Giorgio, *The Time that Remains: a Commentary on the Letter to the Romans*, Stanford, CA: Stanford University Press, 2005

Allen, Douglas, "Phenomenology of religion" in *Routledge Companion to the Study of Religion*, London: Routledge, 2010

Althusser, Louis, "Ideology and the State" in *On Ideology*, London: Verso, 2008

Althusser, Louis, *Philosophy of the Encounter: Later Writings, 1978–87*, London/New York: Verso, 2006

Arens, Katherine, "Mach und Mauthner: Der Fall eines Paradigmenwechsels" in *Fritz Mauthner. Das Werk eines kritischen Denkers*, eds. Elisabeth Leinfellner and Hubert Schleichert, Wien: Böhlau Verlag, 1995, 95–109.

Augustine, *On Trinity*, translation Steven McKennaz, Cambridge: Cambridge University Press, 2002

Augustine, *The Confessions*, translation Henry Chadwick, Oxford: Oxford University Press, 1991

Badiou, Alain, *Deleuze: the Clamor of Being*, Minneapolis: University of Minnesota Press, 2000

Badiou, Alain, *Saint Paul: the Foundation of Universalism*, Stanford, CA: Stanford University Press, 2003

Balmes, Francois, *La nom, la loi, la voix*, Paris: Eres, 1997

Barbaras, Renaud, *Introduction à une phénoménologie de la vie*, Paris: Vrin, 2008

Barthes, Roland, *The Neutral: Lecture Course at the College de France (1977–1978)*, New York: Columbia University Press, 2005

Barton, John, *Understanding Old Testament Ethics. Approaches and Explorations*, Louisvelle: Westminster John Knox Press, 2003

Bataille, Georges, *L'érotisme*, Paris: Minuit, 1957; *Eroticism - Death and Sensuality*, translation Mary Dalwood, San Fransisco: City Lights Books, 1986

Bataille, Georges, *Théorie de la religion*, Paris: Gallimard, 1973, *Theory of Religion*, translation Robert Harley, New York, 1989.

Baumgarten, Alexander Gottlieb, *Aesthetica*, Hildesheim: Georg Olms Verlag, 1961 [1750]

Becker, Oskar, "Von der Hinfälligkeit des Schönen und der Abenteuerlichkeit des Künstlers" in *Dasein und Dawesen. Gesammelte philosophische Aufsätze*, Pfullingen: Neske, 1963, 11-40

Benjamin, Walter, *Selected Writings, Vol. 4, 1938-1940*, Cambridge, MA: Belknap Press, 2003

Benjamin, Walter, *The Arcades Project*, Cambridge: The Belknap Press of Harvard University Press, 1999

Benoist, Jocelyn, *Les limites de l'intentionalité : Recherches phénoménologiques et analytiques*, Paris: Vrin, 2005

Billecoq, Alain, *Spinoza: Questions politiques*, Paris: L'Harmattan, 2009

Blanton, Ward, *Displacing Christian Origins: Philosophy, Secularity, and the New Testament* in Religion and Postreligion, Chicago and London: The University of Chicago Press, 2007

Blanton, Ward, "Dispossessed Life: Introduction to Breton's Paul" in Stanislas Breton, *Saint Paul*, translation Joseph Ballan, New York: Columbia University Press, 2010

Blanton, Ward, "'Reappearance of Paul, "Sick"': Foucault's Biopolitics and the Political Significance of Pasolini's Apostle" in *Journal for Cultural and Religious Theory*, 10.2, 2010

Breton, Stanislas, "Difference, Relation, Alterity," translation Pierre Colin in *Parallax*, 2004, vol. 10, no. 4, 42–60

Breton, Stanislas, *La Pensee du Rien*, Kampen: Kok Pharos Publishing, 1992

Breton, Stanislas, *Philosopher par passion et par raison*, Grenoble: Editions Jérome Millon et les Auteurs, 1990

Breton, Stanislas, *Saint Paul*, Paris: Presses Universitaires de France, 1988; *Saint Paul*, translation Joseph Ballan, Insurrections: Critical Studies in Religion, Politics, and Culture, New York: Columbia University Press, 2010

Breton, Stanislas, *Théorie des Idéologies*, Paris: Desclée, 1976

Breton, Stanislas, *The Word and the Cross*, translation Jacquelyn Porter, New York: Fordham University Press, 2002

Buber, Martin, ed. *Ekstatische Konfessionen*, Leipzig: Insel, 1921 [1909]

Budick, Sanford and Wolfgang Iser, eds., *Languages of the Unsayable: The Play of Negativity in Literature and Literary Theory*, Stanford: Stanford UP, 1996 [1987]

Bueno, Gustavo, *Ensayos materialistas*, Madrid: Taurus, 1972

Bultmann, Rudolf, *Theology of the New Testament*, New York: Scribner's, 1951

Caillois, Roger, *L'homme et le sacré*, Paris, Gallimard, 1939, re-ed. 1988; *Man and the Sacred*, translation Meyer Barash, Urbana: University of Illinois Press, 2001

Caputo, John D. and Michael J. Scanlon, eds, *God, the Gift, and Postmodernism*, Bloomington, Indianapolis: Indiana University Press, 1999

Cassian, John, *The Institutes*, Mahwah, New Jersey: The Paulist Press, 1997

Cavalcante Schuback Sá, Marcia, "On Immensity" in *Phenomenology and Religion: New Frontiers*, eds. Jonna Bornemark and Hans Ruin, Stockholm: Södertörn Philosophical Studies, 2010

Caws, Mary Ann (ed.), *Manifesto: A Century of Isms*, Lincoln, London: University of Nebraska Press, 2001

Cunningham, Conor, *Genealogy of Nihilism: Philosophies of Nothing and the Difference of Theology*, London, New York: Routledge, 2002.

Dahl, Espen, *In Between. The Holy Beyond Modern Dichtomies*, Göttingen: Vandenhoeck & Ruprecht, 2011

Deleuze, Gilles, *Bergsonism*, translation Hugh Tomlinson and Barbara Habberjam, New York: Zone Books, 1991

Derrida, Jacques, "Faith and Knowledge: the Two Sources of 'Religion' at the Limits of Reason Alone" in *Religion*, eds. Jacques Derrida and Gianni Vattimo, Stanford, CA: Stanford University Press, 1996

Derrida, Jacques, *The Gift of Death*, translation David Wills, Chicago: University of Chicago Press, 1995

Diels, Hermann, *Die Fragmente der Vorsokratiker*, Bd 1, Zürich-Hildesheim: Weidmann, 1989

Dominic Crossan, John and Reed, Jonathan, *In Search of Paul: How Jesus's Apostle Opposed Rome's Empire with God's Kingdom*, San Francisco: Harper San Francisco, 2004

Dostoevsky, Fyodor, *The Brothers Karamazov*, translation Richard Pevear and Larissa Volokhonsky, New York: Farrar, Straus and Giroux, 1990

Durkheim, Émile, *The Elementary Forms of Religious Life*, translation Carol Cosman, New York: Oxford University Press, 2001

Duve, Thierry de, *Pictorial Nominalism: On Marcel Duchamp's Passage from Painting to the Readymade*, translation Dana Polan, Minneapolis: University of Minnesota Press, 1991

Eliade, Mircea, *The Sacred and the Profane, the Nature of Religion*, translation W. Trask, New York: Harper and Brothers, 1961; New York: Harcourt Brace, 1959

Engberg-Pedersen, Troels, *Cosmology and the Self in the Apostle Paul: the Material Spirit*, Oxford, UK: Oxford University Press, 2010

Engberg-Pedersen, Troels, *Paul and the Stoics*, Louisville, KY: Westminster John Knox, 2000

Fink, Eugen, *Existenz und Coexistenz*, Würzburg: Königshausen and Neumann, 1987

Franck, Didier, *Dramatique des phénomènes*, Paris: PUF-Épiméthée, 2001

Franck, Didier, *Nietzsche et l'ombre de Dieu*, Paris: PUF, 1998

Franck, Manfred, *Das Problem "Zeit" in der deutschen Romantik: Zeitbewusstsein und Bewusstsein von Zeitlichkeit in der frühromantischen Philosophie und in Tiecks Dichtung*, München: Winkler Verlag, 1972

Franke, William (ed.), *On What Cannot be Said. Apophatic Discourses in Philosophy, Religion, Literature, and the Arts*. 2 volume, Notre Dame: University of Notre Dame Press, 2007

Granel, Gérard, "Far from Substance, Whither and To What Point?" in Jean-Luc Nancy, *Dis-Enclosure: Deconstruction of Christianity*, translation Bettina Bergo, Gabriel Malenfant and Michael B. Smith, New York: Fordham University Press, 2007

Granel, Gérard, *L'équivoque ontologique de Kant*, Paris: Gallimard, 1970; reprinted Mauvezin: Éditions TER, nd

Gurwitsch, Aron, *Marginal Consciousness*, Ohio: Ohio University Press, 1985

Habermas, Jürgen, *Der philosophische Diskurs der Moderne. Zwölf Vorlesungen*, 3rd ed. Frankfurt am Main: Suhrkamp Verlag, 1986

Habermas, Jürgen, *Religion and Rationality: Essays on Reason, God, and Modernity*, Cambridge: Polity Press, 2002

Heidegger, Martin, *Basic Writings: from Being and Time (1927) to The Task of Thinking (1964)*, London: Routledge, 2002

Heidegger, Martin, *Erläuterungen zu Hölderlins Dichtung*; Gesamtausgabe 4, Frankfurt am Main: Klostermann, 1975–; *Elucidations of Hölderlin's Poetry*, translation Keith Hoeller, Amherst, NY: Humanity Books, 2000

Heidegger, Martin, *Gesamtausgabe, Hinweise und Aufzeichnungen, Zu Ernst Jünger*, Frankfurt am Main: Vittorio Klostermann, 2004

Heidegger, Martin, *Grundfragen der Philosophie: Ausgewählte Problem der Logik*, GA 45, Frankfurt am Main: Vittorio Klostermann, 1984

Heidegger, Martin, *The Question Concerning Technology and Other Essays*, translation William Lovitt, New York: Harper & Row, 1977

Heimonet, Jean-Michel, "Bataille and Sartre: The Modernity of Mysticism" in *Diacritics* 26.2, 1996: 59–73

Held, Klaus, *Lebendige Gegenwart – Die Frage nach der Seinsweise des transzendentalen Ich bei Edmund Husserl, entwickelt am Leitfaden der Zeitproblematik*, Den Haag: Martinus Nijhoff, 1966

Henry, Michel, *Genealogy of Psychoanalysis [The Lost Beginning]*, translation Douglas Brick, Stanford, California: Stanford University Press, 1993

Henry, Michel, *I am the Truth*, Stanford California: Stanford University Press, 2003

Hobbes, *Leviathan*, London: Penguin Books, 1968

Hofmannsthal, Hugo von, *Ein Brief* (Brief des Lord Chandos an Francis Bacon), Projekt Gutenberg, http://gutenberg.spiegel.de/?id=5&xid=1247&kapitel=1#gb _found>, 24 April 2010

Holsinger, Bruce, *The Premodern Condition: Medievalism and the Meaning of Theory*, Chicago: University of Chicago Press, 2005

Horrell, David, *An Introduction to the Study of Paul*, London/New York: Continuum, 2000

Husserl, Edmund, *De la synthèse passive*, translation Bruce Bégout and Natalie Depraz, Grenoble: Jérome Millon, 1998

Husserl, Edmund, "Grundlegende Untersuchungen zum phänomenologishcen Ursprung der Räumlichkeit der Natur" in *Philosophical Essays in Memory of Edmund Husserl*, ed. Marvin Farber, New York: Greenwood Press, 1968

Husserl, Edmund, *Husserliana Dokumente: Briefwechsel*, Vol. 7: Wissenschaftler-korrespondenz. Dordrecht: Kluwer, 1994; letter to Hofmannsthal 12.1.1907, translation Sven-Olov Wallenstein, *Site 26-27*, 2009, 2

Husserl, Edmund, *Zur Phänomenologie des inneren Zeitbewusstseins*, Hua X, ed. Rudolf Boehm, Haag: Martinus Nijhoff, 1966

Huttunen, Niko, *Paul and Epictetus on Law: a Comparison*, London: T&T Clark, 2009

James, William, *The varieties of religious experience; a study in human nature, being the Gifford lectures on natural religion delivered at Edinburgh in 1901-1902*, New York, London [etc.] Longmans, Green, and co., 1902

Janicaud, Dominique, *Phenomenology and the "Theological turn": the French Debate*, New York: Fordham University Press, 2000

Jolas, Eugene, *Man from Babel*, eds. Andreas Kramer and Rainer Rumold, New Haven, London: Yale University Press, 1998.

Jolas, Eugene, "Workshop" in *Imagining Language: An Anthology*, eds. Jed Rasula and Steve McCaffery, Cambridge, MASS., London: The MIT Press, 2001: 42–47

Kamper, Dietmar and Wulf, Christoph, *Das Heilige. Seine Spur in der Moderne*, Bodenheim: Athenäum, 1987

Kühn, Joachim, *Gescheiterte Sprachkritik: Fritz Mauthners Leben und Werk*, Berlin, New York: Walter de Gruyter, 1975

Künzli, Arnold, "Irrationalism of the Left" in Judith Marcus and Zoltán Tar, eds., *Foundations of the Frankfurt School of Social Research*, New Brunswick: Transaction Books, 1984

Lagrée, Jacqueline, "Spinoza et la subversion des normes religieuses" in *Spinoza et la politique*, Paris: L'Harmattan, 1997

Landauer, Gustav, *Meister Eckhart: Mystische Schriften*, Frankfurt am Main & Leipzig: Insel Verlag, 1991

Landauer, Gustav, *Skepsis und Mystik: Versuche im Anschluß an Mauthners Sprachkritik*, 2nd rev. ed. Köln: Marcan Block, 1923 [1903]

Laux, Henri, *Imagination et religion chez Spinoza*, Paris: Vrin, 1993

Levinas, Emmanuel, *Autrement qu'être ou au-delà de l'essence*, Paris: La Haye, 1974; *Otherwise than Being, Or Beyond Essence*, translation Alphonso Lingis, Pittsburgh: Duquesne University Press, 2000

Levinas, Emmanuel, *Difficult Freedom. Essays on Judaism*, translation Sean Hand, Baltimore: The Johns Hopkins University Press, 1990

Levinas, Emmanuel, *En découvrant l'existence avec Husserl et Heidegger*, Paris: Vrin, 1982; translation of the essays on Husserl, see *Discovering Existence with Husserl*, translation Richard A. Cohen and Michael B. Smith, Evanston, Ill.: Northwestern University Press, 1998, 135–151

Levinas, Emmanuel, *God, Death, and Time*, translation Bettina Bergo, Stanford, California: Stanford University Press, 2000

Levinas, Emmanuel, *Noms propres*, Fata Morgana, 1976; *Proper Names*, translation Michael B, Smith, Stanford University Press, 1997

Levinas, Emmanuel, *Totalité et infini: essai sur l'extériorité,* Paris: La Haye, 1961; *Totality and Infinity: An Essay on Exteriority*, translation Alphonso Lingis, Pittsburgh: Duquesne University Press, 1969

Levinas, Emmanuel, "Quelques réflexions sur la philosophie de l'hitlérisme" in *Esprit*, XXVI, Novembre 1934; "Reflections on the Philosophy of Hitlerism," translation Seán Hand, in *Critical Inquiry* 17 Autumn 1990, 63–71

Levy, Zeev, *From Spinoza to Levinas*, New York: Peter Lang Publishing Inc, 2009

Marcus, Judith and Tar, Zoltán eds., *Foundations of the Frankfurt School of Social Research*, New Brunswick: Transaction Books, 1984

Marion, Jean-Luc, *Being Given: Toward a Phenomenology of Givenness*, translation Jeffrey Kosky, Stanford, California: Stanford University Press, 2002

Marion, Jean-Luc, *Dieu sans l'être*, Paris: Fayard, 1982; *God without Being*, Chicago: University of Chicago Press, 1995

Martin, Dale B., *The Corinthian Body*, New Haven: Yale University Press, 1999

Matheron, Alexandre, *Le Christ et le salut des ignorants chez Spinoza*, Paris: Aubier, 1971

Matheron, Alexandre, "Politique et religion chez Hobbes et Spinoza" in *Anthropologie et politique au XVIIe siècle*, Paris: Vrin, 1986

Mauthner, Fritz, *Beiträge zu einer Kritik der Sprache*, Vol I. Leipzig: Felix Meiner, 1923 [1901]

Mauthner, Fritz, *Der Atheismus und seine Geschichte im Abendlande*, Facsimile edition. Hildesheim, Zürich, New York: Georg Olms Verlag, 1985 [1923]

Mauthner, Fritz, *Die Drei Bilder der Welt*, Erlangen: Verlag der philosophischen Akademie, 1925

Mauthner, Fritz, *Die Sprache*, Die Gesellschaft, Band IX. ed. Martin Buber, Frankfurt: Literarische Anstalt Rütten & Loening, 1906

Mauthner, Fritz, *Fritz Mauthner – Sprache und Leben: Ausgewählte Texte aus dem philosophischen Werk*, ed. Gershon Weiler, Salzburg, Wien: Residenz Verlag, 1986

Mauthner, Fritz, *Wörterbuch der Philosophie: Neue Beiträge zu einer Kritik der Sprache*, München: Georg Müller, 1910

McCormick, John P., *Carl Schmitt's Critique of Liberalism: Against Politics as Technology*, Cambridge: Cambridge University Press, 1997

Mehtonen, Päivi, "Encyclopaedic Nichts: Mauthner, Mysticism and the *Avant-garde*" in *Nothing Left to Say: Nothingness in Philosophy, Theology, and Literature*, eds. Antti Salminen and Sami Sjöberg (forthcoming)

Montag, Warren, "Lucretius Hebraizant: La lectura de Spinoza del Eclesiastés" in *Spinoza contemporaneo*, eds. Montserrat Galcerán Huguet and Mario Espinoza Pino, Madrid: Tierradenadie ediciones, 2009

Montag, Warren, "Spinoza and Althusser Against Hermeneutics: Interpretation or Intervention?" in *The Althusserian Legacy*, eds. E. Ann Kaplan and Michael Sprinkler, London/New York: Verso, 1993

Montag, Warren, *The Return of the Political*, London: Verso, 1993

Moreno Sanz, Jesús, *El logos oscuro: tragedia, mística y filosofía en María Zambrano*, Madrid: Verbum, 2008

Morgenstern, Christian, *Stufen: Eine Entwickelung in Aphorismen und Tagebuch-Notizen*, München: R. Piper & Co Verlag, 1922, http://www.gutenberg.org/files/ 15898/15898-8.txt 10 April 2010

Mouffe, Chantal, "Politics and the Limits of Liberalism" in Warren Montag, *The Return of the Political*, London: Verso, 1993

Mouffe, Chantal, *On the Political*, London: Routledge, 2005

Nancy, Jean-Luc, *Dis-enclosure: the deconstruction of Christianity*, Fordham: Fordham Univ Press, 2008

Neher, André, *L'exil de la parole*, Paris: Seuil, 1970; *Exile of the Word*, translation David Maisel Philadelphia: The Jewish Publication Society of America, 1981

Nietzsche, Friedrich, *Beyond Good and Evil: Prelude to a Philosophy of the Future*, translation and ed. Walter Kaufmann, New York: Vintage Books, 1966

Nietzsche, Friedrich, *Kritische Studienausgabe*, eds. Giorgio Colli, Mazzino Montinari, Berlin: Walter de Gruyter, 1988, 2nd edition

Oberman, Heiko, *The Harvest of Medieval Theology: Gabriel Biel and Late Medieval Nominalism*, 3. ed., Labyrinth Press, Durham, N.C., 1983

Otto, Rudolf, *Das Heilige: Über das Irrationale in der Idee des Göttlichen und sein Verhältnis zum Rationalen*, München: Verlag C. H. Beck, 1931 [1917]; *The Idea of the Holy: An Inquiry into the Non-Rational Factor in the Idea of the Divine and its Relation to the Rational*, translation John W. Harvey, London, Oxford, New York: Oxford University Press, 1958

Otto, Walter, *Theophania. Der Geist der altgriechischen Religion*, 2. ed, Hamburg: Rowholt, 1956

Peña García, Vidal, *El materialismo de Spinoza. Ensayo sobre la ontología spinozista*, Madrid: Revista de Occidente, 1974

Peña García, Vidal, "Introducción" in *Ética* by Baruch Spinoza, Madrid; Alianza Editorial, 2009

Perloff, Marjorie, *21st-Century Modernism: The "New" Poetics*, Malden, Oxford: Blackwell, 2002

Philipse, Herman, *Heidegger's Philosophy of Being: a Critical Interpretation*, Princeton: Princeton University Press, 1998

Rey, Jean-Michel, *Paul ou les ambiguities*, Paris: Éditions de l'Olivier, 2008

Ricoeur, Paul, *Lectures on Ideology and Utopia*, New York: Columbia University Press, 1986

Ringbom, Sixten, *The Sounding Cosmos: A Study in the Spiritualism of Kandinsky and the Genesis of Abstract Painting*, Åbo: Åbo Akademi, 1970

Ruin, Hans, *Poesins Mystik*, Helsingfors: Söderström, 1935

Ruin, Hans, "Faith, Grace, and the Destruction of Tradition: A Hermeneutic-Genealogical Reading of the Pauline Letters" in *Journal for Cultural and Religious Theory*, Vol 11, 1, 2010, 16-34

Russell, Bertrand, *Mysticism and Logic and Other Essays*, 2. ed., Longmans, Green, 1917

Russell, Bertrand, *Roads to Freedom: Socialism, Anarchism and Syndicalism*, George Allen: London, 1918

Russell, Bertrand, "Mysticism" in *Logic Religion and Science*, Oxford University Press, New York, 1961

Sanders, E. P., *Paul: A Very Short Introduction*, Oxford/New York: Oxford University Press, 2001

Schelling, F.W.J., *Philosophy of Revelation*, 29th lesson, Sämmtliche Werke, volume 14, Stuttgart and Augsburg: J.G. Cottascher Verlag, 1861

Scholem, Gershom, *The Messianic Idea in Judaism and Other Essays on Jewish Spirituality*, New York: Schocken Books, 1971, 1995

Sloterdijk, Peter, *Nicht Gerretet: Versuche nach Heidegger*, Frankfurt am Main: Suhrkamp, 2001

Sodré, Muniz, *A Verdade Seduzida – por um conceito de cultura no Brasil*, Francisco Alves, 1990

Solger, K. W. F., *Erwin.Vier Gespräche über das Schöne und die Kunst*, München: Wilhelm Fink Verlag, 1950

Solger, K. W. F., *Esthétique et Philosophie de la presence*, Paris: Stock, 1934

Sontag, Susan, "Under the Sign of Saturn" in *Under the Sign of Saturn*, New York: Picador, 1980

Spinoza, Benedict de, *A Theologico-Political Treatise*, translation R. H. Elwes, New York: Dover Publications, Inc, 1951

Spinoza, Benedict de, *Ethics*, translation Edwin Curley, London: Penguin Books, 1996

Spitzer, Leo, "Die groteske Gestaltungs- und Sprachkunst Christian Morgensterns" in *Motiv und Wort. Studien zur Literatur- und Sprachpsychologie*, Leipzig: O. R. Reisland, 1918, 53–123

Steiner, Rudolf, *Die Mystik im aufgange des neuzeitlichen Geisteslebens und ihr verhältnis zu Modernen Weltanschauungen*, Berlin: C.A. Schwetschke und sohn, 1901

Steiner, Rudolf, *Chance, Providence, and Necessity: eight lectures held in Dornach between August 23 and September 6, 1915*, translation Marjorie Spock, Hudson: Anthroposophic Press, 1988

Stowers, Stanley, *Rereading Romans*, New Haven: Yale University Press, 1997

Surin, Kenneth, *Freedom Not Yet: Liberation and the Next World Order*, New Slant: Religion, Politics, and Ontology, Durham, NC: Duke University Press, 2009

Taubes, Jacob, *From Cult to Culture: Fragments Toward a Critique of Historical Reason*, Stanford, CA: Stanford University Press, 2010

Thorsteinsson, Runar, *Roman Christianity and Roman Stoicism: a Comparative Study of Ancient Morality*, Oxford, UK: Oxford University Press, 2010

Vries, Hent de, *Philosophy and the Turn to Religion*, Baltimore: Johns Hopkins University Press, 1999

Wasserman, Emma, *Death of the Soul in Romans 7: Sin, Death, and the Law in Hellenistic Moral Psychology*, Tübingen: Mohr Siebeck, 2008

Weiler, Gershon, *Mauthner's Critique of Language*, Cambridge: Cambridge University Press, 1970

Westphal, Merold, "Levinas's Teleological Suspension of the Religious" in *Ethics as First Philosophy*, ed. Adriaan Peperzak, New York and London: Routledge, 1995

Wimbush, Vincent, *Paul the Worldly Ascetic*, New York: Mercer University Press, 1987

Wolin, Richard, *Heidegger's Children: Hannah Arendt, Karl Löwith, Hans Jonas, and Herbert Marcuse*, Princeton: Princeton University Press, 2001

Wolosky, Shira, *Language Mysticism: The Negative Way of Language in Eliot, Beckett, and Celan*, Stanford: Stanford University Press, 1995

Zambrano, María, *El hombre y lo divino*, Buenos Aires: Fondo de cultura económica, 1955 [1953]

Zambrano, María, "La salvación del individuo en Espinosa" in *Cuadernos de la facultad de filosofía y letras*, 1936:3, Universidad Complutense de Madrid, 7–20

Zarader, Marlène, *The Unthought Debt: Heidegger and the Hebraic Heritage*, translation Bettina Bergo, Stanford: Stanford University Press, 2006

Žižek, Slavoj, *The Parallax View*, Boston: MIT Press, 2006

Žižek, Slavoj, *The Sublime Object of Ideology*, London/New York: Verso, 1989

Index of Names

Index of Concepts

Authors

Bettina Bergo

Bettina Bergo is Associate Professor of philosophy at Université de Montréal and the author of *Levinas between Ethics and Politics* (Kluwer, 1999). She is co-editor of several collections, notably *Levinas and Nietzsche: After the Death of a Certain God* (Columbia, 2009), *Trauma: Reflections on Experience and Its Other* (SUNY, 2009), *Levinas's Contribution to Contemporary Thought* (double issue of the New School for Social Research *Graduate Faculty Philosophy Journal*, 1999) and she translated three works of Levinas. She is presently working on a history of the concept of anxiety in 19th and 20th century philosophy.

Ward Blanton

Ward Blanton is senior lecturer in the School of Critical Studies at the University of Glasgow. His first book, *Displacing Christian Origins: Philosophy, Secularity, and the New Testament* (The University of Chicago Press, 2007), was shortlisted for best first book in the history of religions by the American Academy of Religion. His second book is entitled *A Materialism for the Masses: Paul and Radical Philosophy* (UP). With Hent de Vries he edited *Paul and the Philosophers* (The University of Chicago Press, 2012).

Jonna Bornemark

Jonna Bornemark is a philosopher and director of the Center of Practical Knowledge at Södertörn University. Among her publications are *Kunskapens gräns, gränsens vetande: en fenomenologisk undersökning av transcendens och kroppslighet* (Södertörn Philosophical Studies, 2010), *Phenomenology and Religion: New Frontiers* (ed. with Hans Ruin, Södertörn Philosophical Studies, 2010) and *Phenomenology of Eros* (ed. with Marcia sá Cavalcante Schuback, Södertörn Philosophical Studies, 2012).

Marcia Sá Cavalcante Schuback

Marcia Sá Cavalcante Schuback is professor of Philosphy at Södertörn University (Sweden). She has also worked as Associate Professor at the Universidade Federal do Rio de Janeiro (UFRJ) in Brazil. Her field of research is continental philosophy, with focus on phenomenology, hermeneutics, German Idealism, and hermeneutical readings of ancient philosophy. Her latest monographs are *Lovtal till intet – essäer om filosofisk hermeneutik* (Glänta, 2006), *Olho a olho: ensaios de longe* (7 Letras, 2010), *Att tänka i skisser* (Glänta, 2011).

Karolina Enquist Källgren

Karolina Enquist Källgren is a PhD-student in History of Ideas at Gothenburg University as well as a play writer. Her thesis treats the Spanish philosopher María Zambrano, concerning the thinking subject and the limits of knowledge in the concept of poetic reason. She is currently stationed at the University of Barcelona with the Zambrano seminar and working on a translation to Swedish of *El hombre y lo divino*.

Mattias Martinson

Mattias Martinson is professor at the Faculty of Theology, Uppsala University. He has written extensively on religion and secular culture, for example *Perseverance without Doctrine. Adorno, Self-Critique, and the Ends of Academic Theology* (Peter Lang, 2000), *Katedralen mitt i staden – Om ateism och teologi* (Arcus, 2010), and "The Irony of Religious Studies. A Pro-theological Argument from the Swedish Experience" in *Theology and Religious Studies in Higher Education. Global Perspectives* (Continuum, 2009).

Päivi Mehtonen

Päivi Mehtonen, is Academy Research Fellow and Adjunct Professor of Comparative Literature at the University of Tampere and University of Helsinki. Her recent publications include *Obscure Language, Unclear Literature. Theory and Practice from Quintilian to the Enlightenment* (Academia Scientiarum, 2003), an edited collection *Illuminating Darkness. Approaches to Obscurity and Nothingness in Literature* (Finnish Academy of Sciences and Letters, 2007), and articles on medieval and avant-garde poetics (in *Rhetorica, Angelaki* etc).

Elena Namli

Elena Namli is Associate Professor in Ethics and Research Director at Uppsala Centre for Russian Studies. She has recently published a monograph on the Russian critique of Western Rationalism: *Kamp med förnuftet* (Artos, 2009). Earlier publications include *Och på en enda kyrka. Den ryska teologiska etiken och dess ekumeniska relevans* (Artos 2003) She is currently researching different dimensions within the contemporary discourse of human rights (*Human Rights as Ethics, Politics, and Law*).

Jacob Rogozinski

Jacob Rogozinski is Professor of Metaphysics at the University of Strasbourg. His research is focusing on contemporary French Philosophy and on phenomenological thinking of the Ego and the Body. He published recently *Le moi et la chair* (Eng. *The Ego and the Flesh*, Stanford University Press, 2010) and *Guérir la vie – la Passion d'Antonin Artaud*. Some of his essays have been published in English in different collections, as *Bodies of Resistance* (Northwestern University Press, 2001), *Heidegger and Practical Philosophy* (SUNY Press, 2002), *Rethinking Facticity* (SUNY Press, 2008), *Law and Evil* (Routledge, 2010).

Hans Ruin

Hans Ruin is professor in Philosophy at Södertörn University. Recent publications include *The Past´s Presence* (with Marcia Cavalcante), 2006, *Phenomenology and Religion: New Frontiers* (with Jonna Bornemark 2010), and *Rethinking Time* (with Andrus Ers, 2011). He is co-editor for Nietzsche's Collected Works in Swedish and head of the research program Time, Memory and Representation (www.histcon.se).

Muniz Sodré

Muniz Sodré is full professor of Media and Communication at the School of Communication at the Universidade Federal do Rio de Janeiro. His work focuses both on general topics of philosophy and sociology of culture and massculture and further on specific subjects of Brazilian and Afro-brazilian culture. He is the author of 36 books, including a novel, and has some of his works translated into iItalian, French and Spanish. Among his recent publications are *As estratégias sensíveis – afeto, mídia e política* (Vozes, 2006), *Cidade dos Artistas – Cartografia da Televisão e da Fama do Rio de Janeiro* (Mauad, 2004), and *Sociedade, Mídia e Violência* (Sulina/Edipucrs, 2002).

Fredrika Spindler

Fredrika Spindler is a philosopher at Södertörns University. Among her earlier publications are *Philosophie de la puissance et détermination de l'homme chez Spinoza et chez Nietzsche* (Montpellier 1996; Swedish translation. Glänta Prouktion 2005), *Nietzsche. Kropp, konst, kunskap* (Glänta Produktion, 2010), *Spinoza. Multitud, affekt, kraft* (Glänta Produktion, 2009). She edited volumes such as *Estetik och Politik* (with Cecilia Sjöholm, Glänta Produktion, 2008) and *Gilles Deleuze* (Glänta Produktion and Aiolos, 2004).

Jon Wittrock

Jon Wittrock is Dr of Political and Social Sciences of the European University Institute. He is currently working on a postdoctoral project on Carl Schmitt and the borders of Europe. His earlier publications include *Beyond Burgenland and Kakanien? Post-National Politics in Europe: Political Justification and Critical Deliberation* (European University Institute, 2008). His major interests are in critical and political theory and especially concerning the intersection between religion and politics.

Södertörn Philosophical Studies

Södertörn Philosophical Studies is a book series published under the direction of the Department of Philosophy at Södertörn University. The series consists of monographs and anthologies in philosophy, with a special focus on the Continental-European tradition. It seeks to provide a platform for innovative contemporary philosophical research. The volumes are published mainly in English and Swedish. The series is edited by Marcia Sá Cavalcante Schuback and Hans Ruin.

www.ingramcontent.com/pod-product-compliance
Lightning Source LLC
LaVergne TN
LVHW041251080426
835510LV00009B/683